Improving Staffing Practices in Student Affairs

Improving Staffing Practices in Student Affairs

Roger B. Winston, Jr.

Don G. Creamer

Jossey-Bass Publishers • San Francisco

Substantial discounts on bulk quantities of Jossey-Bass books are available to corporations, professional associations, and other organizations. For details and discount information, contact the special sales department at Jossey-Bass Inc., Publishers (415) 433–1740; Fax (800) 605–2665.

For sales outside the United States, please contact your local Simon & Schuster International Office.

Jossey-Bass Web address: http://www.josseybass.com

 Manufactured in the United States of America on Lyons Falls Turin Book. This paper is acid-free and 100 percent totally chlorine-free.

Library of Congress Cataloging-in-Publication Data

Winston, Roger B.
   Improving staffing practices in student affairs / Roger B.
Winston, Jr., Don G. Creamer.—1st ed.
      p.   cm.—(The Jossey-Bass higher and adult education series)
   Includes bibliographical references and index.
   ISBN 0-7879-0851-7
   1. Student affairs services—United States. 2. Student
counselors—United States. 3. College personnel management—United
States. I. Creamer, Don G. II. Title. III. Series.
LB2342.9W56   1997
378.1'94—dc21   96-48334

FIRST EDITION
HB Printing 10 9 8 7 6 5 4 3 2 1

The Jossey-Bass
Higher and Adult Education Series

Contents

Preface

The historic values of student affairs always have shaped the attitudes and behaviors of practitioners and scholars in the field. These values hold individuals in the highest respect and bestow on them certain treasured human assets such as dignity, freedom, justice, and equality. The student affairs profession has taken upon itself the responsibility of continuously reminding the higher education establishment that students are not disembodied intellects by emphasizing the education of the whole person and by organizing itself to contribute to their broader education. Further, these values guide the behaviors of professionals in the way they organize themselves for work, relate to others as they carry out their assigned duties, make decisions about mutual interests, and nurture colleagues and subordinates. They prescribe limits of acceptable treatment of subordinates, and they inform policy development and operational procedures for the student affairs division.

The Need for This Book

Student services emerged and evolved because colleges and universities recognized the importance of supporting and developing students outside the classroom. As the field evolved into a profession, it articulated a set of core values about student development that are still the centerpiece of professional development and practice today. No one, however, has explored the extent to which these values inform staffing practices in student affairs. Now especially, as higher education suffers the continuing shocks of reduced funding, downsizing, challenges to its enrollment and hiring policies, and demands for public accountability in all of its operations, it seems critical to examine whether student affairs still functions in accord with its stated values. Assuming that a field that functions with a clear sense of its values and purposes also chooses and develops staff members who will support those values and purposes, the authors here examine student affairs staffing patterns in different kinds of institutions and assess them in light of the core values of the profession. We also suggest some ways to maintain staff quality amid continuing turbulence and change in higher education.

The Staffing Process

The way an organization structures itself and the nature of the interactions among the people who compose it may be described as its staffing practices. They form a system of policies, procedures, structures, activities, and rewards that govern the way people are hired and managed within higher education. The staffing system includes staff recruitment and selection, position orientation, supervision, continuing education and development, and performance appraisal.

Genesis of the Book

We launched this study because we were concerned about whether the profession of student affairs had progressed sufficiently to ensure appropriate, institutionalized treatment of staff that guarantees continued staff and organization improvement. We suspected we might find certain inadequacies as well as some satisfactory practices, but frankly we did not know what to expect. Almost no evidence of any kind was available; literature in the field was virtually silent about the overall systems of caring for staff; professional associations were mute regarding means of promoting healthy professionalism in these matters, and scholars of higher education have ignored the issues altogether.

Our interest in knowing about the current status of staffing practices in student affairs was whetted by concerns for quality in the field. Before launching the studies that led to this book, we believed that quality education is connected directly to the quality of the people who conduct the operations. Now that the studies are completed, we still believe so. "It's the economy, stupid!" ran one catchphrase of President Clinton's 1992 campaign; likewise, we think, "it's the people, stupid!" who make a difference in the quality of educational programs and services. It is only a small further step then to assert as a corollary that the quality of the people is controlled in considerable measure by the quality of the institutionalized activities and behaviors called staffing practices.

This idea became the focus of the studies that led to this book. We wanted to determine the state of the art of staffing practices in student affairs and to make critical judgments about their levels of adequacy. The former was achieved by careful examination of the literature of the field (and sometimes beyond the field), by conducting a national survey of staffing practices, and by compiling case studies of staffing practices at eight carefully selected institutions. The latter was accomplished by evaluating adequacy through our interpretation of generally accepted organizational standards, values, and principles. Naturally, our own views about adequacy of the practices also served as an interpretive lens in these judgments.

Purposes and Goals

This book informs the student affairs profession about the state of the art of staffing practices as they relate to standards of practice and professional values, and it offers suggestions for improvement. We hope it will also alert professional associations in the field of a neglected domain in which they should be activists, and that it will ignite the interest of scholars such that they conduct, and then publish, serious studies of staffing practices well beyond what we have done.

Overview of the Contents

This book deals exclusively with professional and allied professional staff. By this narrow focus, however, we do not mean to communicate a lack of concern for or underestimate the contributions of the other extremely important categories of staff, such as support and paraprofessional, who are essential to the work done in student affairs divisions.

The book contains ten chapters. Chapters One and Two introduce the essential background and contextual concerns of staffing in student affairs. Chapter One describes the current environmental turbulence in higher education and the historic values of student affairs. Chapter Two elaborates on internal and external institutional realities and presents a staffing model for student affairs.

Chapters Three and Four present the research evidence collected for our studies. Our case studies were taken from research universities, comprehensive state universities, liberal arts colleges, and two-year community colleges. Two institutions in each Carnegie type were selected using a single criterion—reputation for maintaining an excellent overall student affairs operation—and on-site individual and group interviews were conducted with as many practitioners in the division of student affairs as possible. Findings from interviews were compiled into written case studies for each institution and ultimately to a synthesis across institutions.

Current Staffing Practices: Survey Report forms the substance of Chapter Four. The methodology of the survey study and the descriptive findings are presented around the five components of staffing systems—recruitment and selection, orientation, supervision, staff development, and performance appraisal. When combined, these data give a picture of current staffing practices from multiple perspectives because responses were obtained from practitioners at all levels of student affairs operations; as expected, the perception of the overall quality of staffing practices reveals instances of variable adequacy.

Chapters Five through Nine take each component of a comprehensive staffing system one at a time for detailed discussion. In each of these chapters, the relevant aspect of the overall staffing model presented in Chapter Two is extracted to structure a discussion about how to use the model to improve practice. Further, each of these chapters contains an inclusive literature review about the subject. Not surprisingly, most staffing functions have little literature to catalogue actual or preferred practice. Literature about recruitment and selection and about staff development is the most extensive of the functional areas and is contained in journals and books directly related to the field of student affairs. By contrast, literature about orientation of new staff to their positions, supervision, and performance appraisal was skimpy by comparison and often not published in student affairs literature.

Chapters Five through Nine also contain a synthesis of our research findings from literature, surveys, and case studies. These presentations show the most discriminating review of current practice and provide a foundation for the enumeration of staffing principles that are presented in the final chapter.

Chapter Ten summarizes our conclusions about effective staffing practices based on the survey we conducted, case studies, readings from the literature, and over fifty years of professional experience. We also make a number of proposals about how the student affairs field can take decisive actions to improve dramatically the quality of professional practice and thereby the effectiveness of programs and services experienced by college students.

Terminology Used in the Book

Because the student affairs field does not have anything approaching a uniformly accepted terminology, it has been necessary for us to operationally define a number of terms. We refer to the institution-level organizational structure of student affairs as the *division,* which is generally subdivided into subunits that we interchangeably refer to as *departments, functional areas,* or *offices.* The principal, chief, or executive head of the student affairs division is referred to throughout as the vice president for student affairs or simply vice president.

Professional staff are defined as those who hold at least a master's degree in areas such as student affairs, counseling, or higher education, or in another discipline but who because of extensive experience have acquired knowledge of student affairs; who identify themselves as student affairs professionals; and who have responsibility for out-of-class education of students. Some practitioners who completed our surveys reacted negatively to an educational qualification (at least a master's degree) as part of our definition. We do not mean to imply that staff who do not satisfy the educational criterion are incompetent to perform the duties assigned them or lack a sense of ethics and responsibility. There is some feeling in the field that advanced education is not necessary for professional practice in student affairs; we, however, disagree.

Allied professional staff are those with advanced formal education in a specialized profession other than student affairs but who provide services essential to the accomplishment of student affairs' mission. For example, physicians, nurses, accountants, clergy, and attorneys may be considered allied professionals in student affairs.

Other categories of staff are addressed indirectly throughout the book and include *support staff,* defined as persons who perform tasks that enable professionals and allied professionals to provide essential programs and services. Support staff may be full-time or part-time and may be students or nonstudents. Position titles in this category of staff include secretaries, security officers, maintenance workers, and receptionists. *Paraprofessionals* are defined as students who are selected, trained, and supervised in the performance of functions generally performed by professionals. Examples include resident assistants, peer tutors, peer sexuality educators, and orientation leaders.

Suggestions About How to Read This Book

Because this book reports findings of research studies and offers analyses of current staffing practices and practical suggestions for improving practices, various parts may appeal to different readers. Consequently, some may not benefit as much as others from reading it straight through.

The first two chapters provide a contextual and theoretical foundation for the book. Chapter Two presents a model of the staffing process; it seems important to have a grasp of that to understand the remainder of the book.

Chapters Three and Four explain in some detail our research methods and our findings from cases studies and surveys about the staffing process. It is possible that readers interested mainly in practical considerations will want to skip directly to Chapters Five through Nine. However, the concluding section of Chapter Three contains an important synthesis of findings from the eight cases that may provide a foundation for understanding key cultural ingredients in successful student affairs operations.

Each of Chapters Five through Nine deals specifically with one component of the staffing model. Readers who have particular interests in one or more of these topics may find it useful to turn to the appropriate chapter. These chapters more or less stand alone, but all are related to the staffing model and therefore to each other.

Finally, in Chapter Ten we attempt to distill much of what we learned during the course of this project. We offer principles and recommendations that assume one has read the material presented earlier in the book. If readers go directly to that chapter, they may not fully grasp the reasoning that underlies the material there.

Audience

This book was written primarily for those in student affairs who have the responsibility of directing the work of professional or allied professional staff members. That loosely translates to mid- and upper-level administrators. But the book should be of interest also to entry-level professionals who aspire to career advancement.

This book also seems appropriate for use in professional preparation programs. Today's graduate students will be facing a much more complex world than their predecessors, and having a better command of staffing issues and practices is likely to be essential in the next century. Even though this book is written from the unique perspective of student affairs, it has applicability to most areas of higher education administration.

Acknowledgments

We are indebted to a number of individuals who supported our efforts in writing this book. Foremost among those to whom we wish to express our appreciation are Vasti Torres and Sue Stevens, who devoted untold hours in packing and mailing survey instrument packages, preparing data for analysis, providing useful critiques of ideas, and conducting library research. Without their assistance this project would have never come to fruition. We also wish to acknowledge the contributions of Javaid Kaiser at Virginia Tech and Sue Feng at the University of Georgia, who were especially helpful in performing data analyses.

Our great thanks to the College of Education at Virginia Tech and the School of Professional Studies, College of Education, at the University of Georgia for providing financial support that enabled us to conduct the staffing survey.

We also are profoundly grateful to the student affairs vice presidents—Bill Bryan, Jon Dalton, Linda Dayton, Dick Franklin, Len Goldberg, Bob Scott, William (Bud) Thomas, and George Young—and their staffs for participating in the case studies. Their hospitality, candor, and cooperation made that part of this project most enjoyable and a rich learning experience for us.

Finally, we would like to thank Gale Erlandson, editor for higher and adult education at Jossey-Bass, for her patience, support, and incisive critiques.

February 1997   Roger B. Winston, Jr.
                                                 Athens, Georgia
                                                 Don G. Creamer
                                                 Blacksburg, Virginia

The Authors

ROGER B. WINSTON, JR., is professor in the student personnel in higher education program and coordinator of the student affairs administration doctoral program in the Department of Counseling and Human Development Services, College of Education, University of Georgia. He received a bachelor's degree (1965) in history and philosophy from Auburn University and a master's degree (1970) in philosophy and doctorate (1973) in counseling and student personnel services from the University of Georgia. Before assuming a teaching position at the University of Georgia in 1978, he was a residence hall director there and dean of men at Georgia Southwestern College.

Winston is author or editor of eight other books: *Student Housing and Residential Life: A Handbook for Professionals Committed to Student Development Goals* (1993 with S. Anchors), *Using Professional Standards in Student Affairs* (1991 with W. A. Bryan and T. K. Miller), *Administration and Leadership in Student Affairs: Actualizing Student Development in Higher Education*, second edition (1991 with T. K. Miller), *Promoting Student Development Through Intentionally Structured Groups: Principles, Techniques, and Applications* (1988 with W. C. Bonney, T. K. Miller, and J. C. Dagley), *Fraternities and Sororities on the Contemporary College Campus* (1987 with W. R. Nettles and J. H. Opper), *Students as Paraprofessional Staff* (1984 with S. C. Ender), *Developmental Approaches to Academic Advising: Addressing Students' Educational, Career, and Personal Needs* (1984 with T. K. Miller, S. C. Ender, and T. J. Grites), *Developmental Approaches to Academic Advising* (1982 with S. C. Ender and T. K. Miller). In addition, he has authored or coauthored more than thirty book chapters and more than forty professional journal articles.

He is also coauthor of published assessment instruments: *Student Developmental Task Inventory* (1973, 1979, with T. K. Miller and

J. S. Prince), *Student Developmental Task and Lifestyle Inventory* (1987 with T. K. Miller and J. S. Prince), and *Academic Advising Inventory* (1984 with J. A. Sandor).

Winston's honors and recognitions include Outstanding Contributor to Research on Academic Advising (by the National Academic Advising Association, 1984); senior professional, Annuit Coeptis Dinner (by the American College Personnel Association [ACPA], 1987); Melvene D. Hardee Award for outstanding contribution to the student affairs field (by the Southern Association for College Student Affairs, 1989); Senior Scholar Diplomate (by ACPA, 1989–1995); and Outstanding Contributor to Knowledge Award (by ACPA, 1990).

DON G. CREAMER is professor of education and coordinator of college student affairs and higher education programs at Virginia Polytechnic Institute and State University (Virginia Tech). He received a bachelor's degree in American history (1960) and a master's degree in counseling and guidance (1961) from East Texas State University and a doctorate in higher education (1965) from Indiana University. He has held several administrative positions in student affairs including counselor, director of financial aid and scholarships, director of alumni affairs, director of placement, and dean of students. He assumed his current teaching position at Virginia Tech in 1977.

Creamer is author or editor of three other books: *College Student Development: Theory and Practice for the 1990s* (1990), *Opportunities for Student Development in Two-Year Colleges* (1986 with C. R. Dassance), and *Student Development in Higher Education: Theories, Practices, and Future Directions* (1980). He is author or coauthor of more than fifty journal articles and book chapters, and his professional service has included more than 100 consultations with colleges and universities and more than 100 professional presentations.

He is former president of the American College Personnel Association (1978–1979) and has served the association in several other roles including currently as president of the Educational Leadership Foundation, alternate director to the Council for the Advancement of Standards, chair of the Quality Assurance Committee, and Senior Scholar Diplomate. His awards include the

Robert H. Shaffer Distinguished Alumnus Award (1992, Indiana University Department of Higher Education and Student Affairs) and Annuit Coeptis (1989, ACPA Senior Professional), and Significant Contributions Award (1987, ACPA Commission on Two-Year Student Development Programs).

Improving Staffing Practices in Student Affairs

Chapter One

Contexts and Values for Staffing in Student Affairs

The lifeblood of a higher education institution is the individuals who populate it. Without students, faculty, and staff no college or university can exist. Human capital is higher education's principal resource, development of which is its *raison d'être*. Through its staffing practices, an institution acts out its fundamental values about the importance and worth of people and the ultimate purposes of the institution. These practices are embedded within an organized, goal-oriented context and culture that is influenced by the institution's history, mission, customs, myths, rituals, ceremonies, interaction patterns, physical and fiscal resources, and a unique collection of students, faculty, and staff.

Thus we may conclude that an institution's staffing practices are the intentional and institutionalized efforts to locate, attract, organize, and nurture the people who teach courses, conduct research, provide public service, cultivate public and private sources of financial support, furnish support services, and create programs and individual interactions that enrich the educations and personal lives of students.

Because of the paramount importance of the personnel who *are* higher education, it is essential to understand the institutional processes used to select them, to direct, motivate, support, and reward their contributions, and to sustain their personal and professional vitality. The significance of the people in higher education is reflected in the fact that between 75 and 85 percent of the total budget of most institutions is generally devoted to personnel costs (Winston and Miller, 1991). Employees' ability to contribute to the achievement of the goals of higher education is related clearly to their treatment within the organization. When employees are judiciously and properly chosen, assigned, and supervised, they represent the potential of the institution to achieve excellence. Poorly conducted employee searches and selection processes, inhumane or negligent treatment of people, inappropriate work assignments, lack of support for continued personal and professional development, maladroit or no supervision, and failure to reward good performance is the prescription for institutional educational bankruptcy, or at best mediocrity. No institution can achieve excellence unless all of its units—academics, research, service, student affairs, financial, and development—operate in a manner that optimizes its people's contributions to its goals and purposes.

Most colleges and universities, perhaps all of them, strive to achieve excellence within the parameters of their missions. The quality of educational practice is directly related to the creativity and quality of the performance of the people who conduct the work of the institution; the quality of performance over time is inextricably tied to the institution's staffing practices.

These institutional policies and customary modus operandi regarding the management of people are called staffing practices. In the student affairs division, these practices are especially crucial to its ability to achieve its goals for out-of-class student learning and development. Because of the enormity and centrality of the task of facilitating out-of-class learning and development of students, a study of the student affairs division's staffing practices is long overdue and sorely needed. The contributions of student affairs staff to the achievement of learning and personal development goals, and ultimately all goals of higher education, are undeniable.

In this chapter we explain the meaning of *staffing* and relate it to a discussion of organizational structure in higher education and student affairs' role within the multitude of organizational patterns currently found in colleges and universities. Particular attention is focused on how recent financial hardships and changes in the composition of student bodies have affected higher education and how student affairs has dealt with a lack of adequate resources to achieve its goals and mission. Finally, we consider the values that drive student affairs practice and their implications for staffing practices in student affairs.

Staffing: A Definition

The way an organization structures itself and the nature of the interactions among the people who compose it may be described as *staffing practices*. They form a system of policies, procedures, structures, activities, and rewards that govern the way people are hired and managed within higher education. The staffing system includes staff recruitment and selection, position orientation, supervision, continuing education and development, and performance appraisal.

We chose *staffing practices* over other words or phrases to describe this system because we believe the term connotes an integrated approach to the selection, orientation, supervision, development, and evaluation of the people employed within a given organization. It communicates the interrelationships that must exist between people and the processes they use to facilitate their making contributions to the accomplishment of organizational goals. A term such as *human resource management,* by contrast, connotes a primary concern for the organizational oversight of employees. *Staffing practices* also emphasizes the systemic dimension; selecting people to work in an organization is not independent of the kinds of work to be done, how an organization's people relate to each other, the kinds of supervision and support offered them, and what behaviors are rewarded and punished. Each of these aspects depends on the others and is mutually influential. (A model that more fully explains the integrated, systemic nature of staffing activities is described in Chapter Two.)

The Structure of Student Affairs Divisions

Most colleges and universities work toward the goals of student affairs by creating and managing separate institutional units to accomplish them. Normally such a unit is called the *division of student affairs,* although it varies widely across institutions; it is difficult if not impossible to advocate the advantage of one name over another. Where the unit is known by some other label—*department,* for example—the reason is most likely that student affairs is called something else (such as student services or student development), not that the unit actually serves a different function. To be sure, there are many ways to organize student affairs within an institution; almost any imaginable pattern may be found somewhere. Sometimes the functions of student affairs are accomplished through units composed of professional generalists—staff who carry out multiple roles in service to students. In these cases, the organizational unit of student affairs may appear well integrated with other functions of the institution, such as academic support services. This pattern of organization is often seen in smaller colleges, especially private liberal arts colleges.

More often, however, and certainly in the larger colleges and universities, student affairs functions are carried out by specialists—that is, staff who focus on specific functional areas (such as housing, placement, student discipline, or admissions), areas of student need (for instance, health education, counseling, career development, or academic support), or student subpopulations (for example, women, minorities, or international students)—rather than by generalist staff members who deal with students in many different areas of their lives and corresponding institutional contexts. In these cases, the organizational unit of student affairs appears as a stand-alone system of relatively independent services to students.

In this book we refer to the institution-level organizational unit responsible for dealing with the out-of-class lives of students as the *student affairs division*. Although we acknowledge that other terms are in use, this simplifies terminology in these pages; for the same reason, we call the chief administrative officer of this unit the vice president for student affairs, or sometimes simply the vice president. Other titles, such as dean of students, are widely used to designate the executive officer and may be more appropriate in a given institutional context. Here, however, *dean of students* is used to refer to the leader of an administrative unit or department in the student affairs division that often combines somewhat disparate functional areas—such as discipline, Greek life, new student orientation, and disabled student services—that are not large enough to warrant separate organizational units.

Regardless of the specific organizational structure of divisions of student affairs, they almost invariably are structured as bureaucratic and somewhat jurisdictional systems. Thus the division is subdivided into smaller units, each managed by a staff member holding a title such as department director, department coordinator, or assistant (or associate) dean of the given function. Frequently referred to as mid-managers by student affairs professionals, they report to a person with higher authority—often at executive level and with a title such as vice president for student affairs or dean of students—and simultaneously supervise lower-level staff who report to them. This arrangement is hierarchically structured and results in an administratively dominating character for most divisions of student affairs where certain staff—those charged with managerial responsibility—act as leaders for all other staff. This leadership dimension is a crucial factor in successful staffing practices in student affairs.

Such a system of management responsibilities may work remarkably well within most institutions of higher education that are themselves bureaucratically structured into multitiered organizational units with academic departments serving as the foundation of the organizational ladder. In fact, such system arrangements in divisions of student affairs may be very effective in channeling resources toward the institution's priorities and in controlling the flow of professional energy. But in less formal bureaucratic institutions, such an arrangement would be unlikely to work well.

As a general rule there is considerable pressure within institutions toward organizational conformity. As a consequence, a student affairs division's organizational structure, and to some extent its operating philosophy, generally approximates the prevailing structure of other operational units within the institution and the theoretical orientation or style of the institution's executive leadership.

It is precisely because of this that staffing practices are so vital to the achievement of institutional goals, including the goal of high quality in educational services. In these arrangements, staff with administrative or managerial responsibility for particular functions of student affairs or outcomes in students can accomplish their work through a limited number of actions. Fundamentally, management in higher education is the exercise of judgment and the use of authority in controlling two resources: money and people. This reach or span of control of administrators extends in many cases to physical facilities as well, but as important as this function is, most student affairs administrators' actions are limited to the management of fiscal and human resources. Their reach often includes policy promulgation, a very potent form of management, but even here the focus on people and money often overrides other issues.

What an administrator is able to accomplish with allocated fiscal and human resources is the premier test of managerial competence. Logic in most bureaucratic units holds that level of accomplishment is tied to level of access or use of these resources; more money and larger staffs lead to more productivity. But reality often dictates otherwise: accomplishments must be held constant or increased even when fiscal resources do not keep up with system demands and when available human talent is limited because of a lack of appropriate or adequate training, experience, motivation, or professional commitment. In some cases the staff of a student affairs unit has met its limits; it can no longer take on another task or attend to another student need without discarding some present responsibilities. When faced with the necessity of shedding long-held roles or responsibilities, certain ones are seldom considered for elimination. The activities that serve primarily as administrative support for the institutional bureaucracy are frequently considered sacrosanct, which means that cuts frequently end up being made in programs and services that directly affect students' educational and personal development.

Student affairs administrators, especially those at middle and upper levels of the organization, hire and nurture other student affairs professionals. It may be argued that the most important function of any administrative-level professional is to select, assign, supervise, and develop the people who staff the division's units. As will be shown throughout this book and discussed in detail in Chapter Two, conducting these activities is influenced by many factors both within and outside the institutions, but in the end they make the greatest difference to the productivity of student affairs units and divisions.

The Context of Student Affairs Practice

Student affairs is subject to two grand masters: the institution (with its special mission) in which the division functions and the students the division must serve directly to achieve important educational and personal development goals. The success of student affairs divisions always is judged relative to these two sources of influence; both shape the purposes, organizational structures, resource allocations, and expectations of performance.

The influence of institutional purpose on student affairs practice is historically self-evident. Invariably, student affairs divisions justify their actions relative to institutional mission and environment; however, recent conditions—economic, social, and political—have changed this sphere of influence considerably. Institutions both public and private are vulnerable to powerful outside forces that often sharpen or drastically change the precise expectations of student affairs within them. An historical example is the constantly increasing and ever-important flow of financial aid to students from governmental and other funding sources that requires special management behaviors inside the organization. More recent examples include government-mandated programs such as the Americans with Disabilities Act (ADA), which require provision of a wide variety of services but funds them only partially.

Budget Restrictions on Student Affairs Missions

Many societal changes have had direct and very consequential effects on institutions of higher education and therefore on student affairs divisions. The combined effects of revenue shortfalls over the past five to ten years in many states and the erosion of public confidence in higher education has taken a serious toll on institutional capabilities for providing services for students. Politically, in some states higher education has been a relatively easy target in times of revenue shortfalls. In the public sector, tight financial conditions have sometimes forced higher education to compete for funding with other human services such as welfare, health care, unemployment benefits, K–12 education, and public safety. Institutional capabilities also are stretched in private colleges and universities even though their revenues are not precisely connected to political realities of the public sector. Costs of doing business in private higher education have been soaring. For example, expenditures per student rose a dramatic 46 percent between 1977 and 1992 in private universities (*Condition of Education*, 1995, p. 54).

A recent policy analysis (Eaton, 1995) regarding aid to education detailed several parallel conditions concerning public support to higher education and can serve as an illustration of the toll. The analysis reports that support for higher education is diminishing and cites these trends (pp. 6–7):

- The federal government's share of financial aid to students has declined.
- Federal appropriations per full-time equivalent student decreased 9 percent in constant dollars between 1980 and 1993. Federal and state revenues to higher education each declined as a percentage of total current fund revenues between 1980–81 and 1991–92.
- Overall state appropriations to higher education showed an absolute decline in 1991–92 and 1992–93. There has been some improvement in 1994–95, but at a slower growth rate than prior increases.
- State appropriations per full-time student fell 13 percent in real terms between 1987 and 1992.
- The proportion of state and local government expenditures devoted to higher education declined from 23.5 percent in 1968 to 18.3 percent in 1990.

These factors, coupled with rising tuition and fee structures and insufficient private support, raise many policy issues with which higher education leaders must struggle, both immediately and in the long term. One is particularly disturbing and consequential for student affairs: "The public finds itself in the contradictory and unenviable position of escalating its demands from higher education while being reluctant to pay for them" (Eaton, 1995, pp. 6, 7). On the receiving end of this dilemma are student affairs staff members who are constantly under pressure to do more (for students and the institution) with fewer resources (both proportionally and in absolute terms). This situation is not new to student affairs; the history of the profession shows a continuous pattern of escalating expectations and insufficient support to adequately address them.

The seriousness and urgency of this policy issue is being addressed in Virginia, for example, where drastic drops in public revenues and shifting public priorities for funding led to unparalleled reductions in public support of higher education. A Commission on the Future of Higher Education in Virginia was formed to guide public response to the crisis; it recently issued a report that frames the situation for that state and, one suspects, for many other states as well. The chairperson of the commission (Chichester, 1996, p. ii) wrote: "For the past six years, our colleges and universities have gone through an unprecedented period of upheaval and financial insecurity. Six years ago it would have seemed inconceivable to predict that in fiscal year 1996:

- state support has fallen;
- tuition is at an all-time high; and,
- in this fiscal environment, our colleges and universities must absorb 50,000 more students by the year 2007."

The situation cited by Chichester is not universal; some states and some institutions have managed to sustain support to higher education or have shown appreciable gains during the recent past. State funds for higher education operating expenses, for example, were 8 percent higher in 1995 than in 1993 (*Chronicle of Higher Education Almanac*, 1995, p. 5). The broader trend, however, reveals a serious weakening of financial support since 1992. Revenue per full-time equivalent (FTE) student varies substantially according to the type of institution; in 1992, it ranged from $5,743 at public two-year colleges to $30,459 at private universities. Public four-year colleges received $11,785, and private four-year colleges received $14,230 per FTE student.

According to *Condition of Education* (1995), revenue per FTE student (in 1994 constant dollars) increased at all types of higher education institutions except public two-year colleges between 1977 and 1992. At private institutions the increase was particularly dramatic— from $21,538 to $30,459 at universities and from $10,645 to $14,230 at four-year colleges. But while revenue per FTE student increased, government appropriations per FTE fell at all types of institutions over those years. At public institutions the decrease in appropriations was particularly large between 1990 and 1992, and even with significant increases in tuition revenue per FTE student, total revenue fell or remained steady during that period.

Greater Student Needs

Even as tighter fiscal constraints have been placed on student affairs, students now entering higher education have greater need for institutional support than ever before. This was documented by O'Malley and others (1990) in a survey of counseling centers;

85 percent reported an increase in the number of cases of serious psychopathology over the previous five years. Stone and Archer (1990), based on an analysis of the literature, concluded that student-presenting problems at counseling centers had increased in the following areas over the decade of the 1980s: eating disorders, substance (principally alcohol) abuse, sexual abuse and violence (assault, rape, or date rape), dysfunctional family experiences (such as alcoholic parents, physical and emotional abuse, and divorce), and AIDS.

Similarly, Westefeld, Whitchard, and Range (1990) found that the incident of student suicide remains high. Frequently caused by low self-esteem, drug use, and a history of family problems, suicide was seen as increasing in society in general as well as on college campuses.

The increase in the need for long-term psychological services, however, presents an ethical dilemma for many counseling centers. Gilbert (1992, p. 698) cautioned: "It is misguided kindness, as well as being ethically unwise and legally risky, to attempt to carry out a treatment mission with inadequate resources out of compassion for the client."

The student affairs division's leadership is faced with seemingly insoluble problems. As S. R. Levy (1990, p. 617), vice president at a major midwestern university, notes: "Resources are limited; senior administrators may not always understand the needs of . . . [counseling] centers; the demands of students for support and assistance will not likely diminish, and the questions raised by students and others are now more profound and perplexing perhaps than in some previous generations of students."

Other student issues also cry for attention from the student affairs division. For instance, demographers have alerted higher education that in this and the next decade, institutions will have more students from nonwhite segments of the population than ever before. In the past, many of these students have needed greater institutional assistance than their middle-class, white colleagues in order to be successful. As Blimling (1993b, p. 3) noted, "When students come from different racial, ethnic, cultural, religious, or socioeconomic backgrounds, their adjustments are often more difficult," which deserve more and more concentrated attention from the institution.

Student Affairs' Challenge

Thus without doubt, the economic, social, and political forces that have altered the funding patterns for higher education have resulted in major changes within the institutions. Virtually a new language has sprung up in higher education as it adapts to these and other forces. Buzzwords such as benchmarking, best practice, downsizing, rightsizing, outsourcing, reengineering, restructuring, reorganizing, and total quality management are terms taken from businesses that have previously experienced the pressures of change and downsizing themselves (Nicklin, 1995). Each term connotes forced change on higher education systems. Though it may be desirable for all within the organization to be involved in contemplating and analyzing the conditions facing the institution, more likely strategies include top-down mandates for restructuring. One might think of such mandates as facing the future directly and proactively (Guskin, 1996); it is certainly true that circumstances in many institutions require strong leadership to bring about certain operational changes in most organizational units of higher education.

Consequently, student affairs divisions in most colleges and universities are coping with severe shortages in both fiscal and human resources to meet the demands from the institutions and their constituencies for ever-expanding and ever-improving service to students. Some are depending on expanded use of student paraprofessionals, part-time staff, or under-credentialed (in some instances even uncredentialed) staff to save money. Many are cutting staff with no way to make up the shortfall. The consequence has been fewer or lesser-quality programs and services available to students.

Paralleling the new realities in the financing of institutions and the organizational units within them, new student realities also act to constrain the planning of student affairs administrators. Some observers point out that more underprepared students are arriving in colleges and universities today; they will require more direct services if they are to have reasonable chances of success. Often these required services are very expensive, for they take the form of virtual tutorial interactions with students. Observers also note that many students today see themselves as customers, and they have high demands for service; they fully expect institutional responses to their every perceived need. Creating "one-stop shopping centers" to deliver student services, for example, is commonly the result of restructuring efforts within student affairs divisions.

Other substantive matters confront student affairs professionals. Institutions now commonly expect students' out-of-class experiences, as affected by student affairs divisions, to achieve results in student learning. Though professionals have long held that experiences outside the classroom yield lasting benefits to students, only recently has it been demonstrated; research has now shown that the cognitive gains of students are significantly related to out-of-class experiences (Pascarella and Terenzini, 1991). Intuitively, educational leaders know that the role and contribution of student affairs to the student learning objectives of the institution is significant. In practice, however, student affairs has not always been shown respect for its contributions and has not received equitable treatment and resources. As a result, some student affairs practitioners feel like second-class citizens, greatly affecting their organizations' ability to attract and hold talented, well-educated, and competent men and women.

The connection between the quality of staffing practices in student affairs and the quality of educational services delivered to students is direct and powerful. Thus any institutional practice that devalues student affairs will lead to disrespectful treatment of the staff and, ultimately, make it unable to deliver high-quality educational services to either students or the institution. It must be acknowledged also that staffing practices in student affairs are not always directly in the control of student affairs administrators. Often these administrators are compelled to follow institutionally sanctioned practices even where they have been proven ineffective.

Thus the conditions that shape student affairs practice and the forces for changing them are powerful and pervasive. Their effects are nearly omnipresent in student affairs divisions, and any consideration of staffing practices must reckon with these ambient factors. Throughout this book, the reader will be reminded of contextual factors that shape and sometimes control staffing practices that diminish the direct influence of student affairs professionals in this vital area.

The Role of Values in Student Affairs Practice

Of equal and perhaps greater influence on staffing practices in student affairs divisions are the epic values of the profession. Strongly held values of education have long been the hallmark of student affairs practice. Any interaction with a student affairs professional that deals with the purposes of the field will quickly turn to demonstrations of such beliefs as educating the whole person and helping people become all that they are capable of becoming. These beliefs are a beacon for guiding staffing practices, and like the influence of tumultuous environmental factors, the point will be emphasized throughout this book.

One must not claim that student affairs professionals are the only educators in colleges and universities who hold strong values and beliefs about their work. Faculty, for example, hold firm commitments to teaching, research, service, and to the advancement of their disciplines. Despite tumult in the external environment, the commitment of faculty to these purposes has changed little over the past century. Such purposes lie at the heart of the higher education enterprise. Faculty know this, and they have not shirked their obligations to deliver on these commitments. Depending on their discipline, there are important variations in their values and beliefs (Biglan, 1973), but the essential values override the differences.

Many core ideas about higher education are shared by faculty and student affairs professionals. Basically, these shared commitments focus on the goals of higher education, which, as Bowen (1977) illustrated, serve the interests of individuals and society. He articulated goals for higher education that clarify aims for individual students and for society, and he maintained that these should be understood in the context of certain widely held principles about higher education, including education of the whole person, the uniqueness or individuality of learners, and accessibility of higher education to a broad range of persons in society. Bowen's specific goals for individuals included cognitive, affective, and practical purposes and changes in behavior patterns tied to skills, abilities, and competences. He also suggested that personal discovery, career choice, and satisfaction and enjoyment of learning for its own sake are legitimate goals of higher education. Regarding higher education goals for society, Bowen discussed the reality of competing philosophies of education—that is, whether the individual or society is the main benefactor of the process. He saw both clearly and suggested that higher education also plays the important role in society of serving as an agent of change and of social stability.

Student affairs professionals embrace their special form of values for education, values historic in American higher education that have formed an unswerving covenant between student affairs professionals and students. These values serve as a virtual ideology for practice; they form the foundation for educational philosophy for the profession and its practitioners.

Young (1996) placed the essential values of the student affairs profession in an historical context of the profession and showed how they have shaped practice in the field over many decades. He classified the most basic values into two global domains: individuation and community. In the first of these domains, student affairs professionals reveal their historic commitment to "whole person development" and to the uniqueness of each individual. He points to the manner in which the Student Personnel Point of View (SPPOV) (American Council on Education, 1937, 1949) reflected an emphasis on the importance of experience in learning (the "experiencing individual") and of becoming responsible (the "responsible individual"). Young also sees the second of these values, community, in the SPPOV that suggested that self-worth is partly defined by meaningful relationships with others and that mutual empowerment of all within the educational environment is a key to productive, holistic learning.

Earlier, Young and Elfrink (1991) described essential values of student affairs practice based upon survey research of scholars and practitioners in the field. Their consensus-oriented survey yielded eight cardinal values of the profession supported by a large percentage of the respondents as having enduring roles in student affairs practice:

1. Altruism, defined as concern for the welfare of others and associated with attitudes and personal qualities including caring, commitment, compassion, and generosity
2. Equality, defined as having the same rights or privileges and associated with attitudes and personal qualities including acceptance, assertiveness, fairness, tolerance, and diversity

3. Aesthetics, defined as qualities of objects, events, and persons that provide satisfaction and associated with attitudes and personal qualities including appreciation, creativity, imagination, and sensitivity
4. Freedom, defined as capacity to exercise choice and associated with attitudes and personal qualities including confidence, hope, independence, openness, self-direction, and self-discipline
5. Human dignity, defined as inherent worth and uniqueness of an individual and associated with attitudes and personal qualities including consideration, empathy, humaneness, kindness, respectfulness, trust, and self-esteem
6. Justice, defined as upholding moral and legal principles and associated with attitudes and personal qualities including courage, integrity, morality, and objectivity
7. Truth, defined as faithfulness to fact or reality and associated with attitudes and personal qualities including accountability, authenticity, honesty, inquisitiveness, rationality, and reflectiveness
8. Community, defined as mutual empowerment and associated with attitudes and personal qualities including cooperation, commitment, development, participation, and collaboration

Two years later, Young (1993a, 1993b) offered arguments for reordering the eight essential values to reflect the primacy of three values—human dignity, equality, and community. He pointed out that the essential values can be seen as either terminal (desirable end states) or instrumental (desirable modes of conduct to achieve end states), as defined by Rokeach (1973). Thus these three values are suggested as terminal values of the profession, and freedom, altruism, truth, and justice as instrumental values. Following this argument, the essential values of student affairs are:

• Human dignity (including freedom, altruism, and truth)
• Equality (including individuals and groups)
• Community (including justice)

Each of these representations of core values of student affairs points to the centrality of the profession's concerns for people—for their wholeness and their worth—whether seen as individuals or as a community. Likewise, the values are primary whether the concern is for students or for colleagues. Student affairs divisions, when staffed and led by professionals with appropriate academic preparation and practical experience, have been resolute in these value orientations and commitments throughout the history of the profession and, though there seems to be a periodic cyclical swing between emphasis on individual and collective values (Young, 1996), there has been no serious divergence from them for decades.

These are the principles to which the student affairs profession has long been committed, and they serve daily as guides for decision making and action by individuals and group members. We argue in this book that these values should also guide hiring decisions, definition of role expectations, the process of supervision and the conduct and use of performance appraisals, and intentional efforts to nurture continued improvement. It seems illogical and impractical for student affairs practitioners to advocate one set of values for dealing with students and a contrary set for dealing with staff.

Summary

People are every college and university's greatest asset. Quality educational practice is related directly to quality performance, which is dependent on the knowledge, skills, creativity, commitment, and values of the people who work in student affairs.

How institutions locate, hire, and nurture their people is called staffing practices. Student affairs operates within organizational units normally called divisions, which are managed by administrators who have direct responsibility for all staffing practices in the division.

Tumultuous economic, social, and political forces are affecting the landscape for the practice of student affairs. Epic values of higher education generally and student affairs specifically provide long-term stability for practice and powerful illumination for conducting staffing practices in the field.

These are the backdrops for our detailed discussions about student affairs staffing practices in American higher education. They offer special lenses for interpreting our research findings on the subject, and they may guide readers in understanding our findings for their work.

Chapter Two describes a model of staffing in student affairs and demonstrates the contextual conditions that mediate its application. Evidence to corroborate the model and to show vital connections with quality practices is presented in the chapters that follow. Chapters Three and Four form a special section devoted to the presentation of research findings; eight institutional case studies about staffing practices and a cross-case analysis of them are presented, as well as the results of a national survey of staffing practices in student affairs. Chapters Five through Nine discuss separately the staffing practices of recruitment and selection, orientation, supervision, staff development, and performance appraisal, emphasizing appropriate practices for higher education today. Conclusions and recommendations for future staffing practices in student affairs are presented in Chapter Ten, along with some observations about the connection between professional association practices and quality within colleges and universities.

Chapter Two

A Model for Staffing Practice in Student Affairs

Maintaining institutional quality and division vitality is directly tied to an institution's staffing practices. Talented, well-educated, and dedicated people make the achievement of extraordinary results possible; a staff with lesser characteristics allows a student affairs division to aspire only to mediocrity and a future punctuated by crises and make-do solutions. Student affairs divisions that do not have well-integrated and purposive staffing practices will always be forced to play catch-up. This chapter suggests ways that student affairs divisions can promote educational excellence through sound and creative staffing practices. Selecting, supervising, nurturing, and rewarding the staff that composes a student affairs division, however, is a complex activity that requires ongoing attention from the division's leadership both to the people and the demands they face and to institutional and societal expectations and demands of the student affairs organization.

Talent, knowledge, and dedication in staff members may be acquired at the time of initial employment or through intentional developmental activities. Even when a division buys the services of highly skilled, knowledgeable, and experienced practitioners, if they are not nurtured, supported, and challenged once employed, they will generally regress to the institutional norm of mediocrity or leave for a more hospitable professional environment. The process of staffing is vital to the long-term success of a student affairs division and the institution of which it is a part, but it is complex to implement.

This chapter presents an overall conception of the key components of staffing and the conditions and forces that influence the process. Figure 2.1 depicts these components in simplified fashion and makes these points:

- Staffing practices involve interrelationships among recruitment and selection, orientation, supervision, staff development, and performance appraisal.
- Staffing practices reside within and are shaped by the culture of the institution.
- The institution is susceptible to multiple environmental forces that influence staffing practices in both obvious and subtle ways.

Even this simple portrayal of essential elements of staffing practices stimulates the imagination about how many factors may influence them. Some of the influences are direct and in the control of student affairs or other institutional leaders; many others are neither direct nor in the control of the leaders, but they act to fashion what is possible and often necessary.

This chapter begins with a brief depiction of some of the direct and indirect environmental factors that exert influence on staffing practices, then moves to a discussion of how market conditions affect recruiting. Next, the institutional culture is discussed in terms of controlling conditions for staffing. The chapter concludes with a brief discussion of the essential elements of staffing, leaving the details of each to Chapters Five through Nine.

The Environment for Higher Education

Some recent conditions that exert powerful influences on higher education were described in Chapter One, such as lack of adequate governmental financial support, lack of public confidence in higher education, and questioning of the traditional values and missions of many institutions. Such forces are not new, of course, though they seem to have taken an especially harsh turn lately and have raised many troubling policy issues for higher education in America. Tensions between higher education and the agencies or constituencies that govern, fund, and support it have always existed somewhere in the background, and there is every reason to believe that they will continue to do so in the foreseeable future. But these conditions can damage the quality of higher education and make the task of staffing ever more difficult.

Environmental turbulence in higher education is not limited to these quite recent events. Other forces challenge certain core functions of higher education such as curriculum, and certain core resources such as faculty and reward systems. Some of this is most evident in the political life of the institution, where the drama is played out largely in negotiations for policy support and financing, often with state government officials in the public sector.

Other criticisms and challenges are seen in the literature of higher education, where basic changes in philosophy and operations are proposed. For example, some critics want to reform the undergraduate curriculum radically to focus it more closely than today upon concerns thought more central to effective living in a democratic society (Wingspread Group, 1993). There are, fortunately, voices of moderation that call for balance of functions, such as between teaching and research (Astin and Chang, 1995; Atkinson and Tuzin, 1992; Zemsky, Massey, and Oedel, 1993) rather than a complete overhaul of epic proportions. Some critics want to change how teaching and learning occur (Barr and Tagg, 1995), and to promote the use of new methods such as collaborative learning (Matthews, Cooper, Davidson, and Hawkes, 1995). Still others advocate improved faculty productivity (Massy and Wilger, 1995) and changes in faculty roles (Guskin, 1994) and rewards (Bland and Holloway, 1995). In all cases, the arguments are made in a tone suggesting that the goal behind them is the improvement of higher education, but not all agree on the motives.

What do such turbulent forces for change in the larger system of higher education have to do with staffing practices in student affairs? They have several effects, most notably on the power of the institution to attract well-qualified professionals to conduct the work of student affairs. They affect the confidence of the public in higher education. They affect the morale and focus of current staff members. They affect students and their sense of worth and the value attached to their education. They influence the purposes of higher education by turning the institutions toward serving more of a credentialing function and less of a life-enrichment and intel-lectual-exploration function.

Context for a Model of Staffing in Student Affairs

Mindful of these dynamic and sometimes turbulent conditions, the model of staffing focuses specifically on long-term and ongo-ing conditions within the environment of higher education. Staff-ing practices in an institution are directly related to many other conditions and forces, some from outside the institution and oth-ers that are products of the institution's culture. Figure 2.1 identi-fies some of the most important forces and conditions that affect student affairs staffing practices. The outside forces affecting the total institution are symbolized by arrows; these include economic conditions, political influences, academic reputation, and laws and regulations. Aspects of institutional culture also determine how business is conducted and have significant impacts on staffing practices in student affairs; these factors are symbolized by irreg-ular shapes to suggest that they are embedded in the culture and often taken for granted. They include geographic location, work ethos, labor agreements, affirmative action goals or mandates, ad-ministrative culture, institutional resources, and expectations of student affairs.

Economic Conditions

The world and U.S. economies change from time to time, of course, and present new and challenging demands with each fluctuation.

Employment market conditions in student affairs are generally direct reflections of the overall economic conditions in the coun-try and the number of people (especially eighteen-year-olds) seek-ing admission to higher education. In times of relative prosperity, admission applications and enrollments, especially of graduate stu-dents, tend to decline or reflect the population curve of eighteen-year-olds. The reason is that when jobs seem plentiful, potential students have more alternatives from which to select; in lean eco-nomic times, there are fewer alternatives and higher education is viewed by many recent graduates as a preferred alternative to unemployment (and living at home with parents).

Figure 2.1. Context of Student Affairs Staffing Practices.

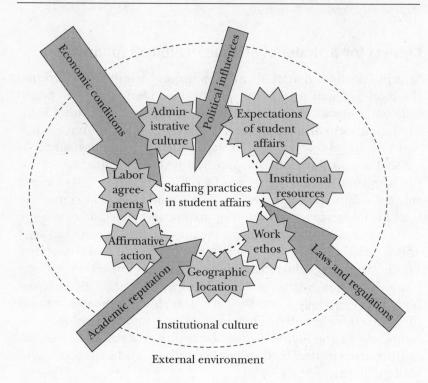

Student affairs preparation programs also are affected by these conditions; in difficult economic times, applications to these programs tend to increase, and consequently there are more entry-level applicants for student affairs positions. The amount of talent and the absolute number of qualified people who could apply for an entry-level position is, therefore, indirectly related to the overall economic conditions. Our observations suggest that there may be a moderately strong negative association between the economy and the number of qualified applicants for entry-level positions.

General economic conditions also have a larger impact on the institution. In most states, when tax revenues decline below projected levels, financial support for public higher education also declines. For many private institutions, an economic decline means that some people who would have been students are no longer able to afford the tuition. These individuals either seek enrollment at public institutions where costs are less or drop out of higher education altogether. In prolonged periods of economic stagnation or decline, public institutions are often faced with fewer resources but more students to be served. On the other hand, some private institutions feel compelled at such times to discount their tuitions through larger scholarships for more students as a means of remaining competitive with public institutions. This, of course, means less revenue for the institution, which in turn necessitates budget reductions through personnel cuts.

From the applicant's perspective, it is often difficult to understand the market conditions that affect recruitment activities. When employment opportunities are limited, whether for external or internal reasons, most persons seeking employment are disadvantaged. When many openings are available, options for the applicants are greatly expanded, but even then location may be the decisive factor for both the institution and the applicant. This is exacerbated by the phenomenon of the two-career couple. Remotely located institutions have the added disadvantage of not being able to provide opportunities for both partners in a relationship. (Some institutions, even in urban areas, have recognized this impediment to recruiting highly qualified applicants and have assumed the responsibility for assisting spouses and partners of applicants in finding employment, either within the institution or elsewhere locally.)

Political Influences

No matter the campus—public or private, large or small—there are those who have no direct legal connection with the institution but attempt to exert influence on various aspects of its functioning. Because these groups or individuals attempt to exert power over the decisions an institution's leadership must make without being directly connected to it, they may be regarded as political influences. Although it is impossible to identify them all, some of the most prominent political influencers tend to fall into several categories:

• Public office holders or would-be office holders who may see political advantage (and publicity) in either criticizing or

praising campus action or inaction, or who attempt to influence hiring or promotion decisions on behalf of constituents
or friends.

- Alumni who feel a sense of ownership of the institution and
believe they have a continued stake in what happens on campus. This concern may be expressed as defense of a beloved
staff member in jeopardy of losing a job or facing reassignment, or as an attack on a staff member who is attempting to
change past practices.
- Religious groups and spokespersons who sometimes find the
activities and beliefs of students to be shocking and worthy of
public condemnation. At religiously affiliated colleges and
universities, some church leaders may feel that they should
have direct input into some staffing decisions, even when not
given the right to do so in the institution's charter or statutes.
Even when they are not directly involved in running the
school, some such leaders may have views that need to be considered when making hiring and promotion decisions.
- Special interest groups—such as those interested in protecting
the environment, opposing the use of animals in research, or
opposing distribution of information about abortion services—
often attempt to influence an institution's policies. Such
causes may become attached to an individual staff member
who is charged with making decisions or being the public
spokesperson.
- Local community members and leaders who attempt to influence the development of programs and services or to sway
decisions about physical plant expansion. In attempts to direct
decisions, individual staff members may be placed under considerable pressure (both legitimate and otherwise).
- Parents who attempt to intercede into normal procedures on
behalf of their son or daughter. Otherwise rational and
upstanding people can sometimes become irrational, vicious,
and vindictive when they perceive that their son or daughter is
in trouble.
- Present or potential donors to the institution, either individuals or organizations, who desire to influence decision making.
- Commercial ventures that attempt to sell their products or
influence purchasing decisions.

The list of potential political influences in higher education is almost limitless; only a few are provided here as examples. Each of these political forces can have a direct impact on staffing practices in student affairs. The attempted influence may be as direct as telephone calls or letters promoting a candidate who has applied for a position, or as indirect as a politician making public statements about how an institution handles certain situations or raising questions about how public money is expended.

Potentially, all staffing practices are subject to outside political influences; they are real and should not be ignored. The integrity of staffing decisions, however, must be protected in the face of external pressure. If illicit political influences are allowed to sway staffing processes, trust in and respect for the staff can be irreparably damaged, which may substantially diminish the morale and productivity of the whole division.

Institutional Reputation

An institution's academic reputation is a major factor in its ability to recruit new personnel. Who among aspiring professionals would not want to work in one of the nation's most prestigious institutions? Being recruited, and certainly being hired, by one of these institutions is a "seal of approval"; it suggests, rightly or not, that the professional must be among the best if chosen by one of the best. It is a win-win situation that works to the advantage of both the institution already possessing prestige and to the aspiring professional craving it.

Likewise, the history of an institution may give it a particular advantage, although this may accrue merely because of the special nature of the institution. If, for example, one is attracted to an environment with a Quaker religious affiliation, relatively few institutions qualify. The range of possibilities is greatly expanded if the search is simply for an institution with a historical commitment to religious values, but even so most would be eliminated from consideration. Similarly, institutions with a military tradition may attract some professionals and repel an even larger number. The point is that academic reputation and historical purpose have powerful effects on the institution's ability to recruit new staff.

Laws and Regulations

As Kaplin and Lee (1995) observe, the laws concerning employment in higher education are quite complicated, due in large part to the fact that there are so many overlapping sources: constitutions, statutes, administrative rules and regulations, common law, and case law at both state and federal levels, as well as academic custom and usage, contracts, and institutional rules and regulations. It is beyond the scope of this work to attempt a detailed treatment of the legal issues associated with staffing in higher education, although more detailed discussions of legal parameters may be found in Chapter Five. Two of the best sources for information about legal issues related to staffing in student affairs are Kaplin and Lee (1995) and Hollander and Young (1991). Administrators should keep in mind that any decision affecting personnel has potential legal implications for the person making the decision and perhaps for the institution as well.

Another major category of regulations affects some public institutions. In some state-assisted colleges and universities, all employees are subject to the provisions of state personnel or merit systems that cover positions as wide-ranging as prison guard, secretary, road machine operator, mental hospital attendant, dietitian, laboratory technician, maintenance engineer, and computer program designer. Usually there is an exempt category of personnel that includes faculty and others, often called administrative or professional staff. The latter category frequently extends only to upper-level, and perhaps mid-level professionals, such as department directors, in student affairs; if so, the remainder of the staff may have to be shoehorned into a classification system that does not recognize their professional status. This becomes even more of a problem when the system has built-in salary ranges and caps.

Effects of Institutional Culture on Staffing

Institutional culture can be thought of as the "collective, mutually shaping patterns of institutional history, mission, physical settings, norms, traditions, values, practices, beliefs and assumptions which guide the behavior of individuals and groups . . . and which provide frames of reference for interpreting the meanings of events and actions on and off campus" (Kuh and Hall, 1993, p. 2). To understand staffing within an institution, one must also understand the context or culture in which it resides and from which it ultimately derives its meaning.

Some organizations, for example, are clearly managed from the top down; direction for work always comes from superiors, and approval for actions from the apex of the organization both formally and informally. Such a person's ideas carry more weight than those of others operating elsewhere in the organizational structure. Further, this person's style of doing business becomes the style of the organization. The reverse hierarchical pattern may be true in other institutions, but either way the manner of orienting, supervising, developing, and appraising staff is influenced or even controlled by this cultural feature.

Another example of the influence of institutional culture can be drawn from the decision-making approach (or style) of an organization. On some campuses, there is a well-known approach to decision making, and everyone knows it must be followed if one is to become an active player in a particular decision. At some Quaker institutions, for example, consensus is necessary from all in order to decide on major campus issues. In other cases, the administration is simply but very importantly committed to a belief that all views are important in any major decision and establishes procedures to guarantee widespread involvement of staff in these important matters. Significantly, these institutions invariably have a reputation for consistency of decision making that is driven in large measure by their respect for the value of each individual in the organization (a classic application of a historic student affairs value!).

Geographical Location

Realtors are fond of saying that selling property is dependent upon three things—location, location, and location. So it may be for recruitment of new staff. From the institution's perspective, location may afford multiple advantages or disadvantages in recruiting new staff, including access to qualified applicants. Potential staff may simply want to live in a certain place or are required by necessity to do so and, of course, this preference can work to the advantage of either an isolated or advantageously located institution. Potential staff often are attracted to either metropolitan areas that provide a variety of cultural amenities or to areas that offer many recreational opportunities. Institutions located near the seashore, mountains suitable for skiing, or other recreational attractions often find recruiting less difficult. As colleagues in Florida have dubbed it, staff who work there are required to pay a "sun tax," that is, smaller salaries compared to other regions of the country that have less desirable weather.

Imagine the difference in recruitment potential between a student affairs division at a major metropolitan research university with a national academic reputation and a high ranking among professionals in other colleges and universities, and one in a small teaching institution in an isolated rural area with only a local reputation. No contest. Identical advertisements for a director of student activities or residence hall director run by both institutions, as an illustration, would likely yield remarkably different results. Only extraordinary effort and some degree of luck by the small school would produce applicant pools of comparable talent and professional experience at both institutions. The result of this unequal competition for new personnel is predictable. The institution with the most favorable contexts for recruiting in most cases ends up with better educated and often more talented personnel. Institutions with better staff generally are more effective in achieving their missions. Thus the sustaining dependence of quality of education on quality of staff is evident and cannot be reversed.

From the applicant's perspective, geographic location may be the controlling factor. Some potential staff are interested only in one general location for personal reasons. Perhaps one's spouse, partner, or immediate family controls the geographical range an applicant can consider; maybe other desires, such as access to urban amenities or a concentration of persons of certain ethnicity, controls the decision. Whatever the reason, geographical location is a major factor that shapes an institution's ability to recruit highly skilled and talented new staff. The attractive locations are likely to attract the most interest by job seekers.

Institutional Resources

Perhaps the most obvious effect on staffing practices is institutional resources. Salary levels, availability of support services and technology, facilities, and staff development opportunities are determined in many cases by the level of resources available to the institution that can be assigned to student affairs operations. There is no mystery about the effect of resources on people. Those who are adequately paid and supported in their efforts through staff, equipment, and at least modest levels of discretionary spending perform better and are more effective than those who are underpaid and unsupported.

In the short run there may be exceptions to this, of course. People work hard for many reasons beyond financial rewards, and as is well known from other evidence (Herzberg, 1968) they may not be motivated by money alone, but in the wider perspective and in the long term, resources must be adequate to sustain high-quality work from high-caliber people. How many resources are available in student affairs directly affects the quality of candidates one can attract to open positions, who will accept employment offers, how long staff will stay in positions, and overall morale. In the short term, staff can often stretch resources to phenomenal lengths, but over a long period doing so is intellectually and emotionally draining and can be a major factor in staff burnout and high turnover.

Affirmative Action

Affirmative action is a complicated subject and still controversial in American society. For many in student affairs the idea of remedying past wrongs or injustices is thought a worthy social goal of education that should be pursued. Without question affirmative action is consistent with (perhaps even mandated by) the values of the profession. There is also an equally pressing pragmatic reason for promoting affirmative action in staffing: the diversity of backgrounds and ethnicity of persons available for enrollment in higher education is increasing and will do so for the foreseeable future. Consequently, student affairs staffs must reflect the composition of the student bodies if they are to be able to affect their lives. Also, as the standards of the Council for the Advancement of Standards in Higher Education state (1986, p. 6): "Where student bodies are predominantly non-disabled, of one race, sex, or religion, a diverse staffing pattern will enrich the teaching/administrative ranks and demonstrate institutional commitment to fair employment practices."

There is legitimate disagreement, however, about how to define affirmative action and what kinds of measures are acceptable in attempting to achieve the goals of social and economic justice for persons and groups who have been the objects of discrimination—specifically racial and ethnic minority group members and women. As Ponterotto (1990, pp. 5–6) notes, *affirmative action* is a widely used term in higher education, but it has no firmly established definition. There is general agreement, however, that these programs are "designed to give minority-group members—primarily racial/ethnic minorities, women, persons with disabilities, and elderly people—greater access to and support in higher education." The concept applies both to students and staff.

How the goals of affirmative action in employment are to be realized is often the source of disagreement. One school of thought argues that institutions should be color blind—that is, all vestiges of past discrimination should be eliminated so that each individual is judged solely on his or her qualifications for employment. Initiative should be taken to aggressively solicit applications from members of target groups who possess the educational backgrounds and experience needed to fill vacancies. Preference or special attention, however, should end there.

Another school of thought argues that a literal lack of discrimination is not sufficient to rectify past wrongs and injustices. This school advocates "using minority status in hiring, promotion, and retention decisions" (Bullington and Ponterotto, 1990, p. 20), which are often expressed in the form of institutional hiring quotas or employment goals. They argue that preferences should be given temporarily to persons from groups that have experienced legal discrimination in the past until the more insidious aspects of discrimination have been overcome.

No matter one's philosophical position about the best means of increasing the proportion of persons from underrepresented groups on the student affairs staff, the ultimate test is whether the approach adopted produces the desired results. If it does not, then obviously other approaches are required. Many institutions will have both official and unofficial positions about the extent to which measures to increase minority staff representation are to be used. Student affairs' staffing practices must be congruent with the institution's official position, but often there is considerable latitude in interpreting guidelines or mandates. (Statutes and regulations concerning affirmative action are summarized in Chapter Five.)

Collective Bargaining Agreements

Most of the 3,600 colleges and universities in the United States do not have collective bargaining agreements. Those that do are most prevalent in the East and Midwest and in community colleges and statewide higher education systems, and the unions tend to concentrate on support staff (such as maintenance workers, clerical and food service staff, and laboratory technicians) or faculty, sometimes both. Because student affairs does not clearly fit into any of these categories of employees, it sometimes is not included in any of the bargaining units.

The defining characteristic of a collective bargaining agreement is that it explicitly, and often in great detail, specifies the terms and conditions of employment; that is, much of what we call staffing in this book is codified in the collective bargaining agreement. Most agreements at the minimum cover hours of work, wages or salary, promotional opportunities, benefits, and job security issues such as seniority and grievance procedures (Fortunato and Waddell, 1981). Where institutions have collective bargaining agreements, a 500-pound gorilla is introduced into the staffing equation; all staffing practices must fit within the provisions of the union contract. Even if student affairs professionals are not covered by the contract, it is important that staffing practices take into account the provisions of the agreement that govern other types of institutional personnel. This restricts the range of staffing options available but also has the potential to advance the cause of the student affairs profession. As Borland (1983, p. 279) notes: "Because collective bargaining is a process that attempts to redefine and assign power, the process may provide an opportunity for student affairs professionals to preserve the integrity of their institutional roles."

Administrative Culture

The administrative culture refers to both what is emphasized by the administration and how it is carried out. It is part of the larger institutional culture, but requires careful attention in order to understand the dynamics that affect staffing practices.

Birnbaum (1988) identified four models of organizational functioning that capture important differences in administrative culture at colleges and universities and that have tremendous influence on how student affairs is structured and even on its assigned mission. He labeled them collegial, bureaucratic, political, and anarchical.

The Collegial Model

This is most evident in small (usually private) liberal arts colleges. Hierarchy within the administration is de-emphasized; interaction patterns among faculty and administrators are informal and frequent. The collegial organization "is egalitarian and democratic, and members of the administration and faculty consider each other as equals, all of whom have the right and opportunity for discussion and influence . . ." (p. 88). Tradition, observance of social conventions, informal status, and the valence of interpersonal relationships play significant roles in the decision-making process. Decision making is by consensus, and though unanimity is not required, it is extremely important that everyone feel that his or her point of view is heard and considered seriously. Such institutions have "administrations to provide support services and to represent the college's interests to its various publics, but the administration is understood to be subordinate to the collegium [the faculty] and carries out the collegium's will" (p. 89).

The Bureaucratic Model

In the public mind, this model connotes all that is wrong with organizations—red tape, slow decision making, blame shifting, and arcane rules and regulations that mask bureaucrats' lack of interest in the people of the organization. A certain level of bureaucracy becomes unavoidable once organizations reach a size such that its members cannot reasonably expect to communicate directly with all other members on a regular basis. As Birnbaum (1988, pp. 106–107) explains: "As organizations grow, the number of subunits (such as departments) increases, these subunits become increasingly specialized, and administrative structures become more complex. . . . Interaction decreases, and norms become confused and no longer serve to control behavior." Bureaucracy seems to be a reasonable response to such conditions.

As with all other organizations, colleges and universities are subject to the same forces that encourage the bureaucratic model. Collegial interaction within a bureaucratic structure can and does still exist, but it occurs in subgroups or units rather than the total organization. Rules and policies regulate interactions and relationships rather than face-to-face communication. "Administrators spend little time with faculty and talk instead to other administrators and to external nonfaculty audiences in state legislatures, professional associations, and boardrooms" (Birnbaum, 1988, p. 107). Faculty also tend to limit collegial relationships to those within their often narrowly defined disciplines or research interests.

The definitive tools of bureaucratic organizations are the organizational chart (which identifies the lines of authority and communication and represents the formal division of labor), specialization into and within functional areas, hierarchical decision making, written rules and policies designed to cover as wide a range of situations and behaviors as possible, and careful record keeping. Research suggests that the forms on which information is stored and the conventions used to analyze data affect the institution's perception of its environment (Pfeffer, 1981) and place parameters on the alternative courses of action an institution will consider (Cyert and March, 1963).

The Political Model

This model of organizational functioning (Birnbaum, 1988) is possible only under certain conditions: when there are multiple semi-autonomous groups that have different (sometimes incompatible) values and interests; when no single group can impose its will on all the others (that is, power is diffuse); when institutional goals are multiple and lack specificity; and when there are insufficient resources available to accomplish all legitimate goals (that is, when choices must be made among competing "goods," not between "goods" and "bads").

Decisions in this model are made through the exercise of power. Power is acquired by building coalitions with other groups in regard to a given issue, which usually requires making trade-offs and compromises. The situation is made more complicated by the fact that groups and coalitions are constantly changing, depending on the issues under consideration. Further instability in coalitions is common because the people who compose the various groups do not always agree.

There are six basic sources of power within an institution that operates as a basically political organization (French and Raven, 1959; Bacharach and Lawler, 1980; Moore, 1993):

- Coercive power is the ability to punish in order to achieve an aim. This kind of power is evident through disciplinary actions (dismissal of an employee, for example), job actions by a union, or withholding funds for a project.
- Reward power is the ability to give something valued by another. For an individual it might be a salary increase or promotion to a higher-level position. For groups it might be willingness to share resources such as facilities or staff or allowing participation in important institutional deliberations.
- Expert power comes from possession of specialized knowledge. People in certain professions such as law, medicine, and computer technology generally hold such power in institutions.
- Referent power is based on identification with another person. Charismatic leaders often possess power through the deference of others. Persons who have established connections with outside funding sources such as government agencies, potential fund donors, or foundations that award research grants also can exert referent power.
- Legitimate or bureaucratic power derives from one's position within the organization. Presidents, deans, and vice presidents have assigned spheres of responsibility over which the governing body (board of trustees, for instance) gives them authority to make certain kinds of decisions and to enforce certain rules and policies.
- Power based on information derives from the fact that certain parts of an organization have responsibility for collecting and disseminating information (about enrollments, available funds, or institutional expenses, for example). There are often many ways that this information can be collected, analyzed, and distributed to others within the organization; how these

processes are handled (or whether or not information is made public) can create advantage for various groups, thus making the holder of the information powerful.

If the definitive tool of the bureaucratic model is the organizational chart, then the budget is the scorecard in the political model. As Birnbaum (1988, p. 136) notes: "The allocation [of funds] decision is primarily a political one of who gets what, when, and how, and in a democratic and pluralistic organization, political processes are appropriate means for resolving such political issues."

Because the political model is based on competition for resources, one might expect such organizations to be in constant turmoil. This is usually not the case, however, for three reasons. First, organizations tend to develop relatively long-lasting dominant coalitions whose established power discourages challenges. Second, individuals belong to multiple subgroups within the organization that necessitates their participating in many political processes involving different people, which creates a system of interpersonal checks and balances. Third, "disruptive conflict is inhibited because power in higher education tends to be issue specific. Different groups develop spheres of influence around issues of concern for them" (Birnbaum, 1988, p. 137), which serves to create tacit agreements among the groups. For example, presidents usually leave faculty recruiting to deans or department heads; faculty leave fundraising to the president; deans leave course development to the faculty; and everyone leaves working with fraternities and sororities to student affairs. To transgress into a tacit sphere of influence is certain to be challenged and may be costly for the intruder. Political models can best be conceptualized as generally being in a state of dynamic equilibrium.

The Anarchical Model

First proposed by Cohen and March (1974), this model is quite different from the other three and is most commonly found at large public research universities. It is counterintuitive because it maintains that there are no cause and effect reactions, or if there are, it is difficult to identify which ones they are.

This model has several identifiable characteristics. Members of the organization have a high degree of autonomy; that is, they do what they think best at the time. Also, according to Birnbaum

(1988, p. 153), "Resources are allocated by whatever process emerges but without explicit accommodation and without explicit reference to some superordinate goals." Indeed, goals are vague and very broad and are often developed after some action has already been taken. For example, an institution receives a large gift for construction of a science laboratory; the gift is accepted and plans for construction get under way; the institution then decides to offer a new doctoral program in the area to attract well-known faculty to the laboratory.

The educational process, or what Birnbaum calls the technology of converting inputs to outputs, is unclear in the anarchical model. Because there is no agreement about goals, educational philosophy, desired outcomes, or creditable evidence about the relative merits of different approaches, the various members of the organization are free to use whatever techniques seem to work for them. Participation is fluid; who is involved in what decisions changes rapidly (especially in the institutional governance structure), membership on faculty committees changes often, and which members are present at any given meeting frequently is a surprise. Issues are frequently complicated by having unrelated matters attached to them. For instance, a decision about whether to increase the student activity fee might have attached to it a decision about remodeling a classroom building that is poorly located, because the faculty senate argues that "academic needs" should be addressed before "extracurricular activities."

None of the four models can accurately describe the organizational functioning of any college or university all the time. Some models may fit better and explain more at one time than another. So, what is their value?

As Birnbaum (1988, p. 83) so cogently notes, models of organizational functioning are abstractions of reality and are useful because they are abstractions. "A model . . . allows us to understand (and sometimes to predict) some of the dynamics of the system that it represents. Models are seldom right or wrong; they are just more or less useful for examining different aspects of organizational functioning. A model serves as a conceptual lens that focuses our attention on some particular organizational dimensions; but in the process of doing so it inevitably obscures or obliterates other dimensions."

Complex organizations in higher education include aspects of each of these cultures; the reality is that they always interact with one another and often conflict and compete. Such interaction of cultures affects styles and content of decisions in direct and indirect ways, influences the manner of orientation of new staff, and may literally control institutionalized staffing practices. The culture may set the pace for work, for example, and determine the standards for judging personal and professional effectiveness of the staff.

Understanding how the organization of which one is a member tends to function (at least most of the time) is essential to establishing effective staffing practices. For example, if one works in a basically collegial institution, it is very important to closely identify with and establish close relationships with the informal faculty leaders. Careful attention needs to be exercised to select staff who can clearly identify with the college's mission and history and who can establish rapport with faculty and students.

On the other hand, if the institution basically operates along the lines of a political model, then student affairs administrators need to pay careful attention to building and maintaining good interpersonal and professional relationships with powerful players in the system, such as the president, academic vice president, chief business officer, and favorably placed academic deans or chairpersons. Moore (1993) also recommends other strategies for the chief student affairs administrator:

- Follow carefully and do homework on the issues the institution faces (whether they directly affect student affairs or not). Doing so "will be helpful in establishing a reputation as an officer or professional with institutionwide interests and roles" (p. 161).
- Strive to be highly competent as a student affairs professional and as a politician. Appearance and reality are both important. It is important to stay abreast of new developments in the field and within the institution and to offer innovative solutions to problems as they arise.
- Maintain high visibility on the campus and in the community. "Being visible simply means attending meetings, socials, and programs of importance to various important constituencies

within and without the college or university" (p. 162). In political organizations staffing practices must be sensitive to select mid-level practitioners who understand and are accomplished at working in such systems. It is also important to establish student affairs as an important player within the institution and to build relationships with other powerful players in order to create tacit agreements that certain areas of institutional life are the legitimate domain of student affairs.

Work Ethos

Work ethos refers to the traditions, beliefs, and commitments toward expending human energy in the completion of responsibilities. The ethos for work varies among institutions and is firmly embedded in the institution's culture. In many institutions, it is not uncommon to hear the comment, "We work very hard around here." But sometimes this borders on the unhealthy, demanding time and energy from staff that, for more balanced and healthful living, should be invested in their personal lives. The point, however, is not whether the ethos is carried to extremes but that it exists in an obvious way and serves very directly to shape staffing practices. These effects are especially evident in the orientation of new staff to their positions and in the supervisory practices sanctioned at the institution. What might be considered going above and beyond reasonable work expectations at one institution may be considered routine at another.

Expectations of Student Affairs

Expectations of student affairs as both a part of the educational process and as an administrative unit are especially variable across campuses. In some cases, student affairs are assigned responsibilities central to everything that occurs involving students. For example, at Gallaudet College, the federally supported college for the deaf, student affairs delivers multiple absolutely vital services directly to individuals and groups of students through such practices as tutoring and extensive peer and professional counseling. But expectations for student affairs vary markedly from such a model. In some small liberal arts colleges, many traditional student affairs functions are incorporated into the activities of faculty and other administrators; that contrasts with large community colleges where recruitment, enrollment management, and the advising of students are handled exclusively by student affairs divisions.

An early career experience by one of the authors illustrates both an institution's work ethos and its expectations of student affairs. Coming from a larger institution into a new position, he was accustomed to attending and directly supporting the activities of the student groups and organizations for which he had responsibility or close contact. Attendance at other student-sponsored or student-led activities was purely a matter of interest. He applied that rule at his new position at a smaller college, but soon began receiving comments many mornings that he had not been seen at the previous evening's reception, play, speaker program, basketball game, or other activity. He finally realized that the expectation of that institution was for senior administrators to attend as many evening student functions as possible—especially if the college's president was scheduled to be in attendance. The norm for student affairs administrators was to be on the campus between forty-five and fifty-five hours per week when classes were in session, and they were expected to be present at most public events.

The cumulative result of these factors and their multiple interactions with the staffing practices of recruitment and selection, orientation, supervision, staff development, and performance appraisal is the delivery of educational programs and services to students and to the institution.

A Model of Staffing in Student Affairs

Firmly embedded within the institutional culture and often affected by events and forces outside the college or university, student affairs staffing practices involve five interlinked and overlapping constellations of activities: recruitment and selection, orientation to new position, supervision, staff development, and performance appraisal. These activities are depicted in Figure 2.2. Each is best seen as a process, often ongoing, rather than as a periodic recurring event. Brief overviews of the components of the staffing model follow; detailed discussions of each component may be found in Chapters Five through Nine.

Figure 2.2. Components of Staffing in Student Affairs.

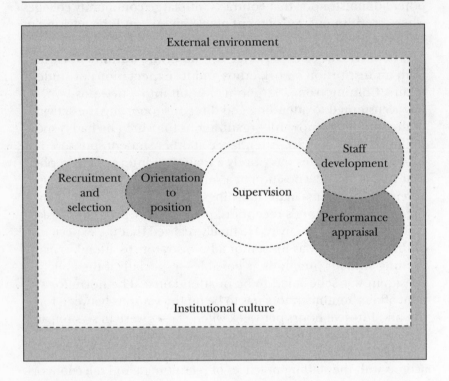

Recruitment and Selection

Probably the most crucial aspect of the staffing process is recruitment and selection of persons to perform the work that needs to be done. Mistakes made at this stage can have widespread and long-lasting effects. Employing a person who is not suited for work in student affairs or in the particular institutional setting can seldom be overcome and can impede the achievement of high quality student affairs operations.

Recruitment and selection include the following processes:

- Determining the purpose of the position.
- Conducting position analysis (that is, determining exactly what the position holder will be expected to do), which is usually formally expressed in the position description.

- Preparing the position announcement, including establishing time frames and application procedures (for example, what in addition to a résumé or vita is required for application).
- Empowering the search committee. This includes providing a specific charge as to what is to be done, conducting an orientation that covers institutional procedures, affirmative action considerations, and facilitating the committee in establishing its own working rules and processes.
- Applying ethical and legal standards.
- Advertising the position. Institutional budgets, time of the year, affirmative action considerations, and institutional tradition generally determine the extent to which positions are advertised beyond the institution.
- Conducting the search. It is essential that applicants have a contact person who can answer questions and ensure that applications are carefully assembled.
- Screening applicants. On most campuses this is the primary duty of search committees.
- Interviewing finalists. Following the work of the search committee, which generally results in a list of recommendations of persons to be invited for interview, the actual decision about who to invite should be made in accordance with the plan announced at the beginning of the search process. It is generally a good idea for a wide cross-section of the student affairs staff, as well as others such as students, faculty, and business affairs personnel, to interview candidates and provide evaluations to the hiring authority.
- Making position offers. Offers and any negotiations that may be required are usually best handled by direct supervisors.

Orientation to New Position

The orientation process actually begins when the new staff member applies for the position. The institution should respond to applications by providing information about the requirements of the position, the goals and general approach of the department and division, and specific information about the institution—its mission, history, people, and culture. During the on-campus interview the candidate should have opportunities to get additional firsthand information about job expectations and the people with whom she or he will work, as well as a sampling of the facilities.

After the person is hired and arrives on campus, a systematic orientation process should be provided. (This may be one-on-one or in small groups depending on the time of the year and whether there are other new staff at the time.) Essential components of the orientation process include educational philosophy and operating procedures of the institution, division, and subunits; institutional and student affairs cultures; detailed exposition of expectations for professional and personal performance (particularly supervision and performance appraisal methods); and introduction to faculty, staff, and students with whom the new job holder will have frequent contact.

Staff who change positions within the division also deserve a systematic orientation to new duties, responsibilities, and relationships. It need not be as extensive as that offered to persons new to the institution, but one should not assume that just because people have been employed at a college or university for some time they have a full grasp of things outside their previous spheres of responsibilities. They seldom do.

Supervision

Supervision is a management function intended to promote the achievement of institutional goals and to enhance the personal and professional capabilities and performance of staff. In our model it is the linchpin that holds the other components of the model together. The functional components of supervision include the following:

- Articulating the unit's mission and needs
- Monitoring and managing the unit climate
- Fostering individual development of staff
- Developing teamwork capabilities and group resources
- Coordinating work activities
- Promoting active problem solving

We propose a somewhat new approach to this task called *synergistic supervision.* An important characteristic of synergistic supervision is that it has a dual focus on accomplishment of the organization's goals and on support of staff in accomplishment of their personal and professional development goals. Furthermore, it is based on joint effort, requires two-way communication, focuses on competences, and is growth oriented, goal based, systematic and ongoing, and holistic.

Staff Development

To be successful, staff development should be directly and obviously tied to the supervision and performance appraisal processes. Through the supervision process the staff member and supervisor should identify areas where personal and professional growth is desired, and it is through the staff development process that these areas can be addressed. Through performance appraisal, accomplishments and areas of needed improvement are documented.

Staff development in this model has a dual purpose: individual staff and organizational improvement. For staff development to be effective it should correspond to a developmental plan for individuals and the organization, and it must be anchored to day-to-day work. Means for reaching these goals, however, should not necessarily be equated with organized programs such as workshops, speakers, or conferences. For individuals important staff development may be acquired through individualized techniques such as coaching, conducting independent research, assuming responsibility for new activities, or working in professional organizations. Organizations are strengthened when the staff who work in them become more knowledgeable or skilled and when they have good esprit d'corps.

Performance Appraisal

To be effective, performance appraisals must be intrinsically tied to both supervision and staff development. In this model, performance appraisal is an organizational system comprising deliberate processes for determining staff accomplishments for the purpose of improving their effectiveness. Though seemingly simple and straightforward, performance appraisal that actually contributes to improved performance is difficult to achieve. Almost universally in higher education, performance appraisal is viewed negatively because it criticizes people's efforts, or indifferently because it is only a paper exercise that has little to do with any other part of organizational life or work conditions.

Performance appraisals demand certain system requirements to be successful. These include a dual focus on staff and organization improvement; a meaningful relationship between institutional productivity and reward systems; recognition of certain contextual standards concerning the contribution of both environment and staff member to effective performance; clear, open, and fair procedures; constant participation and review of position requirements; and recognition of the contribution of certain appraiser attributes in effective performance appraisal.

It is our conviction that performance appraisal can be a constructive process for both individuals and organizations, but it requires sensitivity and integration with the supervision and staff development processes.

Summary

The kinds of people hired into a student affairs division—their personal characteristics and knowledge, skills, values, and motivations—is affected by the institution's culture, geographical location, and political context. The level of skills and the depth of experience staff members possess as they enter the institution determine the extent and content of orientation needed. Similarly, these variables have a direct bearing on the content and intensity of supervision needed. There is a direct connection between individual staff supervision and the staff development program and activities offered by the institution; it is through supervision that the institution can determine the educational needs of its staff. Supervision is likewise directly connected to performance appraisal. Performance appraisal is a formalized extension of the supervision process, not a substitute for it.

Staffing is an integrated and interdependent system of organizational practices. Examining any component of the system in isolation may lead to superficial insight into the practices. The staffing system in student affairs is complex and must be considered as a whole to gain full understanding.

Chapter Three

Current Staffing Practices
Case Studies

As a means of seeking insight into the routines and customs of staffing in divisions of student affairs, we designed a qualitative study that would provide multiple perspectives. This chapter reports the findings from our firsthand study of eight institutions. It presents methods used in the development of case studies at each institution chosen, followed by brief summaries of each case, and finally a synthesis of the cases to identify hallmarks of staffing practices.

This case study method enabled us to observe the campus milieu and to acquire a feel for staffing practices, which is not possible through other methods. The approach allowed us to talk with many practitioners in the course of doing their jobs and learn about their motives for pursuing certain activities as well as about more apparent behaviors. It allowed us to raise questions as they occurred to us, to follow conversations propelled by the interests of practicing staff members, and to make inquiries into the manner in which their staffing practices are driven by policies, institutional culture, force of personalities in leadership roles, or by ad hoc circumstances. Such fortuitous opportunities arose within an a priori plan for data collection; that is, the use of the semistructured interview protocol shown in Appendix C.

Our methods for data collection at each site, therefore, were guided by a plan that was systematically used at each institution and was flexible enough to enable incidental collection of important information.

Case Study Methods

Selection of institutions for study was influenced by the structure of the large-scale survey in the sense that we wanted to examine staffing practices at four types of institutions: research universities, comprehensive state colleges and universities, liberal arts colleges, and two-year community colleges. Thus, we decided to select two exemplary cases from each category according to three criteria: reputation for a quality student affairs program, geographical convenience and accessibility to the researchers, and willingness of the chief student affairs administrator and the staff to cooperate in the study. Initially, the plan was to select institutions for on-site study through a nomination process associated with questionnaires sent earlier to vice presidents inviting them to designate institutions with exemplary student affairs staffing practices. A small number of nominations were received; however, invariably they dealt with a single unit or a special program within a division of student affairs. As our interest was in the totality of student affairs divisions, this approach was abandoned in favor of a process based upon reputation of the overall student affairs operation. In consultation with other scholars and practitioners who have a national perspective on student affairs programs, a consensus list of institutions emerged that met the criterion of "reputation for quality student affairs practice among national leaders in the profession."

Eight institutions were selected: the University of Maryland-College Park and Florida State University (research universities), James Madison University and the University of North Carolina-Wilmington (comprehensive state universities), the University of Richmond and Samford University (small—less than 5,000 students—liberal arts colleges), and Broward Community College and Johnson County Community College (two-year community colleges). Each was nominated more than once as enjoying a widespread reputation for outstanding student affairs programs. The criterion for nomination was overall excellence in student affairs operations and programs for institutions of their type. There was no attempt, however, to identify exemplary or flawless student affairs divisions nor to identify the best or premier student affairs programs at each institutional type. As the staff in each program studied readily admitted, each has areas that need improvement or enhancement and practices that need revision.

Permission to conduct the case study was given by the vice president at each institution. The on-site studies were conducted during March and April 1995, following final approval by the vice presidents of the research methods to be employed at each site.

Data collection methods required at least one of the two principal researchers to visit each campus to conduct individual and group interviews with selected staff members in the student affairs division. Effort was made to include as many members of the staff as possible in the interviews, which were conducted on-site over two days. The first case study was conducted by both researchers, partly as an act of self-training to ensure consistency of methodology in all other case studies. This initial study was conducted at the University of Maryland-College Park, a large, sprawling, complex university with a comprehensive program of student affairs that also is well integrated into other university programs and operations. It proved a suitable learning ground for the researchers, who discovered an openness and seriousness by staff members at all levels of the organization to discuss staffing practices. The interview protocol designed for the case studies worked well, allowing for a natural flow of conversation while issues were systematically explored with staff members interviewed one-on-one or in groups.

The same protocol was used for both individual and group interviews; it was intended to allow staff members to describe their formal and informal staffing practices in their own words. Informants were guided by the researchers to ensure that they commented on all areas of staffing included within the overall research design. They were asked explicitly to comment upon the five areas of staffing practices included in the overall study:

• Recruitment and selection of new staff
• Orientation of new staff
• Supervision of staff
• Staff development activities and practices
• Performance appraisal of staff

Informants also were asked about their perceptions of distinctive features of their institutional practices, both good and bad. Every effort was made to allow informants ample opportunities to provide an accurate picture of their staffing practices without being confined by the researchers' preconceived notions of the type of information they should share. The vice presidents at each site and five to ten other top- or mid-level staff were interviewed individually. The vice president or a member of his or her staff arranged the interviews prior to the researchers' arrival on campus; the only guideline specified by the researchers was a desire to interview department heads or other mid-level staff in the functional areas (if part of the student affairs division on that campus) of enrollment management, campus activities, housing, health services, and student support services.

Group interviews with six to twelve staff members accomplished two purposes. First, they allowed the researchers to hear from as many staff members in the division of student affairs as possible within the two-day format, and second, they allowed for the possibility that a different type of information might be revealed in a social setting with colleagues where one person's comments play off another's. Often the dynamics of group discussions yielded a different type or different level of information from that obtained in individual interviews. In those cases, information obtained in groups tended to serve the important purpose of confirming that obtained in individual interviews. Frequently, group interviews provided insights into the institutional culture and a demonstration of the nature of intergroup dynamics among staff members and departments that in the individual sessions were absent or too subtle for the interviewers to grasp. Group interviews also were used to test generalizations formulated during the course of individual interviews about the nature of the institution, relationships among units in the student affairs division, and the division with other components of the institution; this often dispelled some of the researchers' misconceptions or corrected inaccurate information. The number of staff interviewed at each site depended, of course, on the size of the institution; the range was from thirty at the University of Maryland-College Park to twelve at Samford University.

Publications such as student handbooks, catalogues, descriptions of staff development activities, and staff manuals were examined. Other written documents pertaining to student affairs staffing practices were reviewed when available; however, it was discovered that very few such documents exist at the case study sites beyond the most general, institution-level policies that apply to all persons employed by the institution. With the exceptions of Johnson County Community College and the University of North Carolina-Wilmington, staffing practices at the case study sites are not guided by division-level written policies, but more by informal, though often strongly held and defended, beliefs and commitments of selected individuals within the division.

Verification

Following the on-site visits, a written description of the staffing practices was prepared by the researcher who visited the site. It was read by the second researcher, primarily for coherence and consistency with the chosen style for the study, revised if necessary, and sent to the case site for confirmation of the accuracy of information in it and to get permission to use direct quotes from those who participated in the interviews. This verification process (shown in Appendix C) was followed by the redrafting of the case report into an abbreviated version for presentation in this chapter. Analysis of the cases, searching for themes of commonality and dissimilarities in staffing practices across the sites, was conducted using the full case descriptions, however.

As expected, the institutions chosen for these case studies exemplify high-quality student affairs practice. There was universal recognition of this by participants in the study; the individuals included in the interviews know they work in environments with records of success in student affairs services and programs. They were proud to discuss their practices and to reveal many underlying organizational constructs associated with their practices. Most staff members were candid in their conversations with the researchers and did not seem reticent to discuss crucial, sometimes controversial, issues or to describe some less-than-ideal practices at their institutions.

Case Studies

Brief descriptions of each of the cases studied are presented here by type of institution to provide a glimpse of the essence or the spirit of staffing practices at each site. These vignettes were patterned after the more detailed case studies written for each institution and provide the highlights of the most distinguishing features of each divisional program. The research universities are presented first, then comprehensive state universities, liberal arts colleges, and two-year colleges.

University of Maryland-College Park

The University of Maryland-College Park (UMCP) is a research university located in the metropolitan area of Washington, D.C. The institution's student affairs division and its programs and services to students are considered top-notch in the student affairs profession.

Part of this reputation for excellence is due to William (Bud) Thomas, who has served the institution for more than twenty years and earned distinction within the profession for his accomplishments. Without being dictatorial, Thomas has a reputation within the institution as a firm and clear source of authority about all matters pertaining to student affairs practice. He articulates the mission of the university and sets the standards of performance expectations for all student affairs staff within the context of that mission.

Thomas knows what he stands for and what he expects from his staff. He operates from a position of principle that he can, and often does, articulate with ringing clarity. Examples of principled stances on matters of student affairs practice include his 85 percent–15 percent principle—he seeks to give department heads 85 percent of the decision-making responsibility while reserving 15 percent for circumstances where he must assume responsibility— and his expectation that his staff be "the best in the business." Surprisingly, however, though his signature is everywhere he rarely is heavy-handed in his relations with staff. To the contrary, directors and staff members alike speak of self-responsibility, self-directness, collaboration, connectedness, and goal-oriented actions. They are empowered by Thomas to act in certain ways and they know it.

The hiring decision is crucial at UMCP. All other staffing practices hinge on recruiting and selecting the right person. Following that, UMCP seems geared to accustom the new staff member to the institution and its way of doing business, to oversee his or her actions, and to set high expectations for performance.

Most practices pertaining to recruitment and selection of staff are routine. The university advertises vacant positions, uses search committees, screens for finalists, and interviews them in a fairly conventional manner. It is looking for the person who best fits the announced position, and is fanatic about checking references. Two other things stand out about UMCP recruitment and selection. First, the division is committed to diversity and takes the goal very seriously; each unit of student affairs has its own affirmative action officer. Second, it seems to have an "incestuous relationship" (Thomas's phrase that in this case describes a very positive result) with the graduate preparation programs at the university, which has resulted in a high percentage of current staff holding degrees from the institution.

Orientation practices are not especially visible at UMCP; however, they are present nevertheless. The university conducts orientation programs for new staff; so do units within the division of student affairs. Unit approaches include a "new blood committee" in the Counseling Center, extensive training prior to assuming duties in Residence Life, use of a checklist package of all things to review with new personnel in the Health Center, and cross-training in Records and Registration.

Supervision ranks second in importance only to the hiring decision in staffing practices at UMCP. Though supervision often is customized by units of the division, it is afforded considerable time and energy by those charged with supervisory responsibilities. Some supervisors appear more casual than others about the duty, especially with certain employees, but more seem very structured or organized about it. Some assign very sweeping organizational goals to supervision, including achieving goals, maximizing the use of resources, facilitating the growth of individual staff members, developing ownership among staff about where the unit is going, and promoting close working relationships. For others, the duty includes helping staff members prepare for their next jobs. One supervisor seemed to capture the attitude of many when she said, "Never skip over the fundamentals of supervising."

Opportunities for staff development are plentiful at UMCP. Part of the reason is location; some potentially rich learning opportunity is available every day in the Washington area. Add to this that the university provides many opportunities supplemented by serious commitment and abundant action in the division of student affairs, and every staff member has a plethora of chances to grow on the job. Many actions are intentional, such as bringing in many speakers from outside the university, providing one of the most successful regional conferences in the country on campus every year, expecting staff to participate in professional conferences on and off campus, and seizing every critical moment to learn from everyday experiences. One supervisor underscored a prevailing attitude about staff development in the division when he said, "Staff development is the most appropriate way to demonstrate to staff that the supervisor and the institution are invested in each person's success."

The least well-accomplished staffing practice at UMCP is performance appraisal, though some supervisors use an approach built around conferences with staff and the use of preconference worksheets that they believe works well. There is no hint that appraisal practices are not occurring at UMCP, only that they are less formal than other staffing procedures. Plans are emerging to revamp these procedures for the entire university. When this occurs—according to Thomas it is on the way—student affairs supervisors will follow the university's lead.

In sum, the student affairs staffing practices at UMCP exhibit a self-assured supervisory staff who see themselves as the best in the business. That may seem to smack of cockiness, but in reality it appears more a reflection of individual and collective pride.

Florida State University

Florida State University (FSU) is one of two major state universities in Florida; it is located almost within sight of the state capitol in Tallahassee. It enrolls nearly 30,000 students, primarily from Florida, of which the majority enter as transfer students. Approximately 5,000 of them live on campus.

Because of the proximity to the state capitol, everything that happens at FSU has the potential of becoming a political issue. Students, especially those in the student government association (SGA) that has considerable authority over allocation of activity-fee funds, tend to be politically sophisticated and frequently appeal directly to the legislature or the state higher education governing board to accomplish their goals or satisfy their interests; several staff members commented that some student leaders see SGA as a proving ground for future political careers. Interviewed staff members say they frequently consider the potential political interpretations of the decisions they are called upon to make.

Over the last ten years, the institution has experienced several changes in the positions of president and vice president for student affairs. The current vice president for student affairs, Jon C. Dalton, has been in place since 1989, however, and there has been very little turnover in department head and other mid-level leadership positions in the division.

Several features distinguish Florida State's staffing practices: a tradition of excellence, a symbiotic relationship between the student affairs division and the professional preparation program, high morale and productivity in an era of shrinking financial resources, a high level of commitment to staff development, and an innovative approach to management of the division.

The student affairs division has a long tradition of excellence that has persisted through changes in the head of the institution and the division. As the strategic plan states, the division "enjoys a reputation of being a national leader in quality programs, visibility/leadership of professional staff, comprehensiveness of programs, linkages with academic programs and integration of student development theory and practice." There seems to be a widely held belief across the division that it is the best in terms of programs, services, and personnel. In areas where there are acknowledged problems, staff members view them as temporary conditions that can and will be resolved in the foreseeable future. Longtime staff members often express a high level of loyalty to the institution and report feeling a responsibility to maintain high standards. Pride of membership in a unit that has a distinguished record of accomplishment, however, has not led to complacency or smugness; new problems and issues are not ignored but recognized and addressed with the confidence that comes from a tradition of past success and a belief in the staff's skills, knowledge, dedication, and resolve. One might conclude that the staff has a healthy level of professional arrogance based in optimism and a solid record of achievement.

Another differentiating feature of FSU's staffing practices is the close symbiotic relationship between the student affairs division and the professional preparation program in the department of educational leadership led by Barbara Mann. Graduate students are used extensively to supplement the staff in the division through assistantships and unpaid internships. A large percentage of the staff also has one or more degrees from FSU. The graduate program in higher education, led for many years by the late Melvene Hardee, serves as a magnet to attract talented and promising students; in turn, the division supports students in the program through assistantships, part-time positions, and placements for internships. In addition, a significant proportion of staff members has received graduate training at FSU, either pursuing a degree after joining the staff or being hired full-time after initially coming to FSU to pursue a graduate degree in higher education. Also, a number of senior staff members serve as adjunct faculty in the preparation program; this makes for a high degree of loyalty to and support for the preparation program by the professional staff and provides a pool of eager professionals-in-training who desire to contribute to the division's mission.

Shrinking or stagnating resources for the support of higher education in Florida is a widely recognized problem and cause for concern within the student affairs division. One of the areas most affected by this is entry-level position starting salaries, which are relatively low. Committed to recruiting nationally, the division has experienced some difficulty from time to time in attracting top-notch candidates, especially African Americans, for entry-level positions outside housing. This has been offset to a considerable degree by aggressive recruitment of local and regional minority candidates and the institution's reputation based on high visibility through professional organization leadership. With ever-increasing demands for services by students and increasing numbers of students entering the institution with serious problems, there is grave concern about whether the division can continue to respond to the demands placed on it and still maintain the current level of quality. The optimism the division has traditionally shown when presented with new challenges is being put to the test.

Florida State has a well-established and extensive staff development program. The division's program is overseen by a committee headed by a strong department director; programs involve social events, speakers, and topical issues. Social events include holiday parties, a fall breakfast for all employees, and a spring "Big Top Picnic" for families held in conjunction with the Florida State Circus program that showcases student talent. Each summer an ice cream social is held to which "friends of student affairs" (for example, select faculty members and maintenance workers) are also invited. Speakers include people of national prominence, often appearing in conjunction with other programs offered by the university or other professional association events in the area. Members of the staff also provide information about FSU's students garnered through research conducted on campus. Other programs are planned to address situations identified through needs assessments and in response to active social and political issues. An important staff development activity is the annual Institute on College Student Values conference sponsored by FSU. Some staff members have opportunities to be involved in the planning and presentation of the conference, and most of them attend the sessions. Staff development is also seen as a personal responsibility; to the extent budgets permit, all professionals are given travel funds to allow them to attend national and regional conferences and workshops.

Dalton has an interesting division management approach. Instead of attempting to deal individually with department directors and deans on a routine basis, he divides leaders at this level into three management teams; on a biweekly basis, each team meets with him and with his associate or assistant vice presidents to deal with whatever issues require attention. Dalton describes the process as management team building based on principles of democratic leadership. By dealing openly with issues and problems occurring in one functional area with others in the division, greater creativity is available to solve problems, and collaboration and collegiality across functional areas are promoted. (Day to day supervision of department directors, however, remains the responsibility of assistant and associate vice presidents.) Also, biweekly central staff (department head) meetings are held to share information, hear guest speakers, or discuss broad policy issues; these are customarily much more general in content than management team meetings and are not seen as decision-making sessions.

In summary, many of Florida State's staffing practices are similar to those of other large state universities. Certainly FSU is beset with many of the problems similar institutions face—for example, a lack of resources to successfully compete nationally for highly qualified ethnic-minority staff candidates, greater demand for services but fewer resources, and student bodies that need and expect more assistance than is available. Relatively low pay in entry-level positions in some functional areas makes attracting highly qualified candidates from outside the system challenging.

Florida State's accomplishments seem largely to reflect having attracted staff members who are motivated by things other than material rewards and who have developed a high sense of loyalty to the institution. A potent work ethic seems to run throughout the division; staff are expected to work long and hard, and they do. A tradition of excellence in the student affairs division has established a standard to which current staff members aspire and that serves to help keep morale high. Pride and professionalism seem to be cornerstones of the culture.

James Madison University

Certain artifacts of the culture of the institution govern staffing practices at James Madison University (JMU). In the words of Robert (Bob) Scott, the fifteen-year veteran vice president for student affairs, these include "a caring attitude toward students and a caring attitude toward colleagues." Though these attitudes often are ascribed to Ronald E. Carrier, president of JMU, who richly deserves much of the credit for inculcating the campuswide demeanor of care, the affectionate milieu was evident in Madison College, the immediate ancestor to JMU, and was wisely left intact and nurtured by public proclamations when the institution became a university.

The culture of care at JMU forms a solid core value of the institution and a cornerstone for all staffing practices in student affairs. Staff proudly speak of "the JMU way," which appears to mean putting students first in all actions: "Students are number one here!" As a corollary, faculty and staff are often referred to as number two in the strategy. In public statements, if faculty is not described as second only to students, then "the JMU family" is. However it is stated, the message is consistent: the core value of the JMU culture is caring about students and about staff.

This powerful factor spills over to create a proviso of staffing at JMU: fitting into the environment is paramount in all hiring decisions. Significantly, the sought-after fit is not one-sided; that is, the determination is not made simply to ensure that new staff are comfortable with the institution, but that they will have something to contribute to it in a variety of ways. The doctrine of ensuring that new staff fit in has critics who argue that the institution needs diversity of perspectives, but the vice president is aware of the potential drawbacks to the approach and notes that JMU does not "throw a bunch of people together and see how things work out." One of the effects of Scott's approach is a strong presence of team players in the operational relationships among staff.

Another persistent theme in the JMU way of doing business is the centrality of relationships. The entire operation appears to be erected on the premise that work is best achieved through alliances of staff. "We are all connected with one another," commented one director. Another said: "Collaboration tactics are stressed daily by the vice president." Effects of this tactical focus go beneath the surface into fundamental operational matters such as resource management. An associate vice president claimed that "there is not much competition for resources here. It simply is not tolerated!"— meaning that administrators of individual units know that resources of the unit do not belong solely to the unit alone, but may be used for divisionwide or universitywide purposes. Most staff agree with this assertion even though they may put their own spin on it; one assistant director, for example, said, "There is plenty of competition for resources, but not that pits one unit against another."

There is no doubt that the "students first" mantra is taken seriously at JMU. The leadership of the division is so concerned for student learning and development that it has reorganized the entire division around the issue. A new divisionwide unit, the Madison Leadership Center, was established to help focus resources from the entire division on student learning and development activities. Similarly, concern for staff and their learning and development is equally obvious at JMU. Every aspect of the management of people is "a developmental thing," according to Scott. Self-study and self-improvement, both by individuals and units, is an ongoing activity. Staff feel nurtured by the division leadership. In self-studies, for example, it is as though friends are looking at friends;

even in uncertain circumstances (as currently in Virginia where state-mandated budget cuts are severe), staff express confidence in their leadership: "We don't know what exactly will happen, but we know that we will be taken care of."

Recruitment and selection of staff is viewed "as the most important management decision I ever [will] make," according to one director. Everyone involved in hiring seems to acknowledge this point, including Scott, who stresses, "I am looking for someone with preparation and background but, more importantly for me, individuals who have something to contribute to the institution." On the relative value of background and experience versus credentials, Scott says, "We do not invite folks without credentials." But once that condition is met by all in the final candidate pools, the pendulum swings toward more intuitive judgments about who may have the greatest potential to serve the multiple interests of JMU. In the end, hiring the right person is the most vital aspect of staffing, according to one associate vice president, and often selective personal attributes make one person right for JMU. An associate director argued for hiring persons with certain character traits by saying, "I can teach someone what they need to know about leadership, but I cannot teach character."

Orientation practices at JMU reflect a dual emphasis on relationship building and a developmental method for supervising staff. Staff are expected to attend formal university orientation sessions and to be involved in a unit-directed familiarization process that often takes a "walking around" approach. In each unit, however, there seems to be a plan, an intentional strategy, for acclimating new staff to the mission and purpose of the section. In the more developmentally oriented units, new staff are carefully assessed in terms of their professional and personal status, and plans are drafted for furthering both dimensions while working at the university. One unit is even experimenting with a self-training scheme that appears to be a quasi-self-directed set of activities guided by a mentorlike supervisor.

Consistent with other staffing practices at JMU, supervision is conducted in an atmosphere of care. Scott maintains that "it has to do with improvement of staff," but it also has to do with achieving the larger institutional mission. Whatever the individual approach, and a variety is used in the division, it appears to include frequent meetings and a constant dialogue that in some cases is meant to be "an exchange, an evolving process, and not a time-bound event." Part of this approach is intended to give regular feedback to staff, but it also seems intended as a model of leadership for the supervisors, one of whom summed it up this way: "It is more than things I do. It is providing direction, motivating people, and helping them sort through difficulties." Thus, developmental supervisors have shifted their perspective on activities to focus less on process, as was the case previously, and more on people and unit outcomes.

Staff development is a priority at JMU that is built on the assumption that every staff member wants and needs to grow. Many activities have to do with staff development, including a lot of social activities, and "we have poured a lot of money into travel for staff—even for entry-level staff," says Scott. Retreats are used often and staff meetings are even more frequent, but once again many supervisors treat staff development as a necessary requirement for the development of the division. In these instances, a plan is constructed and all activities are weighed against contributions to the plan. This approach mainly makes participation in staff development intentional rather than opportunistic.

Staff evaluation or appraisal is conducted regularly; Scott expects "evaluation of all staff—no exceptions!" From this premise, however, considerable variation is evident across supervisors. Scott admits that beyond the mandate to do it, staff evaluation at JMU is more "conceptual" than procedural. In most cases, it begins with self-evaluation and takes a developmental form. The evaluation process is closely tied to supervision and the resulting ongoing dialogue that is set up between staff members and their supervisors. The process is therefore formative and intended to result in no surprises during any end-of-year evaluation reports. Mostly, these reports confirm what is already known. "There are no 'gotchas' in our system," maintains Scott.

In summary, JMU's division of student affairs practices what it preaches. It is based on a culture of care for students and for staff and its short-term and long-term staffing practices are consistent with this cultural tenet.

University of North Carolina-Wilmington

The University of North Carolina at Wilmington (UNCW) is a comprehensive public university in coastal North Carolina that enrolls approximately 8,300 students, with about 2,000 living on campus. A relatively young institution, UNCW originated as an extension center of the University of North Carolina at Chapel Hill; it began offering freshmen courses in 1947 and was accredited as a junior college (known as Wilmington College) in 1952. In 1963 it became a senior college offering the bachelor's degree and in 1969 a unit of the University of North Carolina system.

Because of its youth, there is not a great deal of tradition at the university. This is viewed by staff as both a challenge and an asset. The lack of tradition is problematic because considerable time must be spent justifying what is done, and it is relatively easy for institutional leaders to make frequent, dramatic changes in direction. On the plus side, the lack of tradition allows the staff to use creative and innovative approaches in facilitating the development of students and lessens some of the customary barriers between academic affairs and student affairs.

A common theme heard throughout the institution was a lack of resources needed to do the top-quality job the faculty and staff believe they are capable of. There is a shared belief that UNCW does not get its fair share of money within the North Carolina educational system and that student affairs is considerably understaffed and relatively low among the funding priorities at UNCW. This is exacerbated by a bothersome state employee classification system, under which most student affairs staff except senior administrators fall, that was designed principally to regulate personnel practices for clerical and maintenance personnel. The resulting low pay means the student affairs division has sometimes found it difficult to attract highly sought-after, entry-level professional staff members and even more difficult to retain talented and productive ones. A long-awaited revision of the state classification system, which would take into account the professional status and credentials of student affairs practitioners, appears to have become a casualty of state budget cuts.

Given these difficulties, there was very high morale among the staff interviewed and considerable pride expressed in the many accomplishments by the student affairs division since the arrival of William A. (Bill) Bryan in 1982. There was widespread acknowledgment that the high quality of the current programs and professionalism of the staff in student affairs are directly attributable to the energy, creativity, high standards, resourcefulness, and leadership of Bryan. As vice chancellor, he is widely admired by many members of the staff for his championing of the division's need for resources and for acting as a buffer between conscientiously performing staff members and unreasonable expectations and criticisms from others in the university.

Noteworthy features of UNCW's personnel practices include a standardized but flexible recruitment and selection process, a commitment to professionalism at all levels, a structured new-staff orientation process, a well-developed program of staff development, and extensive personal attention to staff members' welfare.

A feature of UNCW's personnel practices unusual in student affairs divisions is the existence of written policies and guidelines. For instance, when a vacancy occurs at the department director or higher level, the vice chancellor appoints a search committee, designates its chairperson, and gives it a specific written charge, part of which might be to "solicit applicants, devise an equitable evaluation system, receive and screen applicant materials, and ultimately present an unranked list of persons recommended for on-campus interviews to the vice chancellor." In addition, a timetable for accomplishing various stages of the search is specified. The chairperson and all committee members are given an outline of responsibilities and a list of things that require consideration, such as legal and ethical parameters, affirmative action goals, and institutional personnel policies. A step-by-step checklist of what needs to be done at each stage of the process is also provided. Particularly impressive is that the chairperson is instructed to train the members of the committee how to conduct a search; essential training topics include confidentiality of materials and permissible and impermissible questions during interviews. (This is particularly important when the committee includes students and faculty members unschooled in the etiquette of the hiring process in higher education or in the student affairs culture.)

Another distinguishing feature of UNCW's staffing practices is the high level of commitment to professionalism. When Bryan arrived as vice chancellor, the division had few staff members with professional preparation or who were involved in professional activities beyond the institution. As vacancies occurred, a top priority was to find replacements who had solid academic and professional credentials. Talented undergraduates who had an interest in careers in student affairs were also identified and hired into entry-level positions; they were then given support in acquiring master's degrees in student personnel. Now it is assumed that new hires will come in with good graduate preparation and solid work (or supervised practice) experience. All professional staff are encouraged to be actively involved in professional associations, which for many means assuming leadership positions.

Once new staff arrive on campus, their productivity is enhanced or limited by how well and quickly they learn their way around the institution, the players' names, their job responsibilities, and the personalities of those with whom they have frequent interaction. Because UNCW is relatively small and generally does not have multiple new staff members in areas other than residence life, new staff orientation is done individually. The supervisor of the new staff member is responsible for organizing and conducting the orientation. To ensure that new staff are not shortchanged, the vice chancellor issued a policy statement in the form of a checklist that details the minimum content of the orientation program; no matter when a person joins a staff he or she will receive a full orientation to the institution and job responsibilities.

Hiring is seen as only the first step in staff development. The breadth and depth of knowledge and skills new staff members bring to their positions directly affects the kinds and extent of staff development activities required. Another hallmark of staffing practices at UNCW is an active, wide-ranging staff development program. Two committees (professional and support staff) are charged with arranging monthly programs or activities. Content may be nationally sponsored teleconferences, presentations by faculty or staff highlighting new university initiatives, programs presenting research findings about UNCW students, training sessions (such as use of computer programs), or speeches by national organization leaders who happen to be in the area. There also are social functions such as holiday parties that include staff and their families and the annual thank-you luncheon for support staff. There is also an extensive system of awards for devotion to duty, innovation, public service, safety or heroism, and outstanding new employees.

As a means of connecting staff development and supervision, each year professional staff members establish personal and professional development contracts in consultation with their supervisors. This is seen as an essential part of the planning process. Its purpose is to assist staff in addressing individual interests and meeting institutional needs, and is a good opportunity for staff to clearly communicate areas in which improvement or new skills or knowledge are needed. At the end of the year, all staff members are called upon to report on the number of staff development activities they participated in and the number of hours devoted to them.

Because personal attention is important for students and staff, Bryan has established the practice of inviting each staff member to a one-to-one discussion with him at least once a year. He sees this as an important way to communicate his concern for the staff member's advancement and welfare and as a way to encourage staff to give the vice chancellor direct feedback and input.

The hallmarks of quality staffing practices at UNCW are the prominence of staff development activities and the shared concern for the welfare of people who make up the student affairs division. Staff are expected to be professional and to use their knowledge and skills to benefit students and fellow staff members alike. This is particularly important given the limits, primarily financial, within when they must work. Most acknowledge that the division bears the stamp of Bill Bryan, who is highly admired and respected. His devotion to creating an outstanding student affairs program and willingness to take hard knocks for the staff is much appreciated.

University of Richmond

The University of Richmond is located in a suburban area of Richmond, Virginia and enrolls about 3,000 undergraduates; it also offers degrees in law and several master's programs. It is selective in admissions, independent (though loosely affiliated with Virginia Baptists), and privately endowed. Its campus is largely residential, with 90 percent of the undergraduates living on campus. Students come primarily from the urban centers of the eastern United States and are largely white, affluent, and academically talented. In recent years, however, Richmond has made major strides in increasing the diversity of its student population through a combination of increased financial aid budgets and increased attention to recruiting international students.

The most striking organizational features of Richmond are its single-sex "coordinate colleges," Richmond College for men and Westhampton College for women. As one of its publications for students explains: "Coordinate college refers to a combination of residential housing, student governance, academic duties, support staff, and programs designed for women . . . and men." Each college has a dean who has a combination of traditional academic duties, such as academic advising, and student affairs functions, such as residential life programs and services and discipline. On academic matters, the deans of Richmond and Westhampton Colleges report to the dean of the School of Arts and Sciences; on all other matters they report to the vice president for student affairs, Leonard S. (Len) Goldberg. At the university level, the student affairs division includes most traditional programs and services—counseling, career services, health services, academic skills assistance, minority student programs, campus recreation, and student activities—offered to all students in the university.

Several distinguishing features of the university have significant impacts on staffing practices in student affairs: a tradition of high levels of student involvement, an overall commitment to excellence, a humane process-oriented style of leadership, and ample fiscal resources and a large, high-quality physical plant.

The University of Richmond is based on the assumption that students should be activists. Students are expected to play active roles in their education, and the student affairs division supports and encourages high levels of involvement outside the classroom. For instance, the student affairs staff justifies the coordinate college structure—acknowledged as sometimes less efficient than coeducational arrangements—as providing greater opportunities for student involvement and leadership development, especially for women, who tend to take advantage of programs in greater numbers.

High student involvement has both positive and negative implications. Because of the implicit expectations of involvement embedded in the culture (especially strong among women), students generally participate in organizations and activities enthusiastically. This gives student affairs staff members many opportunities to influence students' lives and educational experiences, but it can also lead to youthful extravagances, poorly thought out ventures, and confrontations with or attempts to circumvent authority. This sometimes causes tension within student affairs practitioners as they attempt to fulfill the roles of both student development educator and administrator or facilitator and authority figure. But students do find an environment receptive to their personal initiatives, especially in areas that directly affect their residential colleges or daily activities or routine.

Another theme evident throughout the University of Richmond and its student affairs division is the pursuit of excellence. Richmond is fortunate in that it has not experienced the budget crunches of the 1990s; this along with high-quality facilities has allowed the institution to focus on improving and maintaining areas of excellence. The student affairs division is committed to excellence both in programs and services, which is only possible if a competent, energetic staff is in place. Thus the institution's pursuit of excellence is reflected in the attention to staffing decisions and practices in student affairs.

Even though the organizational structure of the University of Richmond is unique, the overall student affairs division is similar to those of other institutions of its type. There is a strong emphasis on professionalism and a desire to create a work environment that can be characterized as allowing freedom to exercise professional judgment and a feeling of collegial support. Goldberg is known as a "process person" who has considerable contact with staff at all levels and with students as well. He shows a concern for the welfare of the staff, mirrored by a concern about maintaining good working relationships throughout the division. Goldberg professes, and the staff confirms, that he gives staff members considerable autonomy in making decisions and structuring their work. Goldberg's humane, process-oriented style helps the division balance the qualitative demands of the institution, the high volume of requests for services from students, standards of good professional practices, and the personal and professional needs of the student affairs staff.

Recruitment and search procedures comply with widely accepted practices in the field, including advertising positions nationally. The student affairs division, however, does not use search and screening committees in filling positions. The supervisor of the vacant position (dean or department director) is responsible for conducting the search, in consultation with others in the functional area and with the vice president. Once candidates who possess the necessary educational preparation and experience have been identified, three to five are invited to campus for interviews. During the course of the on-campus interviews there is extensive involvement by students, faculty, and staff both inside and outside the department or college that has the vacancy. Feedback is sought following the candidate visits to establish a consensus about which best fits the university's needs. Most important is finding candidates with the personalities and personal and professional philosophies that fit Richmond's mission, traditions, and student clientele. Orientation of new staff, beyond information about the benefits package, is conducted by the immediate supervisor of the new staff member and is individually tailored to him or her.

Staff development is highly valued and supported. There are both formal divisionwide programs, such as invited speakers, panels, and teleconferences, and less formal activities often conducted in conjunction with staff meetings. For instance, during the biweekly department directors' and deans' meetings with the vice president, ten to fifteen minutes are devoted to a professional development activity. Many departments employ a similar practice at their unit staff meetings. Other staff development activities include social events, including holiday parties and a large summer picnic for all staff and their families. Involvement in professional associations and attendance at regional and national conferences is valued, and staff are given support in serving professional associations. There also is a program of awards and recognitions for staff, including support staff.

There seems to be no consistent pattern of supervision of professional staff in the student affairs division. The frequency and intensity of supervisory activities tends to be inversely related to tenure at the institution. That is, considerable attention is devoted to new staff members, especially entry-level professionals; the frequency of supervisory sessions tends to decline, except in times of crisis, over the years. The degree of individual attention and assistance in career advancement is largely dependent on the skills and inclinations of supervisors. Because of the size of the institution and the community spirit within the division, most staff members interviewed expressed the belief that they could get what they need in the way of professional assistance somewhere within the division, if not from their immediate supervisor.

Performance evaluation is the most uneven of staffing practices. The human resources unit requires that an evaluation form be completed for all employees annually. This is done, but professional staff tend to place little stock in either the process or the product, and many believe that completion of the forms has no direct connection to salary adjustments. Many supervisors have developed their own procedures for giving staff feedback on performance, which are generally viewed much more positively by the staff being evaluated. Some staff reported finding the process they experienced as helpful; others reported it as perfunctory.

Staffing practices at the University of Richmond are not radically different from many other comparable institutions. There is high morale and a shared commitment to excellence. Considerable attention is paid to recruiting highly qualified staff who share the values of the institution. High standards of professionalism and a commitment to enhancing the quality of students' educational experiences were evidenced throughout the division. It is perhaps attention to detail and doing traditional things well that makes the University of Richmond most exceptional.

Samford University

Samford University, a private, principally liberal arts institution with strong ties to the Baptist Church, is located in a suburban area of Birmingham, Alabama. It is a compact campus with a modern physical plant, mainly because the university moved to its current location in 1957. In addition to its liberal arts programs it also offers postgraduate study in theology and law. There are about 3,100 undergraduates, 1,800 of whom live in on-campus housing.

Samford has maintained a long and historic relationship with the Alabama Baptist Convention and only Alabama Baptists are named to the governing board. The institution has an explicit Christian mission. Unlike some institutions that view themselves as having a strong religious heritage or orientation but few ideological or sectarian constraints, Samford University maintains an assertive religious posture. For instance, with few exceptions, only Christians (though not necessarily Baptists) are hired within the university, including the student affairs division.

Several distinguishing features of Samford University significantly influence staffing practices in student affairs: a clearly articulated educational philosophy and religious orientation, a commitment to professionalism, strong and charismatic leadership, careful attention to selecting staff who fit the institution's culture, and an emphasis on creating a caring, familial atmosphere within the division.

Due in part to Samford's involvement in total quality management approaches, the university has developed nine values statements that embody the basic philosophy of the institution and its approach to education. The process of drafting and adopting these statements helped the entire institution come to a clearer understanding its mission. During the course of conversations with staff in student affairs, references are often made to the Missions, Customers, Process, Visions, and Values (MCPVV) statement as an explanation for why certain practices or policies take the form they do. One product of the process of adopting the MCPVV has been an unambiguous affirmation of Samford's explicitly religious orientation and devotion to high-quality liberal arts education.

The Christian character of the institution is openly communicated to potential staff applicants, and during the course of employment interviews there is open discussion of religious beliefs and background. There is a clear commitment to seeking student affairs staff members who hold religious beliefs and practices compatible with the institution's Baptist heritage. As important as religious orientation is, however, professional competence (acquired through a combination of formal professional education, continuing professional development activities, and work experience) is the absolutely essential prerequisite for serious consideration for employment.

Samford University has undertaken "professionalization" of its student affairs division since the arrival of its current vice president, Richard S. Franklin (affectionately known as Dean Franklin). When he arrived in 1990, no one on the staff had professional experience outside Samford and few had professional preparation for the field. He immediately began to seek new staff from outside the institution and insisted that they have appropriate educational preparation and high levels of professional competence in order to be considered. He also assisted and encouraged staff members in becoming more actively involved in professional organizations and helped many of them make contacts that would facilitate their gaining opportunities for leadership experience.

There is no question in the minds of the staff interviewed that Dean Franklin is the embodiment of student affairs at Samford. As one staff member put it: "He is a man with a vision of higher education and student affairs' role in creating a quality educational experience." Staff have seen him fight and win important battles for the division and credit him with being the primary reason that student affairs' esteem in the university has risen appreciably. He has real influence in the institution and is considered an important decision maker.

Franklin is a charismatic leader who is seen by staff as very empowering. He is soft-spoken and low-key in manner, but puissant. Staff agree that he doesn't "hover," isn't a "control junkie," but is supportive and allows considerable autonomy. A number of staff members indicated that from time to time they were motivated to go the extra mile because they knew it would please Dean Franklin. They were also quick to point out that he personifies caring, setting high standards and working long and hard.

Paramount importance is placed on hiring professional staff who fit Samford's mission and culture. There seems to be nearly equal emphasis on recruiting staff with good professional preparation and appropriate professional experience, and those with a good institutional fit. Being a Christian and feeling comfortable working in an avowedly religious institution are important determinations in the hiring process. Candidates are routinely asked about their religious beliefs and affiliations and are informed of Samford's desire to remain a Christian institution. But religion is not the only topic discussed with candidates in helping to determine fit. Good interpersonal skills, professional expertise, creativity, ability to work collaboratively, and a view of student affairs as a professional endeavor are additional characteristics that predict success in Samford's student affairs division.

There is a conscious effort to create a family atmosphere within the division. A number of staff members acknowledged that the division is really too large to actually function as a family, but family is a metaphor frequently used by staff to describe the division. There are conscious efforts to create a supportive and comfortable work environment. Maintaining a network of warm interpersonal relationships is considered important and is fostered through activities such as the monthly celebrations of everything from birthdays to service anniversaries to personal achievements.

Samford's staffing success seems to hinge on paying careful attention to the selection process, with paramount emphasis on identifying and hiring talented, well-educated staff members. Because of the emphasis on assuring a good institutional fit when selecting new staff, frequent personal contact among staff members in the division, and a personalized approach to supervision and professional development, staff members generally feel comfortable and see themselves as making meaningful contributions. Staff turnover is low and tends to be the result of career advancement, retirement, or decisions to pursue new life directions. Due to the high regard in which the vice president is held, many staff members express a desire to meet his expectations and aspirations for the student affairs division.

The second distinguishing feature of Samford's staffing practice is the atmosphere of caring and interest in individuals that permeates the division. The leadership of the division shows interest in both the personal and professional lives of their staff. Franklin makes a point of helping staff who aspire to positions of greater responsibility to develop the skills and acquire the experiences required for advancement, and actively assists those who are attempting to make career moves. The family metaphor seems appropriate. Staff are respected and cared for while they work at Samford, but when the time comes to venture out, the family provides support and encouragement.

Broward Community College

Broward Community College (BCC) is a large multicampus community college in Ft. Lauderdale, Florida. Its four campuses are located strategically in Broward County to provide access to all citizens. The population of the county is multicultural and diverse and, not surprisingly, so are the college's students, faculty, administration, and staff.

The vice president for student affairs, George Young, has served the institution in the same capacity for twenty-five years and he sets the spirit, mood, and ethos for staffing throughout the system. This is communicated through consistent, reasonable, value-laden messages: "We look for people of real quality, then we empower them." "We look for people who are absolutely committed to students." "We expect our people to get the job done." "We are not interested in someone who insists on working strictly to a job description." "We support our people." "We do not expect perfection, but if you fail, let it not be because you did not work hard."

These simple messages establish an institutional temperament of standards or rules for staffing. Everyone knows the rules (Young repeats them often enough) and they know, too, that they have flexibility in the application of the rules so long as the job gets done. This bottom-line attitude is pervasive among supervisors at BCC.

Certain aspects of staffing in student affairs at BCC span all traditional boundaries of the organization. Leadership is stable, forceful, and humane. Young's views are ever-present, yet they appear to consider kindly the variety of needs of his staff. His expectations are clear to all: work to the mission, serve students, do not let ordinary parameters such as job descriptions get in the way of helping students now. Loyalty to the college is evident in all staff; many are former students who remember the helpful attitude of staff toward them, and they now return the favor. Others seem to recognize that the mission of the college is crucial to achieving many important goals of the community and they are committed to it. Often these commitments stand even when salaries are uncommonly low. (The "sunshine tax" is widespread in Ft. Lauderdale, including at BCC.)

Intuition, or common sense, seems to be the overarching principle of day-to-day staffing operations. Few appear to be trained in staffing responsibilities; rather, they watch others and "do what comes naturally." The college has four campuses so that easy access to college services is available for all Broward citizens, and a full range of student services is hypothetically available at each, yet not every campus has a full contingent of staff. Instead, many staff members located on one campus have collegewide staffing responsibilities, including supervision and evaluation. Also, the use of part-time employees is common in student services at BCC. The practice allows for stretching of limited resources to extend services into more areas, but it is seen as a big problem for supervisors who worry about abusing loyalties to the college by placing unreasonable expectations on some employees.

Recruitment and selection procedures at BCC are routine. Most of the clerical functions are handled by the college's personnel office, where initial screening of applicants also is performed. Search committees interview candidates and make recommendations to the unit director, who usually makes the final decision. Sometimes the vice president is involved in the final choice. In either case, the strategy is expected to yield the person who best fits the work environment. This often means that personal attributes are given preference over formal education and training.

Staff orientation to the job is conducted at two levels. First, the college conducts a formal orientation. Second, the unit employing a new staff member handles its own familiarization process. This latter step often is managed in a mentorlike manner, with an experienced staff member guiding the new member through all steps of the operation. This process appears to extend beyond new staff orientation. Young speaks about his overall attitude toward staff in a similar manner: "When we hire someone, we assume a role model position with them. We push them to further education. We protect them. We criticize them. We cause them to grow."

Supervision of staff takes many forms at BCC. Everyone agrees that it is crucial to success, yet few agree on a common pattern for carrying out the duties. Some see supervision as a daily responsibility, while others see it simply as something they must do. Most would agree that supervision is guidance, but given the multicampus organization and the large number of part-time employees it is difficult to provide close, hands-on direction and to treat all staff the same. The result is that discussions about supervision often take the form of a benevolent, hands-off attitude: "We delegate to intelligent, dedicated, responsible people." "We check them periodically." "Everyone is working toward the mission."

With a specific line item in the budget for it, BCC is able to provide extensive support for staff development activities. Coupled with an attitude from the top that encourages further growth, staff are able to participate in a wide range of on- and off-campus endeavors. They are encouraged and enabled to seek further education, for example. They also are involved in multiple occasions for meetings on campus and retreats off campus. Staff are encouraged to talk with one another often to solve problems and, in a more formal way, ideas are on the table for discussion. Young says "we always are talking about the future," and he wants everyone involved in these discussions.

Formal evaluation procedures at BCC, according to one experienced staff member, are "all very vague . . . and are the least well done of our formal staffing practices." There is a collegewide procedure, but it is almost universally believed to be ineffective. An evaluation form is supposed to be completed, but according to some, doing so is not even enforced by the human resources office, which has formal organizational responsibility for staff evaluation. Instead, Young models another evaluation process that he calls "honoring success." He finds success stories either in student or staff achievement that he plays back to staff, often on formal social occasions. These stories, says Young, "represent our culture" and are "beautiful stuff."

BCC appears to do little that is distinctive in staffing practices, yet it is successful in working toward its mission. In this environment, the best explanations for success may be found not in the procedures themselves, but in the values of the culture as articulated by the vice president.

Johnson County Community College

Located in affluent Overland Park, Kansas, Johnson County Community College (JCCC) is a single-campus college that very much mirrors its community in student and staff composition; it is essentially monocultural but supported by a refined professional operation.

Professionalism in operational policies is patterned after many of the most successful businesses in the immediate geographical area, and this results in standardized policies and procedures for all aspects of staffing in student affairs. Contrary to stereotypes about such an approach, the college demonstrates a very personal, caring attitude about its people. In addition to emulating the most successful businesses, the highly structured approach to staffing was intentionally implemented to solve some inequities of past staffing operations. Top-level administrators are likely to admit that "We have a bureaucracy, yes, but *we* built it!"

Linda Dayton, dean of student services for nineteen years, represents a clear voice of this tailored approach to staffing. She boasts, "We are very consistent here [and] we aren't going to change." Anyone working at the institution or seeking employment there is well aware of the staffing policies and procedures and how they will be applied. Dayton proudly points to this organizational attribute as one of the powerful reasons for the success of the student affairs operation. Some comment that arguments at the college usually are not about policy, but more likely about whether the college is serving students well.

The board of trustees is committed to quality in all operations of the college. Its faithfulness to quality is evident in several staffing practices. All professionals and allied professionals, both full-and part-time, are fully credentialed. Salaries are competitive; the college periodically surveys twenty benchmark schools, then adjusts its salaries to remain in the top one-third of the peer group. Staff members are selected very carefully, trained conscientiously in all aspects of their work, and nurtured plentifully with institutional resources to promote excellence and further growth. The college is generously staffed; to remain a place of high achievement, ample staff are provided to meet carefully agreed-upon work requirements, and they are then expected "to give 110 percent." These practices appear to result in a professional style of operation, a caring approach to education, and a thoroughly dedicated and committed staff.

A persistent staffing issue at JCCC is the wide use of part-time employees. Occupying about 60 percent of the staff positions in student affairs, they are valuable and cost-effective but also present a number of problems: inadequate options for rewarding them, unfair "job creep" (the unintentional and incremental use of part-time staff to perform functions they were not hired and sometimes are not qualified to do), and inharmonious evaluation practices.

One supervisor said, "I feel guilty around my part-time colleagues. I have a full-time job and they do not."

Recruitment and selection procedures are guided by carefully constructed board-approved policies and well regulated by administrators. The policies are written, widely distributed and understood, and followed. Though the procedures for position announcements and for collecting and screening applicants are handled routinely by JCCC's office of human resources, two things stand out about the manner they are applied in student affairs. First, the job descriptions are carefully written in a collaborative environment with those who need the position and then approved by the dean. Dayton says this step is meticulously conducted. Second, recognizing that staff tend to stay at the college for a long time and that a very great deal of money will be spent on salaries and staff development, the hiring decision is treated "like a million-dollar decision!," according to an associate of Dayton who often is involved in hiring staff. Familiarizing a new hire with the college and with the specific unit to which the position is assigned is conducted formally. The office of human resources conducts half-day sessions for both full-time and part-time new employees. Supervisors within specific units are expected to spend whatever time is required, usually about one week, with every new employee to be sure that he or she is comfortable. Shadowing approaches are used in some units. In others, as in the counseling center, orientation is a long-term matter and results in some guided interactions between counselors and teaching faculty about which formal reports must be prepared for the dean.

Supervision is taken very seriously at JCCC. Supervisors meet about once per month for training in supervisory issues, and regular meetings with staff are expected. Supervisory style varies by individual (terms such as "coaching," "teaching," "team-oriented," or "conversational" are common expressions used to describe these variations), but they all show the effects of the regular training. They know that supervision is guidance to help staff do the things required to achieve the mission of the college. Another effect of the seriousness of supervision is an atmosphere of trust and "backing." Staff regularly report feeling supported and trusted without being smothered.

Staff development programs at JCCC reflect the intentional, well-structured approach to staffing found in all aspects pertaining to personnel, and they exhibit the opulence of the college. Guided by a strong board-approved and presidentially endorsed policy, the college publishes a seventy-eight page directory of opportunities for staff development. Almost sixty initiatives are listed in the directory as well as opportunities for recognition awards, research support, resources, and organizational development activities. The president of the college calls this program "comprehensive." No one could quarrel with that assessment. Evidence that staff take full advantage of these opportunities is abundant. Dayton says, "I don't know anyone who does not participate in off- and on-campus [staff development] activities." Like other staffing practices at JCCC, evaluation procedures are formal and structured. They include a fall-term formative evaluation (a conversation about how things are going), student evaluations of program effectiveness, and a spring-term evaluation (a check on how well individual and unit goals have been achieved). Training is provided to help supervisors with evaluation, though many still feel they need to know more to do the job well. Evaluation connotes appropriate rewards, for example, and most supervisors feel that they do not have fitting response options to appraised performance levels.

Staff supervision, development, and evaluation are tightly connected at JCCC. It is difficult to tell where one practice ends and another begins, except that the evaluation role is less comfortably accepted than others. The metaphor of the well-oiled machine might be applied to staffing practices at JCCC—but only if a machine may be said to have a heart, not clockwork, at its center.

Hallmarks of Quality Staffing Practices

A cross-case analysis was conducted of all eight studies. The protocol used in this process is shown in Appendix C and was employed to ensure careful examination of all aspects of staffing practices of concern to our study. The analysis follows a qualitative pattern of searching for commonalities or themes within the evidence contained in each study. At the same time, dissimilarities were noted where found. The results of the analysis follow and are structured around the major themes or commonalities in each case study.

Institutional Culture

Study of these cases shows that their staffing practices are anchored firmly in widely acknowledged doctrines of their respective institutional cultures. Institutional culture is an extraordinarily complex concept in both scope and property, and thus defies simple definition. This examination of eight examples of staffing practices makes no attempt to fully reveal institutional culture in its broadest sense, but lengthy discussions with members of the organizations invariably uncovered certain cultural artifacts upon which staffing practices were built or shaped.

Institutional Identity

Staff members at each location articulate a clear sense of institutional self. They know their institutions well. They respect them and they take pride in them. A result of this widespread awareness of "who we are" appears to reflect organizational health and effectiveness. Doing well what one sets out to do leads to a sense of enhanced self-respect and, in turn, intensification of institutional identity.

Two good examples of the role of institutional identity can be found at James Madison University and Samford University. At Madison, where culturally burdened language is a part of everyday exchanges between staff members, the culture is virtually personified in phrases such as "the JMU way" and "wearing the JMU hat." A "caring attitude toward students and a caring attitude toward colleagues" is the translation of a long-held institutional foundation for James Madison University, even from its earliest days when the institution was called Madison College and served primarily as a teacher preparation and liberal arts college. At Samford University, staff members from vice president to hall directors feel comfortable and quite nondefensive about describing the institution as a Christian college, which has a clearly articulated point of view. The commitment to being a college with a point of view is crucial to understanding how the student affairs division interacts with students and how it conducts staffing practices at the division.

At both Florida State University and the University of Maryland-College Park a belief that "we are the best" pervades the working climate of the student affairs divisions. Staff members at these institutions refer frequently to their commitment to excellence and to their obligation to enhance or maintain a tradition of high standards and excellence. One distinctive result of these attitudes and subsequent behaviors is a very high level of loyalty by the staff to the institution. Thus, healthy arrogance in these cases has the reciprocal effect of contributing to greater functional health within the institution. This shared commitment to basic tenets of the profession, such as the value and worth of individual students and a desire to improve their educational experiences, often seems to motivate staff members to go the extra mile without being directed to do so (or directly rewarded for it) by senior administrators.

Loyalty to the institution exudes from every quadrant at Broward Community College. Many current staff members grew up in the college. They were students there and they remember the assistance they received and now want to pass on the favor to current students. Further, many staff members are long-term residents of the community and take great pride in the work of the college. They like working there even though in many instances they must pay the "sunshine tax" for the privilege.

Clarity of Purpose

Every one of the case institutions is guided by clear purposes. Staff members know the larger institutional purpose of their work, not just the departmental or unit perspective on their job duties, and they can articulate it. In some cases, the operational aspects of institutional purpose become a near-mantra in staff meetings and in task-oriented projects. It is no accident that clarity of aims results in determination by staff to play a meaningful part, to contribute their skills and talents directly. It motivates them to achieve their goals for the good of all.

Intuitively, one might expect such comprehensibility of purpose at a small liberal arts college, especially one with a strong religiously based educational philosophy. Samford University is an example; it has adopted nine values statements to which all units subscribe. Further, all units find ways of operationalizing these value statements, beyond paying homage to them. The value of "openness, truthfulness, justice, and fairness" is translated by the student affairs division to mean modeling desired behaviors, cultivating the art of listening, creating an atmosphere of openness and diversity, adopting policies consistent with desired results, and similar actions.

This level of clarity also can be found in the two-year colleges, Johnson County Community College and Broward Community College. Neither is small, with enrollments near 15,000 and 20,000 respectively. Service to students is the mantra for all staff and it is no mere slogan; "service to students" is meant to impart an absolute faithfulness to help students in all their educational needs and often in their personal needs. Words like *mantra* and *faithfulness* have a religious flavor and describe well the near-saturation level of assistance intended for students at these institutions.

Even the largest institutions in this study count their effectiveness, in part due to the widespread precision of purpose: "Our mission is clear and well articulated," according to many staff at the University of Maryland-College Park. The staff talk about the goals of the division of student affairs and they hear the goals addressed in public settings.

Tradition of Excellence

Staff members at the case institutions take self-satisfaction from historic or in some cases more recently acquired legacies of distinction. Obviously, some traditions have longer tenure than others, but regardless of the age of the tradition, staff members at these institutions feel that excellence of educational practice is ongoing and that they have a commitment to contribute to it.

The University of Richmond has such a tradition arising from its selectivity in student admission and its unique organizational pattern for delivering educational services. It maintains that it is one of the fifty most selective colleges in the nation, and certainly it enrolls many academically elite students. Staff at the university describe their students as "highly involved and very demanding . . . [and holding] high expectations about both the quality and quantity of services provided them." Organizationally, Richmond has created the benefit of both coeducation and single-sex education: Richmond College is reserved for men, Westhampton College for women. These "coordinate colleges" offer some distinct advantages to traditional structures, especially in their ability to deliver on promises of quality through intensive work with smaller groups of students. A certain amount of inefficiency associated with duplication of services in the coordinate colleges is accepted because of the strongly held belief that students are best served by such an arrangement.

Even at institutions without long-held traditions of excellence such as the University of North Carolina-Wilmington, which is a relatively young institution, staff felt pride in the great strides made in recent years under strong leadership from their vice chancellor, who has created high morale and self-satisfaction in the "high quality of the current programs and professionalism of the staff in Student Affairs."

At the University of Maryland-College Park, vice president for student affairs Bud Thomas tells his staff, "There is a high expectation at the University of Maryland-College Park that you are the best in the business." Staff members believe that they were selected from strong pools of contenders and that they are expected to become "stars" in the profession.

Professionalism

From credentials to procedures, all the staffs studied recognize that there is a correct way of doing business. They work to apply the knowledge of the profession of student affairs and to follow the ethical and professional tenets of their institutions and their respective professional associations. A few liken themselves to the best corporations in their geographic area, as is the case at Johnson County Community College, but whatever the comparison, all feel that they know how best to accomplish their work and that they are succeeding because they adhere to proven professional practices.

At Johnson County Community College, the board of trustees acts to demonstrate its commitment to excellence; this is reflected in carefully constructed policies that are meticulously implemented. Written policies, including those for staffing, are the rule at this college. Leaders acknowledge that they maintain a bureaucracy, but they know it was created by and for the people of the organization and they accept ownership of it. Exceptions to policy are rare at JCCC, but instead of feeling enslaved by the practices, staff seem to gain self-esteem from being a part of a well-run, polished organization.

In other cases, such as Samford University and the University of North Carolina-Wilmington, professionalism has been achieved during the last decade. Both institutions have worked diligently to overcome perceived shortcomings often associated with a tradition of hiring uncredentialed or unprepared personnel. These efforts have succeeded because of strong leadership from the executive student affairs officer at each institution, and has resulted in a cultural artifact of loyalty to a professionally run organization.

Ethic of Hard Work

Without exception, staff members at these sites know they are expected to work hard and to contribute to traditions of service to students and to the institution. They also know that their culture will reward them for their hard work, but even where rewards (especially monetary) are inconsistently available, they subscribe to a strong work ethic.

Nowhere is this ethic more evident than at Broward Community College, where the twenty-five-year veteran vice president for student affairs asserts, "We do not expect perfection [from staff], but, if you fail, let it not be because you did not work hard!" Staff often are selected using the criterion of willingness to work hard and long hours as at the University of Richmond, or of high energy levels as at the University of North Carolina-Wilmington. The work at Florida State University is seen as fast paced and demanding and staff are challenged to "do, do, do, do. . . ."

Fortunately, hard work pays off in these institutions. Rewards come, but first there must be achievement and lots of it. Rewards are sometimes realized by career advancement through assuming additional responsibilities or duties within the institution (such as coordination of a professional conference) or positions of greater responsibility at other institutions. The need to "move out in order to move up" is recognized at many institutions where senior administrators take active roles in helping staff prepare for greater responsibilities and then helping them secure new positions when they are ready.

Sense of Family

The language and symbolism of family is used often by staff members at some sites. They are concerned about one another, they come together often to celebrate or socialize, and they work as teams on multiple projects that span the boundaries of organizational structure.

This familial environment is especially evident at James Madison University, where the staff is expected to participate in frequent social events and other activities planned within student affairs. Most sites make frequent use of family metaphors when describing their ways of doing business, but staff at Samford University, where the phrase "family feeling" is commonly used, and at Broward Community College, where the celebration of people is outwardly espoused, seem especially close-knit in their references to one another.

At all sites, staff members exude an ethos of caring, which is reflected by a concern for the welfare, growth, and achievement of fellow professionals. At the larger institutions, however, it would perhaps be possible to speak of a familial feeling, but size and geographic dispersion make this more metaphorical than real.

Powerful, Stable Leadership

It is likely that any division of student affairs that maintains a reputation for quality also will have strong leadership in key positions in the organization. This certainly is true at the case sites studied. In some cases, the leadership of the division is so dominated by the vice president that it would be no exaggeration to say that the essence of the division is personified by that individual. At other institutions the leadership (although no less effective) is more indirect, often emphasizing teamwork and shared decision making. Is the quality of an organizational unit tied to the presence of one person? There can be little doubt that if some leaders of these institutions left their vice presidencies, their absence would be felt throughout, but remarkably, the evidence gathered did not suggest that such a departure would be fatal to the organization nor to its image of quality service. It is a mark of excellent leadership that direction and guidance is institutionalized and that the ongoing effect is not dependent upon the day-to-day actions of the leader.

Omniscient Presence

Most leaders at these sites are credited with being all-knowing and all-seeing within the division of student affairs and sometimes in the larger institution. In several cases, they actually seem omnipotent in a down-to-earth sort of way, though each would reject this label. This self-effacing demeanor, present in all of them, seems to add to their aura of being all-powerful and all-knowing in the eyes of their staff members and, not surprisingly, further increased their effectiveness as leaders. Even in cases where the leader is not seen as ever present, esteem by staff members for leadership and professionalism is universal.

Some of the very special leader attributes discovered in these cases include a pervasive presence throughout the division and sometimes the entire institution, long service in the position, influence on decisions from top to bottom of the division without micromanaging, eloquence of stated purpose or vision, widespread respect by staff, being a "sheep in wolf's clothing" (that is, a hard-headed manager but with warmth and compassion), and promulgating and enforcing informal rules of the workplace. It is noteworthy that staff members at these sites can normally describe unwritten, informal rules of the workplace that they ascribe to their executive-level leader. This is especially evident at Broward Community College where George Young casts a shadow over the entire organization with his rules, mostly unwritten and taking the form of expectations: hard work will be rewarded; commitment overrides procedures; get the job done! All these messages are delivered humanely but leave no doubt as to their importance. Similarly, at the University of Maryland-College Park it is abundantly evident that the underlying assumptions about staffing practices are guided by the hand of Bud Thomas. His influence is everywhere in the division.

Respect for Competence

The vice presidents at the institutions visited for this study show high regard for professional competence, which is reflected in a number of ways. Staff members feel the confidence of the vice president through delegation of decision making and authority. The leaders in this study do not micromanage their divisions, although there is a clear understanding about "what decisions you make, we make, and I make," as a staff member at Samford University put it. A distinguishing feature of the institutions studied is a stress on selecting staff members who possess the necessary educational and professional experience to handle assigned responsibilities. Once selected, oriented to the job, and schooled in the organizational culture, people are left by the leaders to do their jobs.

Long Tenure

Some of the vice presidents at these sites had spent many years laboring at the institution, one twenty-five years and another twenty-two; all had earned the respect of their staff over many years of professional practice at that institution or others. Staff are comfortable with these seasoned leaders. They know what to expect from them. Their effectiveness as leaders seems directly tied to the long-term nature of their tenure; they are known quantities. As Bill Bryan, vice president at UNCW, put it: "Surprises are never welcome; I don't want to be surprised by things my staff did or problems that have arisen which they failed to tell me about. Likewise, staff have a right to expect consistency of action or reaction from me. They need to be able to predict what I will do or what my attitude will be when they consider possible courses of action."

Practical Vision

These leaders possess a talent for articulating the goals of the institution and the division of student affairs in language that is easily understood and that communicates a personal message of responsibility to each staff member.

Bob Scott of James Madison University repeats certain core values over and over in public messages: "Students are number one here. The JMU family is number two." George Young of Broward Community College says, "We are absolutely committed to students. We expect our people to get the job done." "We are consistent [in our application of policies and in our commitment to professionalism]," says Linda Dayton of Johnson County Community College, and these commitments are helpful "in getting the job done." Bud Thomas of the University of Maryland-College Park insists that directors of departments within the division address the issue of contribution to the goals of the division and university by "filling reports with data that are consumer oriented." Len Goldberg of the University of Richmond speaks frequently about "opportunities to have a critical impact on the lives of students."

Reward for Achievement

Leaders at these sites are able to offer rewards for staff achievements. Ability to reward achievements, of course, varies by circumstances of the day or year and by institutional tradition, but in every case there is a strong commitment on the part of leadership of the divisions of student affairs to make appropriate, frequent, and public recognition for productive achievement of staff.

There are extensive and formal rewards programs at Florida State University for both service and outstanding achievements that include awards for developing outstanding student programs, creative approaches or solutions to problems, research and creativity, community service, and long-term contributions. Similarly, the award system at the University of North Carolina-Wilmington recognizes excellence in devotion to duty, innovation, public service, safety and heroism, and outstanding new employees. Samford University holds monthly celebrations designed to recognize staff accomplishments, birthdays, and personal achievements. Leaders at Broward Community College like to "honor success . . . and give lots of positive reinforcement to people," according to George Young, who says that finding many examples of staff helping students achieve success and playing the stories back to staff in public celebrations is a way of "representing our culture." Similarly, recognition ceremonies also play important roles at the University of Richmond, Johnson County Community College, James Madison University, Florida State University, and the University of Maryland-College Park with varying themes and emphases.

Effective Organizational Structures

An axiom of bureaucracy is that if one wishes to ensure the accomplishment of certain tasks, one must organize to make them happen. Organizational structures often become top-heavy and cumbersome, losing their effectiveness. The organizational structures of the institutions studied are readily apparent, but none appears counterproductive. Each in its own way has found a structure to offer the best chance of maintaining quality. Far from being magic bureaucratic bullets, these colleges and universities exemplify variation around core features of their organizational structure.

Conditional Models

Each case site has its own unique organizational structure designed to reflect the contingencies of the particular institution. There are similarities across the case sites, of course. All are organized bureaucratically, for example, with layers of administrative structure beginning at the top with a vice president for student affairs or a dean of students who maintains a staff of associates and oversees departments, each with its own leader. Most staff members in student affairs work for and report to a department director who is clearly responsible for the performance of the unit.

Staff at Johnson County Community College seem particularly content with their very formal bureaucracy. They designed it to reflect the best business practices in the geographical area and the best community colleges, then honed it to a very high level of professionalism in its application. This organization also is unusual in that it carries a strong tone of compassion for people despite its apparent inflexibility. "You have to care about people and we don't want inconsistent practices [regarding our people]," says Dayton.

Broward Community College's organization is responsive to its central downtown campus and multiple suburban campuses. Despite insufficient staff to create a complete management team on each campus, it has found a way to stretch the oversight capabilities of their administrators across several campuses. This system has several notable flaws, but it works at this site.

Distributed Authority

Each member of the student affairs teams at the case sites seems to possess a clear sense of responsibilities and to feel empowered by the assignment of authority to appropriate persons within the organization. Department heads in each case are the key members of the organization from a production perspective. They are the persons looked to and finally held accountable for the achievements of the unit.

Bud Thomas at the University of Maryland-College Park maintains that he hires excellent people, creates a climate for high expectations of superior performance from them, and establishes a relationship with them that allows them to decide the major issues in their departments. He calls this the 85 percent–15 percent principle, meaning he allows them to make about 85 percent of all decisions in their departments but reserves the rest for himself. George Young at Broward Community College prefers to speak about hiring excellent people and then empowering them to do their work. Other institutions studied employ variations of these approaches. Florida State University depends heavily upon the department heads, though they are members of one to three teams who work directly with the vice president in problem solving; Johnson County Community College uses a regularized system of training and supervision to guide their department heads; the University of Richmond employs a dual organization of "coordinate colleges" to capitalize on single-sex configuration and smallness to work with students; Samford University's size and institutional character allows for the best use of charisma in the vice president and collaborative tactics to achieve well-understood goals; the University of North Carolina-Wilmington depends upon standardization of procedures and the strong personal leadership style of its vice president and other senior-level staff to make an otherwise traditional organizational structure work; and James Madison University uses its relationship-dependent staffing practices to create revolving associate vice president–level positions that not only bring periodic freshness to the management of the units but provides internship-like experiences for aspiring staff.

Interdependent Departments

Though the units of the divisions of student affairs, normally departments, are clearly assigned responsibilities, they also recognize their connections to other units and to a larger purpose at an institutional level. This is the organization level that gives rise to collaborative strategies and to a culture of teamwork among all members of the organization.

Without exception, the institutions studied employ collaborative tactics regularly. They re-create expectations for interunit cooperation and in some cases offer tangible rewards for doing business in this manner. Sometimes the rewards are simply access to resources in other departments, but always they include verbal accolades and encouragement from the vice president.

A particularly noteworthy example of collaboration and sacrifice for the greater good occurred at Samford University, where the staff volunteered to forego raises one year in order to employ a secretary in one department. Collaboration is fostered at Florida State University through the workings of three management teams composed of the vice president and collections of department heads. During meetings of each team, issues or problems within a functional area are brought up for discussion and for development of strategies to address them. In so doing, territorial boundaries are broken down and ownership of adversities and resources can be shared.

Striking Practices

Several aspects of the staffing practices at these case sites stand out not so much for their uniqueness but for their commonality.

Commitment to Hiring the Right Person

A combination of good professional preparation and experience plus good fit between staff member and the institution is standard number one at each case site. All recognize that quality performance is tied to the character, skills, knowledge, and experience of the people who deliver the programs and services. But there is no absolute consensus across all schools as to what makes for good preparation. All vice presidents see the value of formal graduate education in the field as preparation for their positions, and all acknowledge the value of experience. If forced to choose between formal education and experience, most vice presidents at these case sites would choose experience. In most cases, the institutions are not forced to choose between experience and professional preparation; they select from an abundance of highly qualified professionals for mid-level and senior positions. Without exception, however, good fit with the institution is the highest priority in choice of new staff members.

Surprisingly, few of these colleges and universities rely heavily on specific written policies. The commitment instead tends to be embedded in the leadership that gives voice to the mandate to hire the right person. Johnson County Community College's position on this matter, however, stands out for two reasons. First, it does have written policies that underscore the value of proper credentials of persons hired, the role of appropriate recruitment procedures, and the role of the office of human resources in coordinating all processes pertaining to hiring of staff. Second, the attitude of top-level administrators who make final hiring decisions is that every personnel decision is a million-dollar decision, underscoring the reality that most professional staff at the college remain in their positions for many years, and the accumulated expenditures for salary, benefits, and further development is very costly to the institution.

James Madison University prefers to emphasize fit with the environment, but this follows an assumption that properly credentialed persons have made the final competition. Even at the expense of diversity, fit with the institution is demanded. Its view of fit is two-sided. First, the new staff member must be compatible with the family-style, students-come-first culture. Second, the new staff member must be able to bring something to the institution. Each is expected to contribute something valuable beyond carrying out the specified duties stated in a job description.

At the University of North Carolina-Wilmington, sets of checklists about what should or must be done at each stage of a search are used divisionwide. These procedures ensure that whoever is responsible for coordinating the search will be reminded of legal, ethical, and professional standards, as well as institutional policies, within which the search must be conducted. They also ensure that people new to the process are given training in appropriate behavior and responsibilities and are made aware of unacceptable practices for committee members that will allow them to make constructive contributions to the process.

Concern for Teaching Institutional Values

While all institutions want a good fit between staff member and the institution, it is recognized that initial fit is only a starting place. Recognizing that staff members have a greater potential for productivity when they fully understand the institution, each college or university is seriously involved in further education of staff about the institution. Sometimes these activities are structured under staff development, but the larger issue is to ensure full knowledge of the institution and its aims.

Samford University, for example, articulates its mission around nine value statements that not surprisingly include a strong emphasis on religious convictions. The statements include such tenets as belief in God as Creator and in the Christian faith; making ethical choices based on the life of Jesus Christ; openness, truthfulness, justice and fairness among persons of both sexes, all races and ethnic identities, all ages, and all levels of giftedness, and respect for opinions, convictions and beliefs different from their own; and a work ethic characterized by diligence, honesty, thrift, and a sincere effort to do one's best. With a mission containing such strong but arguably vague beliefs, the institution must work at teaching how these values can be learned and practiced. In this case, they also require all operations to translate the value statements into operational goals.

By contrast, Broward Community College's core values are not difficult to articulate, but they are so central to everything done by professionals at the college that staff are reminded of the major purpose of the college time and time again. Service to students is a song of conversation as well as of public pronouncement.

Use of Differentiated Management Tactics

Management tactics at these institutions vary from site to site and from person to person. Obviously, no one best system of management of staff can be identified in these cases. What is consistent is the differentiated nature of their approaches depending upon circumstances and the people involved. Supervision of staff, for example, is a universal commitment of the leaders of the student affairs divisions, but each supervisor seems to have her or his own style or approach to the task. They even vary their approaches sometimes by staff member—for example, between a relatively new and untested staff member and a seasoned old hand. In such a case, the absence of a lockstep approach to supervision is seen as a virtue. Thus, quality of staff supervision varies from site to site, from department to department, and from person to person.

While some sites are able to manage staffing practices in very personalized manners, as at the University of Richmond and Samford University, others employ more systematized approaches. Florida State University employs a concept of team leadership among directors and deans structured to achieve management team building and democratic leadership and to encourage creativity in problem solving and greater collaboration and collegiality across functional areas. The University of Maryland-College Park uses a straightforward structure for department meetings with the vice president, but its internal dynamics include openness and genuine opportunity to contribute to decisions, a very appealing management climate to department-level administrators. Still another style is found at Johnson County Community College, where formal meetings are held by the vice president with department heads and they in turn are formally expected to hold similar meetings with their staffs, but training in supervision and performance evaluation still occurs.

Commitment to Staff Growth

It is universally recognized in the schools studied that even good staff members need to grow on the job, and all display serious commitment to staff improvement through institutionally planned and individually determined activities. Some dedicate large financial resources to this end, but regardless of money available, all are absolutely committed to the professional growth of staff.

Opportunities for staff development at Johnson County Community College are abundant. When asked for examples of development activities available to staff, administrators handed over a seventy-eight-page directory of staff development classes, individual development plans, ongoing programs (twenty-four of them), opportunities for working and learning in the Center for Teaching and Learning, personnel exchange programs, programs for professional and personal development, consortium activities with other colleges and organizations, special opportunities, recognition awards, research support, resources available, and organizational development activities. In a masterful understatement, the president of the college called this plan "comprehensive."

Different resources are available at different sites, but all make a serious commitment to further education of staff. All employ ongoing department-level or individually oriented activities. All put money on the line to achieve the goal of constant staff improvement. Most activities are not unusual; retreats, on-campus speakers, participation in institution-level improvement activities, and attending off-campus meetings and conventions are common. Some institutions even have their own professional conferences each year. The University of Maryland-College Park, for example, holds its Maryland Student Affairs conference as a drive-in conference and has been doing so for more than twenty years. All staff pretty much understand that they are expected to attend, and the leadership of the conference is passed from person to person each year. Florida State University conducts its annual Institute on College Student Values. As at the University of Maryland-College Park, most staff attend the conference each year and the planning is shared by various staff from year to year. Both of these institutions also have the uncommon opportunity afforded by a distinctive relationship with nationally recognized graduate preparation programs in their colleges of education. Not surprisingly, quite a few members of both divisions have graduates and current students in the preparation programs among their staff members. Bud Thomas at the University of Maryland-College Park calls this special relationship "incestuous" in a most positive sense and says it reflects one of the truly distinctive aspects of staffing at the university.

Commitment to staff development at Broward Community College is reflected by the important percentage of the college's budget devoted to such activities. This is true as well at Johnson County Community College, but at Broward it is a policy position applied to all community colleges in the state of Florida. Both of these colleges boast of many, many opportunities for staff development and of nearly universal participation by staff in them.

Not only does James Madison University pour a lot of money into travel for staff, in some departments it also insists on a plan for development, not simply for travel, as the money is spent. It also provides multiple internship-like experiences for staff, and gives them the opportunity to change jobs periodically to gain perspective and new skills. Sometimes these opportunities occur on a grand scale; the student affairs division decided, for example, to make a serious attempt to implement the Student Learning Imperative (SLI), an idea promulgated by American College Personnel Association (ACPA) to refocus educational activities and resources on student learning and personal development. To accomplish this feat it reorganized the division, creating one new unit called the Madison Leadership Center to coordinate all on-campus activities that specifically pertain to SLI. Thus, many new opportunities for learning occur for student affairs staff.

All institutions promote involvement in professional organizations beyond just attending meetings and conferences as a means of both promoting professional development and of supporting the profession. At some institutions, such as Florida State University, the University of Maryland-College Park, and the University of North Carolina-Wilmington, involvement is operationally defined as providing leadership for professional associations.

Summary

Many distinctive staffing features were noted in the eight cases studied. Certain cultural artifacts of the institutions are especially noticeable, including strongly held views of institutional identity, clarity of purpose, traditions of excellence, professionalism, ethics of hard work, and a special sense of family in the division of student affairs. Powerful, stable leadership at each of the sites studied are characterized by an omniscient presence of leaders of the divisions and their long tenure, practical vision, and ability to reward staff for achievement. Effective organizational structures also were located at each site and seem to be characterized by conditional models of organization, distributed authority, and interdependent departments. Certain aspects of staffing practices were striking in these cases, especially the commitment to hiring the right person, concern for teaching institutional values to staff, use of differentiated management tactics, and commitment to staff growth.

Two comments should be made about what was not discovered at these sites. First, no particularly unusual procedures were used to recruit new staff, select among the finalists, orient new staff, develop staff on the job, or evaluate staff performance. Procedures seem not to be the key to their success; they do about what most other institutions do. Their distinctive features do not include any procedures uncommon to the profession.

Second, staff performance evaluation is the weak link at all these colleges; none report excellence in this area, and all report concerns about it. Often, leaders report that they are working on a better plan, but the fact remains that none of the schools studied employ performance evaluation procedures that they feel are particularly effective. Similarly, supervision was found to be very uneven across the schools and their divisions of student affairs, although it fared better than performance evaluation. Even where supervision is consciously and meticulously applied, reactions to it are mixed in terms of effectiveness. A common attitude voiced on the campuses is "I was educated to develop students. I know how to do that and I am pretty good at it. I do not know how to supervise colleagues. I have no training or little training in supervision, I am not good at it, and I do not like it."

Most of the schools studied seem to conceptually merge supervision, staff development, and performance evaluation, thus complicating discrete judgments about the effectiveness of each component of overall staffing plans. When this integrated concept is studied, it is not surprising that institutions report doing better with staff development than with the other aspects. Such activities are similar to institutional goals for students and the schools are comfortable with them. Further, many staff development activities are driven by self-assessment techniques, thus freeing supervisors from the task of deciding or helping to decide what is needed for each staff member's further education. In many cases, staff end up deciding for themselves which staff development opportunities they will participate in given the range of opportunity provided by the institution, which may result, from an administrative perspective, in lost opportunities to help staff improve in areas the institution or supervisors believe need improvement. Several vice presidents express reservations about their institutions' committee-run approaches, indicating that perhaps staff were unaware of some areas in which they really needed to improve. Such approaches make it relatively easy to avoid areas that staff feel uncomfortable addressing. Few staff development activities actually address the acquisition of new professional skills.

Thus, the quality of staffing practices at the schools studied appears not to be determined by procedural practices or even policy but by how certain aspects of the larger organization are applied in divisions of student affairs. Institutional culture, student affairs leadership, distinctive organizational features, and a few special commitments regarding the care of the people of the organization point to successful staffing practice in student affairs.

Chapter Four

Current Staffing Practices
Survey Report

A major reason we wrote this book was the dearth of information in the literature about what exactly the staffing practices in student affairs are and should be. The more we became interested in the topic, the wider the information gap seemed to be. For instance, we have been unable to locate a single national study of staffing practices. The most comprehensive study was by McIntire and Carpenter (1981), who studied employment practices in a single National Association of Student Personnel Administrators (NASPA) region a decade and a half ago. NASPA periodically conducts salary surveys of its member institutions and makes aggregate data available.

Student affairs practitioners may be less interested in the survey results than those seeking empirical foundations for practice. If that is the case, we recommend skipping this chapter and going on to Chapter Five, which deals with staff selection.

As a means to answer the very basic questions about actual staffing practices in the field, we decided to conduct a survey that covered the areas of staff recruitment and selection, new position orientation, job satisfaction, supervisory approaches and content, staff development organization and activities, and performance appraisal practices. In this chapter a summary of these results is presented. More detailed information in the form of tables and copies of the survey instruments is included in Appendix A. Additional information from the survey can be found in Chapters Five through Nine, where the different aspects of the staffing process are discussed.

Survey Methodology

The research method was designed to collect comprehensive staffing data from vice presidents and staff members in the full range of institutions of various type, size, and purpose. Because of limited resources, it was necessary to use only a sample; the total population of more than 3,600 institutions and the length and depth of the questionnaires constructed for the study (more than 100 items, many with multiple response requirements) dictated the selection of a manageable sample. Within these constraints, it was decided to survey up to 500 institutions from three geographic regions of the United States. Our goal was to get up to eleven responses from each institution (two from each of five broad functional areas and one from the chief student affairs administrator).

The sampling plan was constructed to allow for the random selection of fifty institutions from four Carnegie classification types—research universities, comprehensive colleges and universities, liberal arts colleges, and two-year colleges (also referred to as community colleges in this study)—in three regions: the Northeast, the Midwest, and the West. The regions were composed of the following states:

- Northeast: Connecticut, Maine, Massachusetts, New Hampshire, New York, Rhode Island, and Vermont
- Midwest: Illinois, Indiana, Iowa, Michigan, Minnesota, Missouri, Ohio, and Wisconsin
- West: Arizona, California, Idaho, Nevada, Oregon, Utah, and Washington

This schema could optimally have yielded 600 institutions. It actually yielded 491, distributed as shown in Table 4.1. The details of the data collection strategies are provided in Appendix A.

Institutional Characteristics

Of the 121 institutions from which we received responses from the vice presidents, 11 percent are research universities, 36 percent comprehensive colleges or universities, 20 percent liberal arts colleges (23 percent of which are affiliated with a church or some

Table 4.1. Number of Institutions and Respondents by Region and Institutional Type.

Region and Institutional Type	Number of Institutions Eligible for Participation	Number of Institutions That Promised Participation	Number of Institutions That Actually Participated	Number of Vice Presidents/Staff That Provided Usable Data
Northeast	167	49	34	28/181
Research university	18	3	1	1/5
Comprehensive university or college	50	18	14	12/80
Liberal arts college	51	13	8	6/43
Community college	48	15	11	9/53
Midwest	167	77	64	54/355
Research university	19	11	10	7/72
Comprehensive university or college	50	21	19	15/113
Liberal arts college	50	18	13	11/75
Community college	48	27	22	21/95
West	157	68	53	39/280
Research university	18	9	6	6/36
Comprehensive university or college	50	26	24	16/149
Liberal arts college	39	17	9	6/51
Community college	50	16	14	11/44
Total	491	194	151	121/816

other sponsoring body), and 33 percent two-year colleges; 61 percent are publicly supported institutions. Vice presidents were asked what proportion of the total institution's budget in academic year 1992–93 was assigned to student affairs; 35 percent reported they received 5 percent or less of the total budget, 38 percent received 6–10 percent, 12 percent received 11–15 percent; and 7 percent received more than 15 percent.

Demographic Characteristics of Respondents

Table A.1 (Appendix A) contains information about the demographic characteristics of the persons who completed and returned usable questionnaires. Almost three-fifths of them are women, but at the higher level of administration the majority are men (64 percent of the vice presidents and 62 percent of the deans). Women are more conspicuous in other roles; 77 percent of the directors and 57 percent of the coordinators are women. The sample is overwhelmingly white (82 percent of the vice presidents and more than 80 percent of the other categories of staff). In terms of age, the majority of respondents were between ages 31 and 50 at the time of the survey, including vice presidents.

Almost all the vice presidents hold either a master's (40 percent) or doctoral (58 percent) degree. The majority of all categories of staff hold either a master's or doctoral degree. The fields in which those degrees are held, however, are varied and often not directly connected to practice. Almost one-third of the vice presidents hold their highest degrees in areas other than student affairs, counseling, or higher education; 30 percent of the deans, 54 percent of the directors, and 46 percent of the coordinators hold degrees from outside the field. The majority of vice presidents hold doctorates in student affairs (14 percent), counseling or counseling psychology (18 percent), or higher education (39 percent).

One sign of professionalism is affiliation with associations devoted to the advancement of the field. Slightly more than three out of four practitioners who responded to our survey report being a member of one or more professional organizations (state, regional, or national). A significant minority of practitioners, however, are not members of any national professional organization directly related to student affairs. Almost one in five of the vice presidents have no professional memberships, along with one-third of the directors and 17 percent of the coordinators.

Finally, the sample is representative of a broad cross-section of functional areas in student affairs. While we may not argue that the sample is representative of the total field in terms of number of professionals in each functional area, it seems evident that the full breadth of areas of practice is represented.

Recruitment and Selection

Vice presidents were asked to describe their institutions' policies and procedures for filling professional staff vacancies. As can be seen in Table 4.2, most written policy concerning employment resides at the institutional level. Interestingly, only two-thirds of liberal arts colleges have written policies that govern recruitment and selection. It also seems to be a fairly common practice for vice presidents to formulate policies ad hoc, especially at liberal arts colleges, but much less frequently at community colleges and research universities. Only at research universities is it common for the student affairs division to formulate and publish its own policies and procedures for recruitment and selection.

Only about one out of ten institutions has developed written statements of ethics (or adopted a professional association's standards) governing selection and hiring of staff. Only slightly more of the student affairs divisions (17 percent of the total sample) have developed written affirmative action policies or plans.

Vice presidents were asked to estimate what proportion of the division's total budget is expended on recruitment and selection of staff in all categories (that is, professional, allied professional, support, and paraprofessional). Institutional type makes a great deal of difference in this regard. Over 20 percent of the vice presidents indicated that none of their budgets are used for recruitment and selection. This is largely because nearly half of community colleges spend nothing and another 47 percent spend less than 1 percent on recruiting. Most institutions (61 percent) spend less than 1 percent on selection processes. Research universities spend the most, with 23 percent spending 1–2 percent of their divisions' budgets and another 16 percent spending 3–6 percent.

Table 4.2. Policies and Procedures Governing Staff Recruitment and Selection by Institutional Type (Percentages).

Policy or Procedure	Total	Research University	Comprehensive College	Liberal Arts College	Community College
Policies and procedures that govern recruitment and selection					
Written institutional policies	87	93	93	67	92
Written student affairs division policies	16	43	21	17	0
Written student affairs department policies	6	14	9	4	0
Ad hoc policies formulated by VP each time there is a search	31	21	37	46	18
Ad hoc policies formulated by the department in which there is a vacancy each time there is a search	18	21	21	17	13
Policies formulated by each search committee	15	14	12	21	16
Have written student affairs division statement of ethics governing selection and hiring of staff	11	21	13	0	13
Have written student affairs division affirmative action policy governing selection and hiring of staff	17	29	15	13	18
Approximate percentage of total student affairs budget spent on recruitment and selection of staff in all categories					
Nothing	22	0	14	13	47
Less than 1 percent	61	62	63	79	47
1–2 percent	11	23	16	8	3
3–6 percent	5	16	5	0	0

Preparation of Job Descriptions

When a vacancy for a professional position occurs and a decision has been made to fill it, who has the responsibility to prepare the job description and announcement or advertisement? At about two-thirds of the institutions, preparation of job descriptions is the responsibility of the department or functional area director; at 20 percent the vice president has the responsibility.

There are, however, substantial differences by institutional type. At almost all of the research universities department directors have the responsibility of preparing job descriptions. In contrast, at comprehensive colleges 79 percent of the department directors and 13 percent of the vice presidents write job descriptions. At liberal arts colleges 65 percent of job descriptions are prepared by directors and 22 percent by the vice presidents. At community colleges 37 percent of the directors write job descriptions, 31 percent of the vice presidents prepare them, 14 percent are written by the collective departmental staff, and 6 percent are prepared by the college's personnel or human resources office.

Preparation of Job Announcements and Advertisements

Institutions' personnel or human resources departments play a much more prominent role in the preparation of job announcements and advertisements than they do in preparing job descriptions. Overall, the responsibility for preparing job announcements falls almost equally on department directors (38 percent) and personnel offices (37 percent), followed by vice presidents (14 percent).

There are significant differences at different types of institutions. At research universities, announcements are most frequently prepared by department directors (71 percent), followed by personnel offices (14 percent) and search committees (7 percent). At comprehensive colleges and universities, department directors (53 percent) most frequently prepare job announcements, followed by personnel offices (24 percent), vice presidents (16 percent), and search committees (3 percent). At liberal arts colleges, the responsibility for preparing job announcements is more equally spread across several persons or offices; 39 percent of the department directors, 26 percent each of vice presidents and personnel offices, and 4 percent of department staff members have the responsibility. Finally, at community colleges, the personnel office (67 percent) most frequently has the responsibility to prepare job announcements, followed by vice presidents (11 percent), others including the president (11 percent), and department heads (8 percent).

The next question was what processes or media do institutions use to search for professional staff applicants. Recognizing that different approaches might be used depending on the level of the position to be filled, we asked vice presidents which media were used to advertise and recruit professionals at the entry-, mid-, and allied professional levels (see Table 4.3).

Entry-level professionals are most frequently sought through house organs such as institutional newsletters or electronic job listings (83 percent), local media (87 percent), regional professional media including newsletters, web pages, listservs, and telephone message listings (50 percent), and professional conferences (49 percent). Mid-level professional positions (for example, department directors and assistant or associate directors or vice presidents) are announced through local media (88 percent), house organs (84 percent), the *Chronicle of Higher Education* (66 percent), regional professional media (61 percent), and professional conferences (53 percent).

A somewhat different pattern is evident in searching for allied professionals; local media (76 percent) and house organs (61 percent) are the most frequently used means of recruiting them. Almost a quarter of the institutions recruit allied professionals at professional conferences of organizations for specialists in the area sought (for example, law or medicine). (See Table A.2 in Appendix A for a breakdown by institutional type.)

Search Committees

The overwhelming majority—97 percent—of all institutions use search committees to conduct or coordinate the search process for professional staff members. There is wide disparity, however, in the responsibilities of search committees (see Table 4.4).

Looking at the total sample of 121 institutions, the most frequent responsibilities of search committees (in descending order from 74 percent to 52 percent) are to screen applicants to deter-

Table 4.3. Advertising and Recruiting Methods for Entry-level, Mid-level, and Allied Professionals (Percentages).

Advertisement or Recruiting Vehicle	Entry-level Professionals	Mid-level Professionals	Allied Professionals
House organ	83	84	61
Local media	87	88	76
National media	8	22	9
Chronicle of Higher Education	25	66	16
Regional professional media	50	61	36
National professional media	22	36	14
Professional conferences	49	53	24
Other	11	14	12

mine if minimum qualifications were satisfied, select who is to be interviewed or recommend to the appointing authority a list to be interviewed, establish screening procedures, coordinate on-campus interviews, and establish selection procedure. There is wide variance in how the search committees conclude their tasks: 45 percent are expected, after on-campus interviews, to recommend a single candidate to whom to make an offer; 35 percent are instructed to submit a rank-ordered list of qualified candidates following interviews; 45 percent are expected to submit an unranked list of qualified candidates following interviews, and 11 percent are instructed to select a single candidate to whom an offer is to be made. (Vice presidents marked all that applied; therefore, it was possible for responses to total more than 100 percent. In written notes some vice presidents indicated that different instructions were given search committees depending on factors such as level of the position and general health of the department in which the vacancy resided.)

As may be seen in Table 4.4, there is considerable variation in search committee responsibilities across institutional types. Inspection of the data suggests that search committees seem to have

Table 4.4. Duties of Search Committees for Professional Staff by Institutional Type (Percentages).

Responsibility	Total	Research University	Comprehensive College	Liberal Arts College	Community College
Prepare position announcement	13	36	12	8	8
Publish announcement	10	29	12	4	5
Establish screening procedures	59	71	52	67	55
Publish screening procedures	17	29	24	13	8
Establish selection process	52	71	41	58	53
Publish selection process	15	29	19	13	8
Screen applicants to determine if minimum qualifications are satisfied	74	79	69	75	76
Select who is to be interviewed	72	50	69	75	82
Recommend a list to be interviewed	60	86	52	58	61
Coordinate on-campus interviews	58	64	57	63	55
Recommend a candidate to be hired	45	29	36	63	50
Submit a rank-ordered list of qualified candidates	35	36	24	63	29
Submit an unranked list of qualified candidates	45	71	48	13	53
Select a candidate to whom to make an offer	11	0	7	21	13
Negotiate hiring terms/salary with candidate	0	0	0	0	0

Note: Vice presidents were asked to mark all that applied.

greater power and authority at liberal arts colleges in influencing who is ultimately hired. Search committees at research universities seem to have more autonomy to structure themselves and to establish the procedures to be followed in conducting the search, evaluating candidates, and selecting which candidates are to be invited to campus for interviews. These search committees, however, appear to have less assigned authority to select or influence the selection of who is actually hired.

Hiring Decisions

Another important aspect of the hiring process is who makes the final decision about whom to offer the position to after the interview process has been completed. It appears to depend on the level of the position and the type of institution.

When hiring mid-level staff such as department directors (in student activities or housing), the vice president was reported at 78 percent of all institutions to be the final decision maker, followed by the president (15 percent).

The picture changes substantially when considering professionals to fill mid-level positions within functional areas (such as assistant or associate department directors). The primary decision maker for this category of personnel is the department director or other direct supervisor (63 percent), followed in descending order by the vice president (26 percent), president (6 percent), and others.

In regard to entry-level staff, the hiring decisions are made by the department director more than two-thirds of the time, followed in descending order by the direct supervisor about 10 percent of the time, the vice president, the collective department staff, the president, and others.

Still another pattern of decision making seems evident when hiring allied professionals. The department director (38 percent) and the vice president (35 percent) make the final decision about equally, followed by the president (11 percent), a committee and the director supervisor (each 4 percent), and others (3 percent).

When considering institutional type as another variable, even more differentiated patterns of decision making emerge. (See Table A.3 in Appendix A for detailed breakdowns.)

When hiring department directors, the presidents at research universities are never the principal decision makers and very rarely are they in comprehensive colleges or universities, but the president makes the decision almost one-fourth of the time at liberal arts colleges and almost 30 percent of the time at community colleges. The vice president (who often is the direct supervisor as well) makes the final decision most often.

Direct presidential involvement drops precipitously for lower levels of staff: at liberal arts colleges 4 percent, for mid-level and 5 percent for allied professionals, and at community colleges 14 percent for mid-level, 12 percent for entry-level, and 17 percent for allied professionals.

The trend is for hiring decisions to be made at lower levels as the level of the position being filled drops within the organization structure. However, there seems to be relatively more high-level involvement at liberal arts colleges and community colleges than at research universities and comprehensive colleges and universities. For instance, only 57 percent and 33 percent of the hiring decisions for mid-level staff members were made by department directors at liberal arts and community colleges respectively, in contrast to 100 percent and 72 percent at research and comprehensive universities.

Inside Versus Outside Candidates

When there are internal candidates for positions, there exists the potential for hurt feelings and questions about self- or professional value on the part of current staff members if they are not selected, and suspicions of favoritism or unequal treatment on the part of candidates from outside the institution when they learn that an internal candidate was selected. Vice presidents were asked how they handled staff on the sometimes delicate issue of filling vacancies with internal candidates. The results indicate that there is no consensus approach. Almost half of the vice presidents stated that in-house candidates are treated exactly as other applicants; about one-fourth indicated that decisions are made about hiring or promoting in-house applicants before publicly announcing vacancies. A smaller proportion (15 percent) indicated that in-house candidates are not given preference in the selection process but are always interviewed; 8 percent indicated that in-house applicants are given preference in the selection process.

Few differences were evident when analyzed by institutional type. The most apparent difference was in making decisions about promoting existing staff before making vacancy announcements: 25 percent of research universities follow the practice, 23 percent of comprehensive colleges, 17 percent of liberal arts colleges, and 28 percent of community colleges. Research universities (58 percent) and community colleges (54 percent) are most likely to treat all applicants exactly alike.

Orientation to New Position

One of the most neglected aspects of the staffing process is the orientation to the new position and institution once a staff member has been selected and arrives for work. Of the staff who had been in their positions three years or less, only 61 percent had any kind of orientation to their new position. When queried further and asked if the orientation was formally structured, only 39 percent indicated it was. Thus, only 23 percent of the respondents who had taken a new job in the past three years had a formal orientation to their new positions.

Respondents to Form B of the staffing survey also were asked who had assumed responsibility for conducting their orientations. They replied that their direct supervisors (38 percent) are responsible most often, followed by their department directors who were not direct supervisors (32 percent), panels of different staff addressing various topics (15 percent), a peer or peers (1 percent), and others (13 percent).

Even though formal orientations were not found to be the general rule, we sought to learn what topics were addressed during the orientation (whether formal or informal) and how well new staff thought they were covered. More than half of the respondents indicated that the following topics were addressed poorly or not at all: job expectations, personnel policies, office procedures and policies, relevant resources, potential or real problem situations, institutional culture, student affairs culture, performance evaluation process, staff development policies, and characteristics of the faculty. Topic areas in which the majority of the respondents reported good or adequate coverage are: performance expectations, benefits plans, introduction to staff with whom respondents would work, and student population characteristics. (See Table A.4 in Appendix A for a detailed breakdown.)

Supervision

The next area investigated was supervision. The issues explored in this area included how often staff receive supervision, what topics are addressed during supervision (both received and given), and the kinds of follow-up that take place after supervision. We also sought to learn the general approach supervisors take in their work with staff.

Staff Supervised and Frequency of Supervisory Sessions

One of the first items of inquiry in this section of the survey concerned the number of staff members supervised by each respondent. The results: 36 percent supervise ten or fewer professional staff members; 28 percent supervise eleven to twenty; 8 percent supervise twenty-one to thirty, and 28 percent personally supervise forty or more professional staff members. For allied professional staff, 83 percent supervise ten or fewer; 6 percent supervise eleven to twenty, and 17 percent report supervising more than twenty. For support staff, 42 percent responded that they personally supervise ten or fewer; 18 percent supervise eleven to twenty; 10 percent supervise twenty-one to thirty, and 30 percent supervise more than thirty. Eighty-seven percent report supervising ten or fewer graduate assistants; 4 percent supervise eleven to twenty, and 10 percent report supervising more than twenty. We are suspicious of these results. Some respondents may have reported the total number of staff members that work in the unit or units for which they have responsibility, not the number of staff they personally supervise, which was the question.

We also inquired of supervisors how often supervision was given to staff. In Table 4.5, the frequency of supervisory sessions given by category of staff is reported. Between 54 percent and 64 percent of all categories of staff reported that they provide supervisory sessions at least monthly. Over 10 percent of the supervisors,

**Table 4.5. Frequency of Supervisory Sessions Given
to Different Categories of Staff (Percentages).**

	Frequency of Supervisory Sessions			
Category of Staff	None	1–2/year	4–6/year	Monthly or more frequently
Professional staff	11	12	14	64
Allied professional staff	12	17	16	54
Support staff	4	22	18	57
Paraprofessional staff	8	13	15	63

however, reported giving professional staff no supervisory sessions
and another 12 percent indicated they give them supervision only
one or two times per year. They also indicated that they provide
supervisory sessions for allied professionals even less frequently.

Topics Addressed During Supervisory Sessions

Table 4.6 reports the topics addressed during supervisory sessions
and the relative frequency with which each was addressed. Very few
topics seem to receive routine or customary attention. Across all
levels of staff, there seems to be relatively frequent attention to
short-term work assignments (things to be done within the next
few days or weeks), new knowledge or information, and little else.
This becomes somewhat more cogent if one remembers that
almost half of all staff members reported having supervisory sessions six times a year or less. It is not feasible to expect that all
these topics should be covered in each session, but topics outside
of the daily functions of the unit seem to receive minimal attention on many campuses. If the field's values include development
of the whole person, then perhaps supervisors need to look at what
they attend to during supervisory sessions. (More detailed suggestions about supervision are presented in Chapter Seven.)

Table 4.6. Topics (as Perceived by Staff) Addressed During Supervisory Sessions by Position Title (Percentages).

Topics	Deans (n = 7)			Directors (n = 52)			Coordinators (n = 185)			Nonadministrative (n = 64)		
	Never	Occ.	Freq.	Never	Occ.	Freq.	Never	Occ.	Freq.	Never	Occ.	Freq.
Work assignments to be accomplished in near future	0	57	43	2	53	45	2	47	51	2	44	54
Short-term personal goals (such as increase exercise)	50	33	17	29	67	4	33	52	15	31	56	13
Short-term professional goals (such as join professional organization)	34	50	17	15	79	6	27	63	10	33	57	10
Long-term personal goals (such as assertiveness)	33	67	0	40	54	6	27	63	10	32	57	11
Long-term professional goals (such as improve report writing)	50	50	0	27	59	14	18	67	15	22	67	11
Personal attitudes (such as cooperation, sarcasm)	17	83	0	16	62	12	29	57	14	27	68	5
Professional skills (such as program evaluation)	16	67	17	11	67	12	12	64	22	50	39	11
Personal skills (such as time management)	33	67	0	31	61	8	25	61	14	28	63	9
Interpersonal relationships	17	83	0	23	69	8	27	56	17	20	67	13
Work attitudes (such as thoroughness, enthusiasm)	17	83	0	27	63	10	30	57	13	19	67	14
Values of profession	43	43	14	31	61	8	25	54	21	30	47	23
New knowledge or information	43	43	14	47	10	43	0	47	53	16	50	44
Professional ethical issues	33	67	0	23	60	16	32	48	20	12	58	20
Progress toward position(s) of greater responsibility		8	30	40	48	12	28	55	17	35	41	24
Mistakes or instance(s) of faulty or poor judgment	17	83	0	31	67	2	34	64	5	30	64	6
Inadequate work performance	33	67	0	61	37	2	31	67	2	67	33	0
Exemplary (outstanding) work performance or production	43	43	14	19	61	20	5	58	37	12	63	25
Short-term career goals	33	50	17	29	65	6	27	60	13	32	52	16
Long-term career goals	53	33	17	31	65	4	39	58	11	33	56	11

Note: Occ. = responses of seldom and sometimes, Freq. = responses of often and always, Deans = staff with titles associate or assistant vice president and dean (not VPSA), Directors = staff with titles department head or director and assistant or associate dean, Coordinators = assistant or associate department director and coordinator. Nonadministrative = staff with titles such as physician, psychologist, accountant.

Satisfaction with Supervision Received

Staff were asked how satisfied they are with the supervision they had received during the current academic year in terms of frequency, skills of the supervisor, and helpfulness of the supervision. (The responses are summarized in Table A.5, Appendix A.) It appears that deans are the least satisfied with the supervision they received. Over 70 percent of staff in all categories seem satisfied with supervision as currently provided. How much of a base they have for comparison, however, cannot be determined from these data.

Training to Provide Supervision

A common comment from practitioners is that professional preparation programs do not place enough emphasis on teaching how to provide supervision. To shed some light on this topic, staff were asked where, if at all, they received training in providing supervision. Only about half of the respondents reported that they had ever received formal training in providing supervision. Broken down by position classifications, 44 percent of the deans, 41 percent of the directors, 55 percent of the coordinators, and 43 percent of the nonadministrative staff have received formal training in providing supervision.

Of those who have, 55 percent received it in graduate preparation programs. Less than half (48 percent) had received training at another institution prior to assuming their current position; about one-third had received (or were currently receiving) training in supervision in their current position.

Staff also were asked about the quality of training that they had received in providing supervision. All the deans rated their training as fair. Over three-fourths (85 percent) of the directors rated their training as excellent or good, 18 percent fair, and 6 percent poor. Coordinators rated their training as excellent (23 percent), good (52 percent), fair (15 percent), and poor (3 percent). Nonadministrative personnel rated their training as 21 percent excellent, 58 percent good, and 21 percent fair.

Staff Development

The goals of this part of the survey were to discover what kinds of activities student affairs divisions provided their staff, what staff development activities student affairs professionals engaged in, and the budget expenditures for staff development.

Staff Development Activities

Vice presidents were asked to identify the kinds of activities available on their campuses and how often they are offered (see Appendix A, Table A.6). More than 60 percent of the student affairs divisions hold social events two to four times per year; when examined by institutional type there seem to be few differences. Most student affairs divisions schedule on-campus speakers once or twice per year. Research universities, due perhaps to size and available resources, have more speakers than other types of institutions; community colleges invite speakers as part of their staff development activities less often (48 percent reported having no speaker in the current year).

Most student affairs divisions do not sponsor division-level workshops for their staff, and when they do, they are held no more than once per year. Department-based workshops seem more frequent than division-level workshops. Most workshops, whatever the base, tend to be of short duration—four hours or less.

We also asked staff to identify the kinds of professional development activities in which they had been engaged during the current year (see Table 4.7). The picture painted by their responses portrays most practitioners as active in furthering their professional development. About 65–75 percent attended one or more off-campus workshops during the year; about 75 percent attended at least one professional association convention; 20 percent participated in preconvention workshops or extended summer programs or institutes. Conversely, about 25–40 percent of staff members did not attend an on-campus speaker program; only about 55 percent attended an on-campus workshop.

Staff development does not always require someone else to provide opportunities. There are many individual activities that can contribute to one's professional development. For instance, 55 percent received coaching from a senior staff member; about 50–60

Table 4.7. Frequency of Participation in Selected Staff Development Activities During Previous Twelve Months (percentages).

Activity and Frequency	Deans	Directors	Coordinators	Nonadministrative
Attended off-campus (not part of a convention program) workshop				
0	35	21	22	26
1	18	7	27	22
2	18	15	21	17
3	12	36	12	13
4 or more times	18	21	18	23
Attended professional association convention				
0	6	24	19	31
1	65	24	41	38
2	12	32	31	26
3	12	8	8	1
4 or more times	6	12	2	4
Attended on-campus professional development workshop (4+ hours)				
0	23	36	43	40
1	47	19	28	31
2	6	24	13	15
3	18	15	8	6
4 or more times	6	4	3	8
Received coaching from senior staff member				
0	25	32	45	38
1	19	0	11	15
2	0	12	7	13
3	0	8	6	5
4 or more times	56	47	31	28
Received personal consultation to solve a specific problem				
0	53	56	36	31
1	6	4	16	21
2	12	4	11	21
3	0	4	7	5
4 or more times	29	32	33	35
Performed independent research on a topic				
0	53	40	47	44
1	6	8	18	18
2	12	4	12	14
3 or more times	29	40	23	24

Table 4.7. *(continued).*

Activity and Frequency	Deans	Directors	Coordinators	Nonadministrative
Authored or coauthored a manuscript for publication				
0	82	68	86	88
1	12	12	11	6
2	6	17	1	4
3 or more times	0	4	2	4
Read a book directly related to student affairs				
0	35	36	40	50
1	6	12	18	22
2	23	12	21	15
3 or more times	36	40	26	12
Read a professional journal article				
0	0	12	7	9
1	18	8	4	13
2	0	0	3	18
3 or more times	82	80	82	85
Participated in summer professional development program or institute				
0	82	79	82	78
1	18	21	18	22
Attended preconvention workshop				
0	71	72	76	79
1	23	24	21	10
2 or more times	6	3	4	11
Attended on-campus professional development speaker program				
0	23	36	40	36
1	41	15	20	15
2	23	24	15	19
3 or more times	12	25	24	29
Enrolled in graduate class directly related to the field				
0	88	85	84	86
1	6	3	8	4
2 or more times	6	11	9	10

Activity and Frequency	Deans	Directors	Coordinators	Nonadministrative
Volunteered to assume responsibility in an area in order to get new or additional experience				
0	41	28	32	35
1	53	24	29	31
2	6	32	21	19
3 or more times	0	16	21	14
Conducted data-based research study				
0	71	64	74	67
1	23	12	17	24
2	6	8	5	8
3 or more times	0	16	14	8
Attended program or workshop to enhance personal growth				
0	12	33	43	40
1	41	29	23	18
2	35	13	16	18
3 or more times	12	25	20	24
Attended program or workshop to develop personal skills (such as time management, speaking, writing)				
0	53	56	59	59
1	12	28	18	15
2	35	4	16	14
3 or more times	0	12	7	12
Acquired new technical skills (such as use of computer program)				
0	53	53	40	37
1	18	36	35	10
2	18	0	14	3
3 or more times	12	8	10	16

Note: $n = 448$. Deans = staff with titles associate or assistant vice president and dean (not VPSA). Directors = staff with titles department head or director and assistant or associate dean. Coordinators = assistant or associate department director and coordinator. Nonadministrative = staff with titles such as physician, psychologist, accountant, nurse.

percent received consultation in solving a specific problem. Only 20–30 percent, however, authored or coauthored a manuscript for publication; over half conducted independent research on a topic, but only 20–25 percent conducted data-based research. A large majority (over 75 percent) read four or more journal articles, but only 50–60 percent read a book directly related to the field.

Funding and Organization of Staff Development

As can be seen in Table 4.8, only about half of the student affairs divisions have a budget or budget line specifically for staff development. (At liberal arts colleges only 11 percent and at community colleges only 19 percent have such a budget line.) Overall very little of the average division's budget is devoted to staff development; 10 percent reported spending nothing and about half devoted less than 1 percent of the division's budget to staff development activities.

Most institutions use committee structures to organize and plan staff development programs. About 25 percent of the responding vice presidents indicated that staff development is handled solely by a division committee, another 26 percent are coordinated joint efforts between division and department committees, and 12 percent assign staff development to departments. A small minority (5 percent) responded that staff development is solely the responsibility of the individual. Only 10–20 percent of the institutions have written policies that govern staff development activities.

Performance Appraisal

Respondents to Form B of the staffing survey were asked about their experience with performance appraisal: how frequently it took place, what information was used in the evaluation, and what kind of follow-up took place after completing the performance appraisal.

From 26 to 35 percent of the responding staff members indicated that they had received no formal performance appraisal the previous year. A majority (52–55 percent) reported they had a single annual appraisal. Informal appraisals tended to take place somewhat more frequently. From 25 percent to 45 percent of the respondents indicated that they were unaware of any informal appraisals being conducted; if informal processes were used, they tend to take place one or two times per year. (See Appendix A, Table A.7 for a more detailed breakdown.)

In Table 4.9 one may observe that the supervisor's observations are the most frequently used data in making performance appraisals. Examination of accomplishment of previously established goals (44–67 percent), evaluations of programs for which the staff member was responsible (41–60 percent), and self-evaluations (for all except nonadministrative staff) were all frequently used. For staff with the titles of dean and assistant or associate vice president, budget information was an important part of the performance appraisal. Student and staff evaluations were little used for any category of staff as part of the performance appraisal data.

The final set of questions asked about performance appraisal concerned follow-up to the appraisal process (see Table 4.10). The most prevalent kinds of change that follow performance appraisals are recommendations for professional development activities (about one-fourth of the time), establishment of new goals for the position (10–34 percent of the time), establishment of new personal or professional goals (35–41 percent of the time), and annual salary adjustments (about 25–35 percent of the time). Very infrequently do follow-ups take the form of changes in supervision or position responsibilities, or recommendations for behavior change. Considering these data, one is led to wonder whether performance appraisal is taken seriously in student affairs as a means of improving staff performance.

Job Satisfaction

The last area explored through our surveys was job satisfaction. In particular, we were interested in learning about the degree of satisfaction student affairs practitioners have with their current positions. In response to that straightforward question, 2 percent indicated they are very dissatisfied with their jobs, 10 percent dissatisfied, 6 percent neutral, 60 percent satisfied, and 22 percent very satisfied. This produced a weighted mean of 3.90 on a 5-point scale (1 = very dissatisfied and 5 = very satisfied). Overall, it appears that student affairs practitioners are quite satisfied with their positions.

We next asked about the single most rewarding aspect of their jobs. Overwhelmingly, staff responded that working directly with

Table 4.8. Expenditures for Staff Development by Institutional Type (Percentages).

Budget or Expenditures	Total	Research University	Comprehensive College or University	Liberal Arts College	Community College
Student affairs division has budget specifically for staff development	48	57	40	11	19
Approximate percent of 1992–93 student affairs budget spent for *on-campus* staff development activities					
None	10	0	10	13	11
Less than 1 percent	52	64	45	48	57
1–2 percent	26	29	26	30	22
3–4 percent	8	7	10	0	5
5–6 percent	3	0	7	0	3
7 percent or more	2	5	0	0	3
Approximate percent of 1992–93 student affairs budget spent for *off-campus* staff development activities (excluding attendance at professional association conventions)					
None	11	7	10	13	11
Less than 1 percent	42	43	44	42	40
1–2 percent	39	50	37	38	37
3–4 percent	6	0	5	8	9
7 percent or more	3	0	5	0	3
Have written division policy about staff development	10	21	12	8	5

Budget or Expenditures	Total	Research University	Comprehensive College or University	Liberal Arts College	Community College
How staff development is managed					
Division committee plans and organizes	25	33	40	13	13
Division staff member responsible for student development activities	8	17	8	13	13
Staff development is solely the responsibility of departments	12	25	3	17	15
Staff development is solely an individual responsibility	5	0	5	0	10
Staff development is a coordinated effort between the division and departments	26	17	23	35	28
Staff development at division and in departments is conducted independently	16	8	15	22	15

Table 4.9. Data Used in Performance Appraisals (percentages).

Type of Data	Deans	Directors	Coordinators	Nonadministrative
Supervisor's observations	83	88	91	92
Students' evaluations	33	24	26	10
Support staff evaluations	17	12	22	15
Evaluations of programs for which responsible	50	41	60	60
Data provided by staff member related to pre-established goals	67	44	59	55
Peers' observations/ evaluations	0	41	30	32
Budget information	67	6	36	21
Self-evaluation	50	74	62	22

Note: n = 246.

students is the greatest reward they receive from their jobs; a distant second is being a member of an educational community. Nothing else rivaled the significance of working directly with students, but as can be seen in Table A.8 in Appendix A, a number of other rewards were attractive to small subsets of practitioners.

Finally, we asked staff if they were planning to change positions within the next twelve months. Thirty percent responded "yes." That group was then asked whether their plans were to seek a position inside or outside the student affairs field. Almost two-thirds (64 percent) plan on remaining in student affairs. Their primary reasons given for seeking a new position were increased pay and desire for a position of greater responsibility.

Table 4.10. Follow-up of Performance
Appraisals by Position Title (*n* = 241, percentages).

Action Following Appraisal	Deans	Directors	Coordinators	Nonadministrative
Recommendations for professional development activities	0	29	26	26
Changes in supervision procedures or process	17	0	8	4
Salary adjustments for next year	33	29	34	26
Establishment of new position goals	0	32	34	10
Reassignment of position responsibilities	17	3	11	2
Establishment of new personal and professional goals	0	41	35	36
Recommendations for behavior change	17	3	10	11
Nothing related to performance	17	35	20	38

Note: Respondents were requested to mark all that applied.

Of those seeking a new position, 36 percent plan to look outside of student affairs. No single reason was identified for leaving the field that was endorsed by more than one or two persons. Some of the reasons given included poor prospects for advancement in student affairs, inadequate pay, lack of prestige for student affairs professionals, inflexibility of work requirements (incompatibility with raising a family), and desire to work in another area of higher education.

Summary

These data provide a single-dimension practitioner perspective on staffing practices in student affairs. The perspective is limited, of course, by the nature and content of the questions asked in the surveys, but overall one senses that staffing practices in student affairs are not monolithic. There are in fact many staffing patterns, sometimes associated with type of institution or level of position, but more often with local institutional preferences and styles of upper- and mid-level administrators.

Multiple interpretations of the data presented in this chapter are possible. As the staffing job is getting done—that is, some level of functioning was reported in each area—one might interpret the data to support a view of the generally adequate nature of current practices. By contrast, as needed improvements were noted in every area of staffing included in the survey, one might interpret the data in a manner to highlight the generally incomplete form of staffing in each area. Needed changes to current practice seem evident in each area of staffing, and the most serious deficiencies were noted in orientation to new position, supervision, and performance appraisal staffing functions.

Further interpretations of findings from the surveys are presented in Chapters Five through Nine, which are devoted to detailed discussions of each staffing area. These interpretations are in synthesized or combined form so as to include evidence from case studies and literature reviews as well as survey data in the form of conclusions that can be reached from all research conducted for this study. Our conclusions, therefore, are related contextually to each staffing area.

Chapter Five

Recruitment and Selection of Staff

An excellent student affairs staffing program begins with hiring the right people and placing them in positions with responsibilities that allow them to maximize their skills, knowledge, and talents in the pursuit of student affairs' purposes. There are no equivalent substitutes for talented and professionally competent staff in a student affairs division of excellence. The first commandment for student affairs administrators, therefore, is to hire the right people. The second commandment is to do it the right way.

Both of these rules or standards for achieving excellence in staffing are discussed in depth in this chapter using literature, original research, and some voices from the field. The application of both rules is consistent with the values of the profession as described in Chapter One and with the model of staffing detailed in Chapter Two. From the inception of a need for a new staff member through a careful analysis of the position and a successful search for the right person, the values of human dignity, equality, and community must guide every action. The actions are, of course, tempered by the institutional culture and constraints imposed by the environmental context, but above all they must reflect a vision for educational excellence to be achieved in a humane atmosphere.

Student affairs divisions are faced with several significant problems in recruiting and selecting the right staff:

- Staffing practices often are determined by institutional- or governing-level agents and not by division-level policy.

- Thorough position analyses often are not conducted prior to launching searches for new staff.
- Many institutions are handicapped in their recruitment of excellent staff by market conditions beyond their immediate control.
- Searches for new staff often are burdened by ethical breaches by both institutional representatives and applicants.
- Many student affairs divisions fall short of achievement of their goals for diversity.
- Recruitment and selection procedures across levels of staffing, including professional, allied professional, support staff, and paraprofessional staff may not be sufficiently differentiated to achieve the best results.

Our research highlights these issues among other discoveries of generally effective recruitment and selection practices in the field. A brief discussion of some of them is presented for context, then an in-depth review of literature is presented, followed by a synthesis of our findings from case study and survey research on staffing practices. Next, we discuss our overall findings in the framework of the staffing model presented in Chapter Two and conclude the chapter with some recommendations for practice.

Persistent Issues in Recruitment and Selection of Staff

The practices that govern the hiring of new staff often are not determined by division-level policy. Instead, a philosophy of hiring is present at the division level (and in the cases we studied this was a distinguishing feature of the hiring practices), but nothing beyond the personal commitment of administrators to hire the right person seems to be in place in most of the institutions. Likewise, little attention is given to this issue in the literature reviewed. If the recruitment and selection of new staff is as high a priority as it seems to be, it is remarkable that so few institutions have committed themselves formally to policy positions on the issue. Though policy statements alone might not ensure adherence to carefully followed procedures in every instance, they surely would help at least with consistency; coupled with commitments by managers, they might offer some tangible evidence of commitment to hire the right person every time. Very little money is spent on hiring, according to our survey data, and this too seems inconsistent with stated beliefs that hiring the right person is priority number one in staffing practices. The presence of policy might further ensure that budgeted resources for recruitment and selection of new staff are available. The need for resources to hire new staff seems self-evident in an institution committed to high-quality educational service to students.

A related matter that seems unresolved or unclear is the absence of careful job or position analyses prior to launching searches for new staff. This is a case where the literature is clear: conducting a job analysis is an essential prerequisite to recruitment and selection of new staff. Case data, however, suggest that such practice is nowhere near universal or consistent. It may be assumed that job analysis is likely when a new position is created, but little evidence suggests that such analyses are conducted routinely when staff members are replaced. This seems an important matter for further attention by administrators committed to delivering quality service to constituencies on a dependable basis.

Not surprisingly, many institutions have severe limitations on their searches for new staff. These may be caused by geography, resources, or the mission of the institution, but whatever the cause, the playing field simply is not level for all institutions in their recruiting efforts.

There is evidence of ethical breaches on the part of hiring officials and applicants for positions. A fortuitous exchange of messages on a listserve [studev-l@uconnum.uconn.edu] in late spring of 1995 pointed to multiple abuses on all sides of the issue. Responding to a simple request from one professional for examples of ethical lapses in hiring, dozens of other professionals responded. Here are some examples of responses highlighting lapses by hiring officials. (Identifying information has been removed.)

> I have to admit that I've experienced more unprofessional treatment in job searches than I care to remember, and for a while it made me wonder what I was getting into. The most egregious example I recall is when I participated in an on-campus interview for an entry-level position. I went through a day and a half of interviews, from students to the CSAO and included making a presentation. As I was leaving the hiring authority's office to return home, I remember

very clearly being told, "If you're the person for the job, and I think you are, we'll be in touch in about a week." I never heard from them again. The hiring authority refused to take my phone calls and didn't respond to my status check letters. This was in 1987, and I still don't know if I'm getting the offer.

I interviewed at a large Southern institution. In a telephone conversation with the director, I asked about the presence of internal candidates with strong credentials and was told that there were none. (We "know" how this goes.) I got to the interview and the first thing the director told me was that there was an internal candidate. In fact, this person, whose position reported to the position I applied for, was an alum and had eighteen years in the office. Guess who was my tour guide for the next hour or so, asking me how I might improve things?

I am waiting from institutions to hear if I got the job or not—one was twelve years ago. But what really irks me is when schools notify unsuccessful candidates with the infamous form letter. I don't see a problem using this device when someone doesn't make the first cut, but when you are a finalist?! At one institution, I was one of two finalists. I didn't get an offer, but did receive a dittoed letter (with purple ink and all) saying that there were hundreds of people who applied and we couldn't respond to all. . . . Excuse me, but I was one of two.

One of the things that concerns me most are illegal questions. A candidate finds him/herself in a Catch–22. If you respond, "I'm sorry, that is an inappropriate question and I don't feel comfortable answering it," it doesn't look very good. If you respond with 100 percent disclosure, that may not look good either.

I've had the terms of the job offer changed once the offer was made. On another (an internal position), I was passed over for the other applicant (also internal) who had no experience for the job, and I had six years. I wondered if it had something to do with the fact that I was over four months pregnant at the time, and she had no intention of having more kids? How do you prove that? A rejection letter I received once didn't really reject me; it was a general announcement that went like this: "We at 'such and such institution' are pleased to announce our new hall director staff for the upcoming year," and then listed their names and institutions the newly hired came from. Nope, my name wasn't on the list. Guess I didn't get hired. (At least I don't think so. That was fourteen years ago!)

It seems that each time I have been involved in a job search I have encountered unethical situations. In my first search, I was contacted by a school where I had an on-campus interview and was told that I did not get the job. OK, so this was a good thing and I was given feedback upon which to improve my performance. After I had time to absorb this and come to terms with not getting the job, they called me back and offered me the job!!! I must admit I was flabbergasted to say the least. Being young, desperate, and naive, I accepted the position. I worked there for three years and always felt mediocre.

I interviewed for a position and was the unanimous choice of the selection committee and the dean. I was told not to worry, that the rest was paperwork. I received a call a week later asking if I was considering other offers, and was told to wait and call them prior to accepting any other offer. A week passed and another call comes, informing me that there was some difficulty in the Affirmative Action Office, but not to worry, I would definitely be offered the position. A week later, I was told that I would not be hired.

On the other hand, many instances were cited in the exchange of messages of ethical or professional etiquette breaches by candidates. Here are some examples:

- A candidate's mother was brought to an interview. She waited in the receptionist's office all day.
- One candidate received a speeding ticket on the way to an interview and wanted reimbursement from the institution to pay for it.
- Another candidate asked for reimbursement of a headlight replaced during the trip to the interview.
- Still another candidate brought pets to the interview and wanted the institution to arrange hotel accommodations that would allow pets.
- One candidate gave five references, all with the same address and phone number.
- A candidate was offered and accepted a position, but did not show for work on the first day. She had taken a position elsewhere. The institution had to try to contact her to find out what happened.
- A candidate accepted a position without resigning from the one currently held and wanted to work both jobs, even though they were in different states.

An additional issue in recruitment and selection is that most institutions simply are falling short of their goals for diversity among new staff. Underrepresentation of minorities in higher education and women in senior leadership positions places a special burden on student affairs staffing specialists, as they often are assigned extraordinary expectations for creating climates for out-of-class learning characterized by multiple perspectives. Case study data suggest that most student affairs administrators are fully aware of these shortcomings and want to do better but, for whatever reason, have been unable to fully achieve their goals.

Finally, recruitment and selection procedures across levels of staffing, including professional, allied professional, support, and paraprofessional staff may not be properly differentiated. Intuitively, one would expect that different procedures are appropriate for specialized staff functions with the division; yet most recruitment practices we observed in our research show only minor differences. On the other hand, we observed a consistent application of recruitment principles (perhaps an indication of the effect of student affairs values) in all searches conducted.

Perspectives from Literature

Student affairs books and journals contain helpful material about recruitment and selection of staff and offer substantiation and support for the staffing model presented earlier and for the principles of hiring the right person using the proper procedures. Snyder (1989, p. 300), for example, provides an argument that supports the basic tenet of this book: "Central to delivering a quality program are competent, well-trained, and personable employees. Consequently, it follows that *the most successful student service programs tend to be those where the managers select, hire, and retain competent and caring individuals.*" Snyder's views are consistent with the findings of this study and the perspectives of the student affairs staffing model. Available literature will be used to extend and provide more details about the principles and prerequisites introduced earlier.

Authors who write about recruitment and selection of staff often focus on such concerns as the use of standards of admission to the profession (Stamatakos, 1981) and for the clarification of skills and competences at entry level (Hyman, 1988; Ostroth, 1981), at mid-manager level (Gordon, Borders Strode, and Mann, 1993), and at senior level (Sandeen, 1991). Similar perspectives are presented on the employment of paraprofessionals (Winston and Ender, 1988). Other authors specifically address recruitment and selection efforts for minority candidates (Sagaria and Johnsrud, 1991) including for executive-level positions (Haro, 1991). Other contextual literature includes discussions of institutional systems where, as Sims and Foxley (1980) point out, some institutions have fully operational employee classification systems that govern position analysis and all other personnel matters. Many do not, however. Where the systems are in place, student affairs administrators should, of course, implement them as prescribed. Where they are not in place, student affairs administrators should put into effect their own systems of personnel management that fully consider all the contexts and issues involved in staffing in the field. In either case, it is desirable to base the implemented system on the precepts of development (Sims and Foxley, 1980). Just as student affairs administrators generally adhere to the principles of student development in their educational programming for students, Sims and Foxley argue that similar principles for staff development should form the basis of major personnel decisions.

The literature on recruitment and selections includes some expressed concerns about the overall approach to personnel selection generally used in higher education. Cooper and Garmon (1990), for example, point out that most administrators of American higher education agree with the views of nationally acclaimed management educator Peter Drucker about the preeminence of management decisions and that the decision to hire the right person tops the list of decisions to be made. Observing that behaviors often do not follow beliefs, they ask, "Why then do colleges continue to treat hiring as an esoteric exercise which, somehow by magic, will always accurately identify, attract, and secure the best qualified personnel—in a very unscientific way?" (p. 2). They call for a modern procedure that they refer to as a "holistic approach to hiring" (p. 3), which rests on a careful consideration of multiple perspectives on candidate qualifications and which does not hurry a process that is absolutely vital to the success of the college or university. This view is consistent with the principles enunciated earlier about hiring.

Position Analysis

Authorities generally agree that the recruitment and selection process begins with an effective position or job analysis (Sims and Foxley, 1980; Stimpson, 1993; Upcraft, 1988; Winston and Miller, 1991). "Position analysis is the process of reviewing the duties, responsibilities, and qualification requirements of a position and relating the results of the review to other facets of the personnel function . . ." (Fortunato and Waddell, 1981, p. 43). Other facets include setting of standards for performance evaluation, determining needs for further training and development, and nondiscriminatory employment practices. Stated simply, position analysis allows employers to "know what the job is" (Upcraft, 1988), the debut concern for recruiting and selecting staff.

Position analysis may be accomplished using a variety of methods. These methods are reviewed in Sims and Foxley (1980) and in Winston and Miller (1991) but essentially entail the collection of data, such as obtained from observations, interviews, questionnaires, narratives or logs, and expert analysis, to prepare position descriptions, salary schedules, training and development programs, performance evaluation standards, and standards for equal employment opportunities.

A crucial outcome of position analysis is data upon which position descriptions are prepared and subsequent searches conducted. A position description normally is thought of as the formal statement of duties that defines a position. Position descriptions also may include less formal statements, but equally important, such things as letters of agreement between staff and supervisor (Fortunato and Waddell, 1981). However, the more formal approach is most applicable here.

Fortunato and Waddell demonstrate the many uses of position descriptions. Position descriptions often are used to help avoid the creation of unnecessary positions, to serve as a check against hiring unqualified or overly qualified staff, to plan work for the position, to determine which positions are exempt from the Fair Labor

Standards Act, to set pay rates, to determine standards for evaluating staff performance, to help settle grievances regarding the scope of positions, to conduct salary surveys, and to identify training needs.

Position Descriptions

Authorities agree generally on the content of position descriptions, though some variations are noted. For example, Winston and Miller (1991) include position title, division in which the position is located and title of the supervisor for the position, goals of the position, work activities and procedures of the position, position requirements including minimum education, knowledge, and experiences needed, and conditions of employment. Fortunato and Waddell (1981) list position title, department, date of review, code number, supervisor, functional statement, most significant duties and responsibilities, catch-all duties statement, position requirements, and statement on scope of supervision received. Sims and Foxley (1980) add physical environment and social environment to these lists while Stimpson (1993, p. 136) goes even further to suggest that the position description "should reflect a clear understanding of (a) the mission of the institution and the student affairs division, (b) the contribution of the staff position in question to the accomplishment of that mission, (c) the responsibilities assigned to the position, and (d) the activities a person holding the position will be expected to complete in meeting those responsibilities."

Recruitment Procedures

With the position description in place, authorities turn their attention to recruitment procedures. As a rule, to accomplish this step most institutions employ a search committee, which may be charged with multiple assignments. Bloland and Moore (1982) confirm this practice, but note that "literature on this pervasive phenomenon in higher education is surprisingly meager, long on opinion and short on data" (p. 252). Though it may be entirely legitimate that the specific functions of a given search committee be indigenous to a particular search within a specific institution, it is imperative that the functions be clear from the outset. Such clarity is necessary to achieve the goals of hiring the right person using the proper procedures, but it also is necessary to avoid misunderstandings that sometimes may lead to legal disputes. Dalton (1988), for example, warns administrators of the consequences of ambiguity and unclear procedures. Reminding administrators that the courts often are more concerned with the procedures of personnel searches than with the substance of them, he advises: "Search committees must be clear about their role in selecting finalists and making the job offer. As a rule, it is usually best for the supervisor to reserve final authority for the hiring decision and to make sure at the outset that the committee members know that the supervisor has this authority, so that there is no misunderstanding" (p. 336). Hollander and Young (1991) offer guidelines for student affairs administrators regarding employment responsibilities, and these may serve as appropriate knowledge for all committee members. This argument is carried further by Stimpson (1993), who contends that whatever the assigned role of the search committee, individuals on the committee should be allowed to ask questions of the assigning authority "to minimize the chance of a misunderstanding as the process draws to a close" (p. 139). Stimpson also points out that search committees are the guardians of important standards such as those for affirmative action, that they invariably are involved in handling sensitive information about candidates, and that they should be briefed on issues of confidentially about this information.

Often search committees are asked to prepare announcements for the position vacancy and to advertise for suitable candidates in various media. The goal is to develop a large pool of candidates to enhance the chances of recruiting the right person for the position (Fortunato and Waddell, 1981). The announcement should contain the essential elements of the position description but also information such as the starting date for employment, application deadlines, and application procedures (Stimpson, 1993; Winston and Miller, 1991).

Once prepared, position announcements should be distributed as widely as possible. The breadth of recruitment and thus the reach of public announcements may depend on the nature of the position and the availability of suitable candidates within the geographical area. In most cases of professional or allied professional position announcements, however, widespread use of professional and public media is used. Such practices appear to vary by type of institution. McIntire and Carpenter (1981), for example, note that two-year institutions make much more use of local and regional newspapers for these advertisements than do four-year institutions. They found also that the supervisor was far more likely than the search committee to have prepared the position announcement for many positions; however, the search committee involvement in the announcements increased with the level of the position. Further, composition of the search committee appears to be influenced greatly by the person who forms the committee.

Other functions of the search committee include reviewing applications to determine the final pool of candidates, keeping candidates informed of their status, checking references by telephone, interviewing, and making recommendations for employment (Stimpson, 1993). Each of these functions may vary from committee to committee or across institutions (McIntire and Carpenter, 1981), but some decisive involvement by search committees is inevitable on each of these matters. Sometimes initial screening of applications occurs in the institution's personnel office, but at some point in the screening process, the search committee will be the primary judge of who makes it onto the final list of candidates. Sometimes screening forms are employed by the committee (Stimpson, 1993) to structure the process and to attempt to achieve consistency among committee members. Stimpson also offers advice on the remaining common duties of the search committee. He gives particular emphasis to preparations for and conducting of on-campus interviews, where he stresses quality over quantity of time spent with candidates, and to checking references, where he accentuates the need for accurate information. Both he and McIntire and Carpenter (1981) admit that written letters of reference may not be especially helpful. In the end, the search committee will forward recommendations to the administrator with hiring authority. The list forwarded may be an unranked or ranked list of qualified candidates.

Selection Process

Rickard (1981) offers some helpful ways of thinking about the actual selection process, including variations in how search committees are used (and even what they should be called, such as selection committee, candidate review committee, or screening committee, depending on the functions to be performed), the place of affirmative action goals, what should be included in an application, hiring procedures, reference checks, and interview preparation. These issues and some of the more common problems in recruitment and selection are addressed by Rickard (1984), which also offers advice on what to do about each problem. The most common problems, he maintains, are lack of clarity about decision making and hiring authority, imposition of inappropriate application requirements, lack of commitment to affirmative action principles, impersonal hiring procedures, incomplete and untimely reference checks, inadequate preparation for interviewing, unclear criteria for evaluating candidates, and failure to provide closure in a selection process. Generally, his solutions to these problems include being clear about philosophy, goals, roles, and authority, specifying requirements for the position clearly, contacting finalists personally and handling arrangement carefully, checking references at appropriate times in the selection process and doing them thoroughly, being prepared, being consistent with existing practices, and being candid about the institution.

Bloland and Moore (1982) offer advice on the use of search committees based upon their study of almost 100 executive-level student affairs officers' practices: keep the size of the committee small; assign appropriate support staff (especially for senior-level positions); select a chair who is senior-level to those serving on the committee; allow candidate nominations; begin the selection process as soon as suitable candidates have been identified, and promote political sensitivity in the committee.

Upcraft (1988) provides a candid and helpful summary of these hiring issues in general that may apply to both search committees and supervisors acting in recruitment and selection roles. Succinctly, his advice is to know what the job is, know what you are looking for, act affirmatively, check references, develop a screening process that is clear to everyone, determine the scope of the search, make sure candidates are fully informed, develop an interview plan, share information and decide, make an offer and then negotiate a contract with and hire the winning candidate, and inform unsuccessful candidates as soon as possible.

Perspectives from Research

Research conducted for this study examined staffing practices currently in use and is presented globally in Chapters Three and Four. It is useful here to highlight certain findings regarding recruitment and selection of staff found in those studies to underscore supportive evidence for the staffing principles or standards suggested at the opening of this chapter. The evidence from these studies strongly supports the following conclusions about current practice.

1. *Hiring the right person is the preeminent staffing concern for student affairs.*

Evidence from case studies shows the strongest support for this claim. Institutions studied proclaimed the absolute importance, or the preeminence, of "hiring the right person" to fill vacancies. All institutions treated this staffing phase with the highest respect, with many claiming that it is the most important decision any supervisor ever makes. One administrator at Johnson County Community College proclaimed, "Every personnel decision is a million-dollar decision!" Consistent with this viewpoint, the college also boasts, "Once hired, a lot of systems are in place to support [the new staff member]." Many similar comments could be cited from other institutions where the same views are held.

Survey results focus more on procedures than commitment, but the evidence shows the centrality of recruitment and selection in staffing practices in all colleges and universities studied.

2. *Written policies governing recruitment and selection are sustained at the institutional level. Divisional written policies about recruitment and selection are rare, yet adopted procedures are used unwaveringly.*

Survey results show clearly that recruitment and selection practices are guided by institution-level policies, not student affairs division-level polices. In some cases, especially in community colleges, an office within the administration is formally charged with overseeing these functions, often called the office of human resources. Such offices exist in other institutions and play some important role in the application of policy about recruitment and selection, but they play an especially prominent role in community colleges.

A sense of consistency of practice is revealed in the survey results across all types of institutions and is strongly supported in the case studies. All institutions studied employ recruitment and selection procedures that are carefully followed though not necessarily alike; some minor variations were found in them (though it is difficult to tell from the survey results how much variation exists), but informants at all the schools report that they follow their adopted procedures carefully. Extraordinary care was given to job analysis and to the preparation of position descriptions at only one case site, but this may have reflected the institution's unusual zeal for the use of written policies and procedures. One senses that everyone involved in the recruitment and selection phase of staffing knows how very important the hiring decision is, and they commit themselves firmly to an agreed-upon process.

3. *Procedures used in recruitment and selection are ordinary, conventional, and strikingly consistent.*

In no case, from either the survey or the case studies, were extraordinary procedures discovered; rather, well-regulated, systematic, routine procedures are used. Differences across case sites were exhibited mainly in terms of variable roles for institutional personnel offices and for search committees. In one case, search committees were not employed at all. Significantly, this institution was private.

All institutions reported that they advertise position vacancies, collect applications, screen candidates, check references, bring candidates to campus for interviews, and choose the "best fit" for the job. Variations in each of these steps in recruiting and hiring can be found but they mostly are in emphasis, not formal procedure. For example, one vice president said he would consider firing a supervisor who did not check references carefully! Reflecting on the importance of being well organized, another administrator at the same institution said of their procedures, "[It is important] to look like we know what we are doing." In another instance, consistency in use of policies and procedures was given extraordinary attention to achieve a goal of ensuring that applicants have a clear sense of what they will find if hired by the institution. Though these attitudes and practices may appear exceptional, some form of them was found generally throughout the cases studied, and one suspects they exist in all student affairs units.

Beyond a strict adherence to an institutionally sanctioned process, the procedures used for recruitment and selection of staff at these institutions are not uncommon. Rather, they seem to accomplish routine things well, knowing that such routine procedures matter.

4. *The hiring decision most often is assigned to department heads in student affairs, especially for mid- and entry-level staff, and to vice presidents for decisions about department heads.*

The important role of department heads in the hiring process often begins with preparing the position description. It is not clear from survey data whether a careful job analysis is conducted prior to writing the description. Only in a few cases was such practice noted in case studies, but it is clear that the department head or supervisor of the person to be hired occupies an important role from the beginning of the search process. The department head may appoint the search committee and give the charge for specific requirements of the committee. Naturally, in many cases the vice president is involved in this process, but the department head's role is most obvious.

These hiring authorities also seem to be the keepers of the student affairs divisions' philosophy of hiring, an important feature of the actual hiring decision. Particularly in the cases studied, it was noted that a well-articulated philosophy guides the final employment decision. In these cases, great care is taken to reveal the institutional culture to candidates and to determine whether the candidate would fit within the culture. Even where concerns exist about enhancing diversity of staff, this concern was predominant. As one vice president said, "[We do not believe that we should] throw a bunch of people together and see how things work out." The same view also is evident at another institution where administrators see the task of finding people who can join existing staff by "embracing a sense of organizational purpose," and at another where "being Christian and feeling comfortable working in an avowedly religious institution" are important determinants of the final hiring decision.

5. *Written policies governing ethics and affirmative action are rare in student affairs.*

This condition is surprising given the nationwide interest in institutional diversity and civil rights. The absence of written policies does not mean an absence of concern about the issues, of course, but it is interesting to note how informally this concern is applied to such fundamental practices as hiring. A notable exception was found at one case site, where every unit in the division of student affairs has its own equity officer to oversee hiring and other procedures to be sure the division's goals for affirmative action are achieved whenever possible. Still, the overwhelming fact is that only about 5 percent of the reporting institutions in the survey attend to these concerns by sustaining written policies.

6. *Surprisingly little money (proportional to total budgeted funds) is spent on recruitment and selection of staff.*

Another surprise finding from survey results is that very few budgeted funds are spent on recruitment and selection of new staff. In 1992–93, student affairs divisions appeared to spend a minuscule proportion of their budgets on recruitment and selection of new staff. Almost one-fourth of the reporting institutions (22 percent) spent nothing on recruitment and selection of staff and 61 percent spent less than 1 percent of their budgets for this function. Could this be because so little hiring has been possible in recent years due to fiscal constraints on the institutions? Two-year institutions spent the lowest percentage of their budgets on recruitment and selection (a function of the role of institutional personnel offices?) and comprehensive state colleges and universities spent the highest percentage, but none reported spending more than 6 percent of the budget on these functions.

7. *Most hiring authorities in student affairs choose experience over formal preparation as the most important qualification for employment,*

though the decision normally is balanced between experience and for-mal preparation.

If forced to choose, decision makers usually opt for experience over formal preparation when selecting new student affairs personnel. In most cases, however, the choice is not forced; candidates increasingly are likely to have both. The greatest preference for experience may occur for entry-level candidates, where many newly credentialed candidates do not have significant full-time professional experience. It also may occur when salaries for positions are low. In these cases, the employer may be able to better afford an uncredentialed candidate over the credentialed one.

The Role of Professional Preparation

Throughout our studies, the special role of professional preparation programs in providing qualified and credentialed candidates to employment pools was affirmed time and again. As just reported, hiring authorities may give precedence to experience over formal preparation if the choice is an either-or alternative. But most of the time such is not the case. In most cases today, the final pool of candidates for professional employment are graduates of formal preparation programs, although of perhaps widely variable quality.

In some instances in our case studies we found an absolute commitment to hiring only "fully qualified" candidates, meaning the application of a standard calling for hiring only persons holding master's or doctoral degrees from legitimate (or as one person put it, "pedigree") graduate preparation programs. Such commitment often accompanies a widely held view within the employing institution that the college or university is a highly professional place and that only highly professional people should be hired into it.

Such attitudes have not always been so prevalent in student affairs. In decades past, many were hired into student affairs roles with "appropriate" personal attributes, but there was little concern about whether the person was a graduate from a student affairs preparation program. In fairness, these persons may have held legitimate graduate degrees in some field appropriate for higher education, but they may not have studied the theories, research, and practice that undergird a professional preparation program in the field. The result was, of course, that even twenty years ago most staff working in student affairs roles were not graduates of the field's preparation programs.

This condition surely is changing. Today a clear majority of student affairs practitioners enjoy the benefits of master's degrees in the field and, increasingly, of doctoral degrees. To be sure, allied professionals in the student affairs field hold graduate degrees from their respective disciplines or fields, but taken together, a significant majority of practicing professionals in student affairs today hold graduate degrees in directly related fields—that is, counseling or higher education-based programs with significant student affairs components.

We take special note of this condition in the field of student affairs because it represents a clear trend over several decades toward hiring persons with strong, directly related graduate-level degrees. We also note it, however, because it still is not a controllable gateway of entry into the field and needs to be sustained through diligence and planful behavior by hiring officials. We believe, and think the weight of evidence from our studies supports the contention, that candidates for positions at all levels of student affairs who have graduate degrees in the field are better qualified in both the short and long term than those without such degrees.

We further contend that employers have an ethical and moral obligation to ensure full professional qualifications in all staff. It is our belief that when circumstances require employing someone without graduate professional preparation, it is incumbent upon the employer to provide the necessary educational experiences (on a par with that offered in good master's degree preparation programs) to ensure full qualifications in the staff member in the near term. The option is to hire fully qualified candidates to start with or to provide necessary and appropriate on-the-job and continuing professional education to permit parity of knowledge, skills, beliefs, and values among all staff after they arrive on the job. Our research suggests that most student affairs divisions do not have the resources, especially the time, to assure that underprepared staff acquire the basic skills and knowledge needed to provide optimal levels of services and programs in addition to the duties for which they were hired.

A final comment about graduate programs in the field addresses the appropriate place for doctoral degrees. Just as master's-level preparation is becoming increasingly prevalent in the field, so is there a growing need for advanced study to occupy the increasingly demanding leadership roles in the field. Mid-to upper-level administration is heavily encumbered in today's higher education with multiple requirements for knowledge and skill that only a decade ago might not have been imperative. Research, assessment, and evaluation skills represent only a portion of the mandatory skills needed today. Couple with these abilities the need to know and use legal intelligence, managerial talents, conflict resolution, budget handling, and political negotiation and one has a demand for advanced education and training. The need for more doctoral-level education is already established; leaders within both student affairs divisions and graduate degree programs need to respond with deliberate positive action to prepare the field for the demands of tomorrow.

Some cynics in the field, however, recognize doctoral preparation as only a "union card" required for advancement to senior administrative positions, but see *any* doctoral degree as acceptable. In some cases, they shop for the nearest doctorate-granting university to find the program that is least expensive in terms of time, academic rigor, and personal effort. While this may be convenient, the time has come for employers to begin asking what relationship the content of the degree program has to the work in student affairs for which the person is being considered. Possession of the doctorate should be weighted in employment decisions by the degree to which its content applies to the work of student affairs professionals.

Using the Staffing Model in Recruitment and Selection

There is no one best way to recruit new staff members, and there are no magical tricks in any of the processes. There are, however, certain ideals for practice that pervade any particular archetype or designed structure for accomplishing the task of finding and hiring new staff. The application of the values of the profession, for example, constitutes a near-inviolate rule for successful recruitment.

Locating and hiring the right person by the proper means is consistent with the values of the profession and with the standards for recruitment and selection discussed earlier in this chapter. Concern for the college community, for example, motivates employers to seek the very best person available who can carry out the duties of the position while strengthening the bonds of camaraderie and comity in the existing community. The very best person may be someone who can add diversity or a fresh perspective to the community, but the goal of the employer and the value being expressed is "concern for the community." This process also is concerned with individuation. Employers want to hire only those who can flourish in the position and in the existing community. Such concern is another expression of respect for the dignity and worth of the candidates and for their abilities to contribute to the existing community with an equal chance of success as others already functioning in the culture.

The staffing model presented in Chapter Two should be remembered to envision the role of recruitment and selection in the overall staffing process within the institution. Recall that recruitment and selection is firmly embedded within certain environmental conditions that help to make the institution what it is. The fluctuations of market conditions, the institution's location, and its reputation and history combine to set general parameters for hiring—who is available and the nature of their professional and personal attributes.

Recruitment and selection of staff occurs within a student affairs culture shaped by many external and internal forces as depicted in Chapters One and Two. The process of recruitment and selection comprises several interdependent steps or components: assessing the need and establishing the purpose of the position, performing position analysis and preparing the position description, empowering the search committee, applying legal and ethical standards, preparing the position description, advertising the position, conducting the search, screening the applicants, interviewing finalists, and recommending the hiring authority.

Assess the Need and Establish the Purpose of the Position

In addition to concern for environmental conditions, organizations must have a clear sense of purpose and understand how each position contributes to the accomplishment of that purpose and of other assigned responsibilities if they are to make the right decisions about new personnel. Thus the student affairs division must know what it is trying to accomplish if it is to expect its people to help achieve the mission.

Generally, the clarity of student affairs purpose is associated with the clarity of purpose of the entire institution. Both typically are problematic in higher education. Many institutions have multiple goals that tend to be stated vaguely, making it difficult to know when or whether a goal is achieved. (In some cases, institutions have purposes that though not incompatible with one another are inharmonious or rivals for attention, which can create competition for limited resources and among functional units.) Student affairs divisions operating within these ambiguous environments are inclined to follow suit, describing their purposes with language that is admirable but indeterminate. In these conditions, even the best people may have difficulty being completely successful. It is very difficult to achieve a goal, to be successful, if one does not clearly understand the goal. Likewise, it is difficult to hire the right person if one does not know precisely what job needs to be done.

Perform Position Analysis and Prepare the Position Description

The first step in the sequence leading to hiring the right person is to perform a position analysis. Whether the position is new or recently vacated, there must be a careful determination of why the position is needed, precisely how it will assist the division and the institution to achieve its goals or mission, how it relates to other positions in the division, and what skills and other abilities are necessary to carry out its responsibilities. The position analysis also should include a judgment as to whether other positions in the division should be reconfigured in light of the vacancy. Thus the position analysis is a broad-scale study of division needs, ideally involving all members of the existing staff and examining how this and other jobs function to meet the needs.

Preparing the position description is the next prerequisite to the hiring decision. It must be prepared with great care. Benefits of determining distinct position descriptions in advance of the hiring decision accrue to the institution, to the student affairs division and unit where the position exists, to the search committee and others involved in the hiring process, to the candidates for the position, and to the supervisor of the position. There are five major reasons for carefully preparing the position description:

- Composing a clear position description requires the organization to conduct some type of position analysis that ensures the need for the position in light of institutional goals.
- The position description makes clear to other members of the unit in which the work is to be performed what is expected of a new member.
- It helps the search committee (or other mechanism that might be used) to know what it should search for and what screening procedures should be put in place.
- It helps candidates for the position understand institutional and divisional performance expectations and know what questions to ask about the work expected prior to making a decision about whether to accept the position if it is offered.
- It helps shape the quality of subsequent staffing practices, including the orientation, supervision, staff development, and performance appraisal of the staff member.

The specific content of the position description may include position title, credentials or position specifications, administrative location of the position, physical and social working conditions, goals for the position, work activities and procedures, and conditions of employment (Sims and Foxley, 1980; Winston and Miller, 1991).

Empower the Search Committee

A third step in the hiring process is determining how the decision will be made. Though not used universally in colleges and universities, search committees are most frequently the mechanism used to carry out the recruitment and selection process. Care should be taken in their composition to ensure that crucial constituencies are represented on the committee. Generally, two committee membership approaches can be taken: select members from the unit or units most affected by the search, or select members from diverse units within and sometimes outside the division and the institution. The choice may be related to the level of the vacant position. It makes sense to select persons who represent broad perspectives on search committees for higher-level positions, but it may not be so essential for lower- or entry-level positions. The choice of approach also may be related to the division or institution position on affirmative action. Anticipating that hiring decisions may be influenced by the official or unofficial position on affirmative action of the institution and division, it makes sense to consider wide perspectives when appointing persons to serve on search committees.

Search committees often are political in makeup and purpose. Care should be taken when composing a search committee to include (or at least make conscious decisions about) persons who represent the major educational and political constituencies of the division or institution. Regarding mid- to upper-level positions, it may be crucial in most institutions to include members of the faculty on search committees, as most student affairs divisions have agendas that suggest working more closely with faculty and academic affairs units. No search committee membership choice should be made, however, that excludes the possibility of appointing persons with appropriate professional perspectives. It is a balancing act to get the right persons on a search committee, but it is important.

Instructing the search committee is vital. As they tend to be ad hoc committees, members may not know precisely what is expected of them. Even if members have served in other searches, the rules or requirements for a particular position may change from one search to the next, leaving them to grope for procedural expectations. The duties of the committee should be made clear by being stated in written form by the administrator who appoints the members. It is an essential part of the empowering process. As is the case at the University of North Carolina-Wilmington, we strongly recommend that each division develop a short (one- to two-hour) orientation program in which each committee member participates before the search begins. Included in this orientation should be discussion of ethical and legal issues; detailed explanation of the position's anticipated duties; identification of essential skills, experiences, affirmative action requirements, and educational background; development of the rules that will govern the functioning of the committee; delegation of responsibilities among committee members; establishment of deadlines; and clear definition of the committee's charged responsibilities.

Directions given to search committees vary from institution to institution, sometimes from search to search. Some of the more common issues and decisions to be made by empowering officials are the following:

• *Preparing the position description.* Generally, this is accomplished by the intended supervisor for the position or, in some cases, by the supervisor's supervisor. We recommend that all members of the related staff assist in this process.

• *Setting the complete application framework.* Both the search committee and the applicants need to know the various steps in the application process; they should be reflected in the position announcement and, subsequently, in the position advertisement. This framework will make clear the relationships among various offices and officials in the process, such as the role of the institution's personnel office and of the executive officer of student affairs.

• *Determining the minimum requirements of the position.* This determination should be made as a part of the position analysis process, but without fail the search committee should be clear on it from the beginning of the search process. It should include noting whether special credentials, such as for certain counselors, are required and whether there is a preferred balance between the formal education, background experiences, and personal attributes of candidates.

• *Preparing the position announcement.* This duty often falls on the search committee and should take the form of a written statement that includes a description of the institution and its environment; the title and role of the position achieving institutional and division purposes; the qualifications required of candidates for the position, including especially any that will be given special weight or consideration in the final decision; the process that will be used to conduct the search, including deadlines for application and for the beginning of the review process; requirements for a completed application, such as whether references are required for all applicants or whether, for example, only names, addresses, and phone numbers are desired to permit gaining formal references later in the process; to whom the application materials should be sent; and any institutional affirmations such as commitments to affirmative action and diversity.

• *Advertising the position.* This process includes determining the media to be used to get the announcement before the widest possible audience of potential candidates. For most professional positions, the *Chronicle of Higher Education* is used to run ads about the position. Similar publications, such as those run by professional associations (NASPA and ACPA, for example), are frequently used. Postings at conferences may be accompanied by conducting interviews at the conferences in some cases. Local media such as newspapers and newsletters are used regularly in this process, as are special mailings. It may be especially crucial to send special announcements directly to certain institutions, such as historically black institutions, women's colleges, and small and sometimes isolated colleges.

• *Managing the overall search process.* Committees may be asked to receive applications, log them for official records, inform applicants when materials have been received and when a decision is rendered about each application, collect references for finalists, determine who will be invited to campus for interviews, schedule the on-campus visits of candidates, and handle all correspondence associated with the search.

• *Determining the finalists.* Sometimes committees may be told at the outset the number of finalists who can be brought to campus for interviews. This may be associated with the amount of money available to conduct the search and certainly is related to the level of the position within the divisional hierarchy. Preferred practice is for the committee to invite three to five candidates to campus, interview them, and make decisions about who is preferred for the position. Alternative approaches are sometimes used. For example, especially when resources are tight, the committee's top choice may be interviewed on campus and, if found acceptable, recommended for hiring to the appropriate institutional official. If the candidate is not found acceptable or turns down the offer of the position, the committee's second-ranked finalist is invited to campus and the process is repeated until a suitable candidate is located and hired. In either approach, committees very often will interview semifinalists by phone prior to making a determination to bring someone to campus for face-to-face interviews with many staff.

- *Making arrangements for interviews.* Committees must acquire appropriate funding for bringing candidates to campus for interviews. This is sometimes handled by others, such as the department head, but committees should ensure that the funds are available early in the search process. On-campus interviews often occur over more than one day and include staff within the unit of the position and many others outside it. The candidate's potential supervisor and that supervisor's supervisor normally are included in the interview process. A host for each candidate should be provided, and all arrangements including lodging and meals should be handled by the host.

- *Making the final decisions.* The process of making the final choices between candidates should be established early. All feedback available from campus interviews must be collected and analyzed. Criteria for choosing finalists must be applied, and decisions must be made about top candidates to be recommended to the hiring authority. The form the recommendation takes should have been specified by the committee's appointing authority: an unranked list of acceptable candidates, a ranked list of acceptable candidates, or recommendation of a single candidate. The final decision about whom to make a position offer to, however, will generally be made by the committee's appointing authority, perhaps in consultation with higher-level administrators.

Ethical Standards

Another vital step in the hiring decision is the application of appropriate legal and ethical standards. Ethical standards are published by leading professional associations (such as the ACPA Statement of Ethical Principles and Standards, 1993) that should be applied to the hiring process to assist in the achievement of social justice goals within the student affairs division and the larger institution.

Legal Parameters

There is a maze of statutes, regulations, presidential executive orders, and constitutional provisions, in addition to contracts and common law, that potentially apply to the employment process in higher education. No student affairs administrator should attempt to negotiate this minefield without the aid of competent legal counsel.

Fortunately, on most campuses the basic framework for recruiting and employing new staff have been codified in sets of institutional rules and procedures that assure compliance with the relevant legal provisions. Most institutions have personnel (or human resources) and affirmative action (or Equal Employment Opportunity Commission) units that can assist in preparing for and conducting staff searches. In the sections that follow, we identify the principal areas of law that apply in this area.

The Threshold Question

Whether an institution is public or private determines which legal provisions apply (Hollander and Young, 1991; Kaplin and Lee, 1995). Public colleges and universities are required to guarantee their employees' rights as specified in the U.S. Constitution, such as freedom of speech, religion, and affiliation. Private colleges, because they are not extensions of the government, are not covered by the federal constitution and can legally "engage in acts of private discrimination" (Kaplin and Lee, 1995, p. 46). There are other legal protections, however, that do apply to private college staff members that often effectively blur this distinction.

Contracts

Frequently, although not always, student affairs professional staff members have a written contract with the institution, whether public or private, that specifies the terms of employment. Hollander and Young (1991) recommend that the following be specified in the contract and other documents (such as staff handbooks and institutional procedures manuals) provided to staff at the time of employment: position description, salary, fringe benefits (including leave policy), term of office (contracts are usually for one year in student affairs), process of performance appraisal, date of notification of action regarding continuance of employment, due process procedures regarding review of institutional actions affecting employment, and other relevant employment-related issues, such as funds for professional travel and permissible or prohibited outside employment.

The contract is a useful document that can prevent misunderstanding later in a staff member's tenure. It is important for any contract to be approved by the appropriate institutional authority so it will be enforceable. This frequently means that contracts do not go into effect until approved by the institution's governing board.

Nondiscrimination Statutes

In the past forty years there have been a number of federal statutes passed to protect employees from unlawful discrimination on variables such as race, national origin, sex, disability, and age. These statutes apply to all public institutions and to private institutions that receive any form of federal financial assistance (including student financial aid); this covers all but a very small number of private colleges and universities (fewer than twenty). Table 5.1 identifies relevant statutes and the areas of discrimination prohibited.

There are, however, important areas in which discrimination has taken place in the past and is still not federally prohibited, namely sexual orientation and alien status or citizenship. Also, private religiously affiliated institutions are exempt from the religious discrimination prohibitions of Title VII of the Civil Rights Act.

Affirmative Action

As discussed in Chapter Two, affirmative action programs are still politically controversial. Kaplin and Lee (1995, p. 254) note that

Table 5.1. Selected Federal Antidiscrimination Statutes and Regulations Affecting Higher Education Employment.

Statute	Prohibition
Title VII of the Civil Rights Act of 1964	Discrimination based on race, color, or national origin
Title IX of the Education Amendments of 1972	Discrimination based on sex
Section 504 of the Rehabilitation Act of 1973	Discrimination against "otherwise qualified" handicapped persons
Americans with Disabilities Act of 1990	Discrimination against qualified individuals with a disability
Equal Pay Act of 1963	Discrimination based on sex
Age Discrimination in Employment Act as amended in 1986	Discrimination against persons at least 40 years old
Pregnancy Discrimination Act of 1978	Discrimination on the basis of pregnancy, childbirth, or related illnesses
Equal Employment Opportunity Commission regulations of 1980	Sexual harassment

Sources: Gehring, 1993; Hollander and Young, 1991; Kaplin and Lee, 1995.

affirmative action in employment is even more controversial than in student admissions because there are more regulations and requirements involved and because "beneficiaries of affirmative action in employment may be more visible because they compete for often-scarce . . . openings."

Affirmative action as a remedy to past discrimination was put into action by two Executive Orders (11246 and 11375). Aside from prohibiting discrimination based on race, color, religion, sex, and national origin, they require adoption of employment category goals. Student affairs administrators should consult the unit charged with implementation of the institution's affirmative action plan for guidance before beginning a search process.

Prepare the Position Announcement

Preparing the position announcement follows in the process. This crucial step informs all who are interested in the position precisely what the search committee is looking for in clear and unambiguous language. The announcement may include such information as title; organizational location; supervisor; mission of institution and division and contributions expected by the staff member toward the accomplishment of these missions; goals and work requirements of the position; minimum educational, experience, and knowledge requirements; and conditions of employment. This information is critical in enabling a candidate to evaluate the position relative to her or his qualifications and interests. If stated clearly, the information may ease the overall process by self-elimination of candidates who clearly do not fit the announced requirements.

Advertise the Position

Next, the position should be advertised widely in a variety of media. The purpose, of course, is to inform the widest possible audience of the availability of the position. Often the scope of the announcement may be limited by resources or other constraints; therefore, it is very important to think carefully about which audience is most important to reach. The *Chronicle of Higher Education* generally is thought to be the most helpful medium in higher education, though it may not be read at all institutions. Extra care should be taken to ensure that the announcement reaches potential minority candidates. It is the responsibility of the search committee to determine targets for special attention, but direct mailings to small institutions, historically black institutions, and women's colleges should be made. A sidebar issue: some announcements specify that written letters of reference are required from every applicant. This is a clear waste of effort for many people. Generally, search committees are interested in references only from the finalists, and even then reference letters tend to be the least valuable of the documents received about applicants. A preferred strategy is to ask for names of references in the original application. If the candidate makes the final pool, the search committee can exercise its option to get full references, taking the time only when the information may prove useful in making final decisions.

Conduct the Search

The search process is continued by collecting applications from all interested parties. This process should be handled with meticulous care. Applications should be received by the office listed in the position announcement, acknowledged to the applicant, recorded in a log to permit careful tracking, and referred to the search committee for review. The chair of the search committee, or perhaps a special initial screening subcommittee, should monitor the applications to determine whether the committee's goals for attracting qualified candidates are being achieved by the announcements. If not, the chair should launch additional procedures to widen the reach of the announcement. Without fail, the chair should conduct or oversee an active recruitment process for qualified individuals. Use of the Internet to post general announcements or to inform specific colleagues and making telephone calls to alert others of the availability of the position are minimum steps to be taken. The richness of the final pool of applicants may be dependent upon these extra steps.

Screen the Applicants

Screening of applications may be conducted from the beginning of the search process but, certainly, immediately following the announced date to begin the reviews. Some institutions require that the position announcement include a deadline date—that is, a date after which no further applications will be reviewed. It is recommended, however, that the announcement include a date for the beginning of the review process and that the application period be left open until a final decision is made.

Some ethical issues are germane here. First, application material should be handled as carefully as any confidential information. Committee members should be briefed on the handling of the information in a manner that underscores the potentially sensitive nature of the materials in the applications. Second, committee members should be trained to review applications. This is especially vital when students are members of search committees, as is often the case in student affairs. Students may not know what to look for in professional applications, and they should be carefully informed about what to expect and how to evaluate what they read. Third, applicants should be kept informed of the status of their applications. If the process is taking longer than might be expected, all applicants should be notified of the fact. When applicants are eliminated from the pool for whatever reason, they should be notified immediately that their applications are no longer being considered. Naturally, applications should be held so long as the applicants are being seriously considered as finalists, but as soon as the committee knows that an individual is out of consideration, he or she should be informed immediately.

The final screening process will depend upon the original empowerment of the committee. For example, the committee may have been instructed regarding the number and composition of the finalists to be interviewed. For higher-level positions, it is common for three to five candidates to be selected for on-campus interviews, but there are many reasons—some of them financial—why these numbers may be lower. Telephone interviews with candidates believed to merit on-campus interviews should be conducted prior to the on-campus interviews. This normally is the last step before actually inviting candidates to campus.

Interview Finalists

The search committee generally is responsible for inviting candidates to campus and for hosting them during their stay. They also generally set the interview schedule and make all necessary arrangements to carry it out smoothly. This may include making travel, lodging, and meal arrangements and ensuring efficient reimbursement of candidates for all expenses incurred in the campus visit. Interviews should be arranged for all persons with whom the new staff member might interact in carrying out the duties of the position. Some of the interviews may include group discussions and formal presentations, but they certainly should include ample opportunity for the candidate to interact with the supervisor for the position and, in most cases, with the administrator at the next highest level beyond the supervisor in the organization.

The search committee should have determined how it will make its decision among the finalists. A commonly used approach is to allow all persons who interviewed the candidates and all members of the search committee to evaluate each candidate on a form especially designed for the purpose. It is important that the form be tailored to the specific job search, as it is crucial that the evidence collected from observers be germane to the position requirements. Even an open-ended form may work well if the evaluators are instructed about what comments the committee wants. Following the collection of all individual evaluations, the search committee must arrive at its best judgment of which candidates to recommend to the hiring authority. Again, this process may be dictated by the original empowerment of the committee. The hiring authority, perhaps the department head or the vice president, may have asked for the names of three candidates to choose among, for example. The committee may have been asked to rank the finalists to aid the hiring authority in reaching a decision or, equally likely, to provide an unranked list of finalists.

Recommend to Hiring Authority

Following the instructions of the original empowerment of the committee, the final act generally required of the search committee is to make its recommendations to the hiring authority. Once a decision is made and the terms of employment are agreed upon between candidate and hiring authority, the search committee is disbanded.

Distinctions may be made in recruitment and selection of professional, allied professional, and support staff. Normally, however, these distinctions vary in procedures, not in principle. All staff, for example, are viewed as crucial to the success of the division or else they should not be hired. The issue of clarity of unit purpose remains the same across staff levels and types. The place of appropriately prepared position descriptions does not vary by type of position. Search procedures may vary by type of position, but the intentions are similar. Formal search committees may not be employed for some support position vacancies, for example, but concerns for fairness and effectiveness are imperative for all searches.

Recommendations for Practice

From the evidence presented in this chapter, including perspectives on the profession's values, a proposed model of staffing, research in literature, case studies, and surveys of vice presidents, several suggestions for practitioners can be offered about their recruitment and selection practices.

First, practitioners should be attentive to the guiding role of professional values in framing their recruitment and selection behaviors. Knowing that the profession stands unwaveringly on beliefs about dignity, equality, and community, policies and procedures should be put in place that honor these commitments in whatever actions are taken to recruit new staff. We should give no less attention to these historic virtues when dealing with staff than when dealing with students.

Second, student affairs divisions should formalize their recruitment and selection practices by promulgating written policies and procedures to be sustained at the divisional level, and they should provide extensive and ongoing training in the application and use of these policies. Too many searches for new staff are based either on ad hoc procedures or on policies of the institution that may only remotely reflect the values and needs of student affairs. This is not an argument for abdication of the institution's policies but for the refinement, commitment, and professional use of precisely tailored policies designed to produce the desired result every time they are applied. It also is an argument for determining in advance of emergent need how one of the most important decisions ever made in the division will be carried out. When need for a new staff member is justified, there should be no mystery within the division about how the need will be addressed.

Third, every aspect of the staffing model discussed in this chapter—assessing the need and establishing the purpose of the position, performing a position analysis and preparing the position description, empowering the search committee (if one is used); applying legal and ethical standards; preparing the position announcement, advertising the position, conducting the search, screening the applicants, interviewing finalists, and making recommendations to the hiring authority—should be followed in some thoughtful fashion. Though there are neither perfect designs nor any magic for applying these steps, each step should be considered in whatever approach is taken to recruitment.

Fourth, care should be exercised in recruitment and selection processes not to confuse experience with qualifications when making hiring decisions. Applicants may be eliminated from consideration for a position because they have not performed the duties specified in the job description before. Without denying the worth of experience, talented and well-educated but less experienced professionals frequently can quickly acquire new skills and move programs and services to new levels of effectiveness, whereas less talented but more experienced practitioners can adequately meet current job expectations but will be unable to go beyond present requirements to meet changing conditions. The best candidate usually is the best-qualified professional, not necessarily the most experienced one.

The ethics of the profession should be behind every action taken to recruit and select staff. A premier value and ethical principle of the profession is respect for the individuals involved in the process. There is no excuse for sloppy or inattentive procedures in recruiting. Every person who applies for a position is making something of themselves public and open to scrutiny by others. Persons charged with scrutinizing credentials or dealing directly with applicants should be especially sensitive to the self-esteem issues involved in the application process. Search committees (or others handling the process) should be trained and constantly reminded of the crucial matters involved in administrative processing of materials, reviewing of professional credentials, interacting personally with applicants, and making decisions about applicants. A simple rule should suffice to guide these actions: do unto others as you would have them do unto you.

Fifth, more effort is justified in recruitment of staff to achieve divisional and institutional goals for diversity. The barriers to the successful achievement of these goals in the environment are well known and do not need to be restated here; many times they are beyond the control of student affairs administrators. But other barriers are within the institutions as well, and these often can be overcome. Training of search committees is crucial, of course, and it may include asking for reviews of professional credentials that have a different focus. Current practice tends to reinforce the existing norm for what constitutes an adequate background for candidates. At the very least, a heightened sensitivity to alternative forms of professional background seems justified. Perhaps the work of Haro (1991) and Sagaria and Johnsrud (1991) might be applied to help remedy this situation. Both of these sources claim that their approaches to recruiting and selecting minority candidates can move organizations "from rhetoric to results" (Sagaria and Johnsrud, 1991, p. 105).

Finally, achieving fit with the environment is at once a highly desirable goal for recruitment and selection of new staff and a conceptual trap for sustaining the status quo within an organization. Final decisions about fit of candidates with the environment of the institution should balance both concerns. At different times in the life of a student affairs division, yielding to either perfect fit or optimal misfit may be justified. In the end, however, fit between the new staff member and the environment is a conditional, not an absolute, virtue.

Summary

Staff recruitment and selection practices in student affairs divisions are guided by two complementary standards: hire the right person; use the right procedures. These standards are consistent with the historic values of the profession and the cultural contexts of the institution.

The right person usually has credentials acquired through formal training (though there are exceptions), possesses background experience suitable for the vacancy, manifests values and personal attributes consistent with the institutional ethos, exhibits integrity, and shows potential to make substantial contributions to the goals of the division and the institution.

The proper procedures for hiring staff usually are to follow institutional and divisional policies and guidelines, adhere to fundamentals of job analysis, prepare position descriptions, empower and instruct search committees on their precise responsibilities, post or advertise vacancies, apply appropriate legal and ethical standards, carefully screen applicants, conscientiously interview candidates, and prudently select the person with the best fit to the institution and the position.

This chapter also presented findings from literature and research on the subject of recruitment and selection of staff. The main findings include the following: (1) Hiring the right person is the preeminent staffing concern for student affairs. (2) Written policies governing recruitment and selection are sustained at the institutional level. Divisional written policies about recruitment and selection are rare, yet adopted procedures are used unwaveringly. (3) Procedures used in recruitment and selection are ordinary, conventional, and strikingly consistent. (4) The hiring decision most often is assigned to department heads in student affairs, especially for mid- and entry-level staff, and to vice presidents for decisions about department heads. (5) Written policies governing ethics and affirmative action are rare in student affairs. (6) Surprisingly little money (proportional to total budgeted funds) is spent on recruitment and selection of staff. (7) Most hiring authorities in student affairs choose experience over formal preparation as the most important qualification for employment, though a balance between experience and formal preparation is usually preferred and increasingly easy to find.

These findings are reflected in the recruitment and selection portion of the staffing model presented in Chapter Two.

Finally, the chapter presented several recommendations for practice that may serve as extended standards for practitioners who wish to ensure the success of their recruiting and selection processes.

Chapter Six

Orienting Staff to New Positions

Orienting new staff to a specific position begins during the recruitment and selection process and proceeds through an intentional process of acclimation at the beginning of employment. As inquiries about candidate qualifications are made by search committees and administrators with hiring authority, information is exchanged between candidate and institutional officials about the vacant position, about the institution and the department in which the position is located, and about the people and the culture of the environment of the position. At or near the actual assumption of position duties, this introduction process is continued, either formally or informally, to ensure full awareness of duties and expectations by the new staff member.

This familiarization or introduction process is crucial to setting the new staff member on a course of productivity and accomplishment that will lead to success in the position. Thus, the orientation task is to acclimate staff fully to the educational and operational philosophy of the institution and of the division of student affairs, the institutional and student affairs division culture, expectations for the position and for personal and professional performance, and relationships among faculty, staff, and students.

It is crucial to orient new staff intentionally, explicitly, and thoroughly. Hiring new staff is a major institutional investment of resources and deserves every warranty of success. Orienting new staff members is an act of welcome into the professional community that embodies the profession's values of respect, fairness, and community. The goal is to ensure that every new member of the community is accorded full opportunity to contribute to the achievement of institutional, departmental, and personal goals.

There are important differences between orienting staff who come from outside the institution, especially staff members new to the field of student affairs, and staff who assume new positions within the same institution. Information about the culture of the institution, including its principal policies and procedures, are vital to the former and less necessary to the latter. Introducing an outsider to an institution and to a division of student affairs is different from reassigning or promoting an insider. Some requirements for familiarization to new roles are common to both, however, and these are discussed in detail in this chapter.

Yet these standards are not always achieved in the profession. Student affairs must cope with certain unrelenting problems in the orientation of staff to new positions:

- Orientation of staff to new positions is universally recognized to be a vital staffing practice but often is assumed rather than guaranteed.
- Informal orientation practices dominate the field; thus there is no assurance that meaningful orientations actually take place, or that if they do that they are conducted thoroughly.
- Orientation of staff is more likely when the member is hired from outside the institution. Persons receiving new assignments within the institution are too often assumed to be fully prepared for the new responsibilities without transitional briefing on new tasks and expectations.
- Staff appointments to mid-level positions, such as department heads, often receive no assistance in orienting themselves to their new roles beyond cursory social introductions.
- Orientation activities for new staff often focus on routine matters and ignore more substantive and vital matters.
- Orientation activities often are not conducted well or cogently.

This chapter presents multiple perspectives on how student affairs prepares its members for new positions. Some of the enduring problems of orientation are outlined, followed by perspectives from literature and research. The staffing model presented in Chapter Two provides a framework to illustrate how orientation might be improved on many campuses. Finally, recommendations for practitioners are offered.

Persistent Issues in Orientation of Staff to New Positions

Despite general acceptance of the importance of orientation to new positions, too many supervisors give inadequate attention to the process. As certain activities almost always occur to brief new staff, such as informational sessions conducted by the institutional human resources office and business and social meetings with supervisors and colleagues, it often is assumed that the process is completed in a fully acceptable manner. Beyond these few formal activities, many divisions of student affairs leave the orientation duties to the immediate supervisors. The result often is an incomplete orientation, not necessarily lacking in quality but leaving new staff members feeling unprepared to confidently assume their new assignments.

Informality seems to be the rule, not the exception, in the processes used to orient staff to new positions. In many cases this may very well be the best approach, especially if only one person is the recipient of the familiarization activities, as is the case in all but the largest units at large institutions. Such an approach may communicate genuineness and inclusiveness: "You now are one of us; let us handle this task as routinely as we will handle many other tasks together." The downside to this approach is obvious: without formality of structure and content it is difficult to determine if all important matters are adequately addressed. The best-intentioned supervisor who does not have a well-conceptualized, concrete plan may overlook important areas, especially if the new staff member arrives at a busy time, such as near the beginning of the fall semester.

It is less likely that persons from within the institution who are receiving new assignments will be accorded as satisfactory an orientation to the new position as those hired from outside. There are many reasons for this; some may argue that there is no great need for explicit or formal orientation to a new position for someone who has been employed at the institution for a year or more. It is true that staff who assume different responsibilities within a division do not need the same orientation as do persons unfamiliar with the institution, but evidence suggests that they do have a need and that it is often unsatisfactorily met.

This situation often occurs with the appointment of department heads or other mid-level administrators. Assumptions about their lack of need for explicit orientation to their new positions are widespread. By virtue of their prior education and experience, they are presumed to know all they need to know to do their new work well. They may contribute to this feeling by their own acts of confidence: "Yes, I am prepared for the new responsibilities." Such a sentiment, expressed or not, does not necessarily mean that the person actually feels no need to know more about the institution or about expectations for performance in the new role. Even when explicit orientation is provided, it may be offered with less preparation and thoroughness than that offered a person new to the profession or the institution. Staff at mid-management level often need more thorough briefings about the history of issues and problems, some of which are quite sensitive.

Orientation activities intended to inform new staff about benefits and institutional policies occur almost everywhere. Indeed, all staff do need to know about the institutional rules they must live by, and they all must make crucial decisions about their long-term economic futures. Information sharing about these and related matters generally is handled well on behalf of new staff. The problems arise through inadequate treatment of other matters that carry equal or greater importance to individual success on the job. Knowledge about matters such as institutional cultures, including the faculty and student cultures, is vital to new staff members. They most certainly will learn of the dominant cultures of the institution sooner or later, but in the meantime crucial mistakes may be made and future success at the institution jeopardized because of well-meaning but ill-informed actions.

The quality of orientation practices is notable. Whether staff receive formal or informal orientation, they often point to inadequacies in it. Information may be presented insufficiently or inaccurately; often, needed information is not presented at all. It perhaps is a testament to the durability of student affairs professionals that they manage to acquire the necessary perspectives on their new roles in due course of carrying out their responsibilities. There is a significant question, however, about loss of productivity, damage to morale, or even derailment of professional progress when necessary information is denied by the absence or inadequate handling of orientation activities for new staff. How much better might a staff member perform if comprehensive information about the institution and about expectations of personal performance is clearly and effectively presented at the beginning?

Perspectives from Literature

Rarely can one assert that there is a genuine dearth of literature about any topic in the student affairs field. The field is old enough, diverse enough, and populated by enough scholars and seasoned practitioners who recognize the importance of accumulated knowledge that literature of some type is available to at least describe most topics or phenomena. But orientation of staff to new positions may qualify as an exception; literature on this topic is scant.

That this is so, however, does not necessarily suggest a consensus that staff orientation is unimportant. Rather, one gains an impression from the literature that the topic is a given—something that everyone knows or should know about. The perceived logic seems to be that when one hires a new staff member, she or he should of course be guided to a thorough understanding of duties and responsibilities. The problem is that all too often this vital step in staffing is overlooked, and the result is destructive to the capacity of the staff member to succeed in the job, especially in early stages. If treatment of the subject in the literature of the field does indicate the level of thought and consideration given to orientation of new staff to their positions, then the field is neglecting this important staffing procedure to its peril.

Upcraft (1988) and Stimpson (1993) offer more direct advice on the subject of orientation of new staff than any other authors. Both appear to treat the subject essentially as a given, however. Upcraft builds upon the principle of "hiring the right people" and contends that "the supervisor should take direct responsibility for helping a new employee get oriented to the new job and should present a plan, on the first day of work . . ." (p. 43). His advice to develop an orientation plan coincides with the principle of intentionality common to the field of student development and asserted in the beginning section of this chapter. Upcraft further suggests that the orientation plan is crucial to "help staff get to know key people in the organization" and "help new staff learn about the organization" (pp. 43–44). He suggests familiarization of new staff with expectations for relationships and definitive clarity on the nature of the institution and its culture.

Recognition of the place of orientation activities in the selection and training of staff is provided by Stimpson. He suggests that following the final decision on choice of candidate, the successful candidate be given the phone number of the person who will assist in the transition of the new staff member to the organization along with "a description of the assistance that will be provided to facilitate transition and orientation to the institution and position" (Stimpson, 1993, p. 145). He further advises: "Orientation activities should include reading materials, an overview of benefits and other campus employee programs or services, and an opportunity to meet key people with whom the new employee will work" (p. 145). Finally, Stimpson recognizes new-employee orientation as a preservice function of the division of student affairs, but casts most of the necessary activities as coinciding with the recruitment process. He does suggest that the preservice functions conclude with "some form of well-structured class, retreat, or set of sessions on campus designed to furnish new employees with information about organizational expectations and the chance to develop the skills and perspectives needed to assume assigned responsibilities effectively" (p. 146).

Just as one might see orientation of new staff as something of a last step or as an integrated process with recruitment and selection, others might see the process as the beginning step or as a vehicle for staff development. Baier (1985, p. 223) claims that "well-run orientation activities set the proper climate for more in-depth staff development programming." This spirit then leads to rapid acclimation of new people to their new environment and introduces them to the constantly changing organization. Baier makes a good point: that student affairs professionals have long argued the benefits of new-student orientation to their success in college. The same argument applies to new staff; their chances of success on the job are improved by a quality new-staff orientation experience.

Perspectives from Research

Evidence about orientation of new staff members to their positions is mixed: our survey data show minimal execution of the responsibilities and general satisfaction with them even though not all important topics were addressed. Case study evidence shows strong and universal commitment to the practice. Still, a few generalizations about the practice are justified by the available evidence.

1. *Orientation of new staff generally is viewed as an important aspect of staffing responsibilities and is accomplished jointly by institutional-level personnel and by personnel within the division of student affairs.*

Orientation is a joint obligation of some institutional office—perhaps a personnel office—and by the supervisors in the division of student affairs. In the cases studied, all vice presidents indicated their support for participation in institutional orientation activities. In some cases, participation was mandatory. Survey data support the multilevel nature of new-staff orientation. Certain functions are performed at the institutional level, such as explaining general personnel policies of the institution and employee benefits. Others are handled at the divisional or departmental level, such as performance expectations and descriptions of students at the institution.

All institutions studied on site are concerned that new staff members get the "big picture." It was frequently noted that orientation to the job begins during the recruitment and selection process. In some cases, new staff are fairly familiar with the institution and many of its personnel by the time they accept position offers. Still, attention is given to ensuring that new staff fit the environment in fact and not just in perception. Everyone acknowledged that while a lot of information is transmitted during the recruitment and selection process, there always seem to be important matters to learn. Because so much information (some of which may not seem relevant at the time) is offered applicants during their campus visits, much may not be retained by the time the new staff member arrives to begin work. At Florida State University, for example, one staff member commented, "It is easy to fall into hidden political traps here. Everything isn't as it seems on the surface." At the University of North Carolina-Wilmington, the vice president established a policy statement that is used much as a checklist that outlines the minimum content for the program, which guards against missing some important aspects of orientation of new staff. This minimum content is expected to be covered whether the orientation is for a single new staff member who arrives mid-year, or for several new staff members in housing who arrive well in advance of the academic year.

An interesting approach to orientation was found at James Madison University where, in addition to other programs at the university and division level, one department head conducts his own assessment of the new staff member much as one might imagine occurring in a strict application of a student development approach to teaching and learning. Using interactive means, this department head makes an initial determination of the professional developmental status of the new member and drafts a beginning plan for helping the new staff member achieve optimum achievement and growth. Beyond this personalized developmental purpose, his stated goal for employing such a strategy is to help the new member fully understand the institution, including what it has been, how it is changing, and what are its likely alternative futures.

Many units of student affairs seem to have some practices that require a very high level of precision in the new employee. Examples include offices of admission, financial aid, and counseling. Anywhere external regulations are formally implemented, such as in the application of the Americans with Disabilities Act (ADA), the Family Educational Rights and Privacy Act (FERPA or Buckley Amendment), Title VII of the 1964 Civil Rights Act (prohibiting discrimination based on race, color, and national origin), or Title IX of the 1972 Higher Education Amendments (prohibiting discrimination based on sex), a high degree of conformity to the regulations is expected of new staff; therefore careful orientation activities are conducted to ensure compliance to the regulations or to important office procedures associated with them.

2. *Supervisors and department directors have the most at stake and are the most likely divisional personnel to carry out the functions of new-staff orientation.*

It is logical, of course, that supervisors and department directors perform this duty. They are the ones most directly responsible for fashioning the environment in which work is performed, and they will eventually be called upon to judge how well the duties of the position have been performed. Possessing considerable self-interest in having the position responsibilities handled well, it seems reasonable that supervisors would either orient new staff thoroughly and expertly themselves, or insist on a carefully planned, thorough orientation delivered by others.

All evidence collected at case sites supports this notion. There are many reports of how serious this activity is considered to be. In one case, new hires often do not hold full credentials for the positions because the school offers low salaries and has a custom of hiring "home-grown" staff into student affairs positions. Supervisors at this college readily acknowledge that orientation is therefore a very important aspect of all staffing practices for them. They recognize that people must be prepared to accomplish the assigned work, and when preservice preparation is insufficient, orientation is the route to begin bringing new staff up to speed quickly. (Orientation, however, cannot replace good professional preparation. Extensive, intensive, long-term staff development would be required to bring such a staff member up to the level of many entry-level professionals who graduated from creditable preparation programs.) In other cases, orientation of new staff seems to have an air of bragging about it; existing staff really want the new member to know all of the good and effective qualities already operational on campus. Existing staff take pride in telling these stories to new staff.

Given the case study evidence that strongly supports orientation of new staff, it is surprising to discover in survey evidence that not all supervisors and department heads carry out their responsibilities for new-staff orientation in a conscientious manner.

3. Orientation of new staff is most likely to be handled informally.

Orientation of new staff is conducted in various ways. Some approaches are formal, of course, such as one discovered in a large counseling center where a "new blood" committee exists explicitly to conduct initial and ongoing new-staff orientations. More likely, however, the activity is arranged with little or no structure or formality in a literal sense. Any activity taken seriously might be seen as formal, but in the case of orientation of new staff the evidence points to seriousness of motive and intent in an atmosphere of casual, ongoing routine. One suspects that informal approaches are preferred by many administrators for a variety of reasons, including that the task generally is carried out for one person only, a pedagogical situation hardly suitable for formal instructional tactics. Sometimes the function is handled as a reasonably intensive period of close supervision, looking over the shoulder of the new staff member as the actual duties and responsibilities are carried out and coaching along the way. This can be, and often is, arranged with little formality. New staff sometimes are assigned "buddies" who have similar responsibilities and can talk and walk them through all the duties of the position. When this option is chosen, the buddy tends to be a peer associate rather than the supervisor or department head.

At Johnson County Community College, supervisors are expected to meet with new staff frequently during the early stages of employment and to employ shadowing approaches to orientation, but there is no formal requirement that these activities be carried out. At Broward Community College, "walking around" approaches to new-staff orientation work effectively; the orientation thrust appears to be groundbreaking for establishing the type of division-staff relationship that assists the division in achieving its major goals for further staff development. According to the vice president at Broward, "When we hire someone, we assume a role model position with them." This relationship-building intent is evident at James Madison University also, where the relationships are intended to set the stage for supervision, staff development, and evaluation of staff.

4. *Though seen as important to successful performance on the job by staff and supervisors alike, appropriate orientation to positions is not received by many new staff members.*

Only about 60 percent of staff in our surveys reported receiving an orientation of any kind to their positions. This matter is further exacerbated by a consequential number of respondents who received some form of orientation but indicated that certain important topics of orientation were not included, at least in their cases. It is especially crucial to note that some of the topical areas not handled well were subjects such as job expectations and procedures for performance appraisal. What an oversight! How can new staff ethically be held accountable for their position responsibilities when they have not been informed of the standards to be applied in judging their performance?

5. *The content of new-staff orientation often deals with the most routine matters and ignores or handles poorly some of the most crucial issues of success on the job.*

Routine matters of orientation, such as teaching office procedures, may be handled by relatively effortless tactics and are easier for busy supervisors to prepare for and execute. Other matters, such as helping new staff fully appreciate the extent and richness of the institutional and divisional cultures and carefully laying out performance appraisal standards, require more concentrated effort and time by the new staff member so as to fully comprehend them, and focused and exact methods by the supervisor. This distinction may partially explain why many new staff report receiving inadequate or incomplete orientations to their positions.

Routine matters are important also, of course. New staff need to know about office procedures, benefits, who they will be working with, and student characteristics. But when placed in topical priority order, most staff—new and old—will agree that some topics of orientation are more directly related to their success than others.

6. *The quality of new-staff orientation is questionable.*

Of the 60 percent of respondents to our surveys who received any form of orientation, about half of them reported that the topics of their orientation were handled well. Thus, for some new staff—perhaps 30 percent—orientation may be judged of reasonable to high quality. This means most new staff receive something less, or in many cases nothing at all.

It should be noted that this tilted judgment about new-staff orientation does not fit our case data well. From the perspective of case-based information, orientation of new staff is performed at least adequately and perhaps much better. In fact, many informants at case sites gave testimony not only to the importance of the function but to the skill with which it is executed in their units. It should be remembered, of course, that these institutions were chosen because of their reputations for excellent student affairs programs.

Using the Staffing Model in Orientation of Staff to New Positions

Orientation of staff to new positions should include certain content, including the educational and operational philosophy of the unit, division, and institution, institutional and student affairs division culture, expectations for professional and personal performance, and relationships between faculty, staff, and students. The approach to orientation may be formal or informal. Formality is a secondary issue in orientation of new staff; explicitness and thoroughness are primary issues.

Educational and Operational Philosophy

New staff need to know more than the specific duties associated with a position to ensure that they are fully prepared to assume the role. Indeed, knowledge of routine functions of the position may have been acquired sufficiently during the interview and hiring process and may require only detailed reiteration during the orientation period. However, new staff need to know what underlies the divisional and institutional approach to education, including what is to be achieved (the aim of education) and how it is to be achieved (the methods of education). Beliefs about educational practice may vary even when expected outcomes are the same, leading to an emphasis on one approach and a corresponding de-emphasis on others. Some educators believe strongly in the pre-eminence of student development as the aim of education; others prefer a broader goal of student learning. As similar as these goals may appear, each calls for a slightly different emphasis. The former may highlight psychosocial outcomes of education such as identity achievement and quality of interpersonal relations whereas the latter may stress intellectual forms of growth. It also is possible that the prevailing concern of the division is for the delivery of certain services to students without much overt concern for the form of learning that may result from the benefits of the service.

Belief systems also vary by institutional focus such as the balance between concerns for preparing students for life (perhaps through a broad liberal arts education) and for work (as might be found in a technical or vocational college). In the former type of institution, acceptable programs within a particular student affairs area might be much broader than those appreciated in the latter type, where most educational programs are focused on career choices and the fulfillment of vocational or career goals. Understanding such differences may lead a new staff member to imagine very dissimilar programs intended to facilitate achievement of each outcome and, thus, to imagine alternative ways to succeed in the new job. Conversely, if the staff member misunderstands the overarching institutional purpose, completely inappropriate programs and services might be planned, thus leading to an unsuccessful experience by the staff member, which of course directly affects the functioning of the unit.

Institutional and Student Affairs Division Culture

The new staff member also needs to understand the precise nature of the institution, especially its cultural components. In some institutions, the facilities, services, and even opportunities for face-to-face contact with students may be fragmented, as might be the case in a multicampus community college with a high proportion of students enrolled part-time. This environment might lead to a style of education analogous to a shopping center or cafeteria. The student may shop for services when and where they are needed in this environment. Student affairs in such an institution may be required to accentuate accessibility, flexibility, and responsiveness in all educational programs and services. It is likely also that this type of organization will emphasize service delivery above all else and will focus on environmental and organizational standards of quality. It is vital for new staff members to realize from the beginning of their new positions explicitly which standards will be used to evaluate their performance on the job. If they are to be held accountable for primarily organizational effects (perhaps contributions to institutional efficiency and responsiveness) they need to conduct their operations in a manner to yield such effects, and this must be made explicit during the orientation process.

In other institutions the culture may allow educational opportunities that resemble a close and interactive family, as might be the case in a small, residential, liberal arts college with almost all of its students enrolled full-time. In this environment, programs and services may be patterned more around common interchanges among faculty, staff, and students. Seeking out services in these cases may seem foreign to students who can take advantage of everyday involvement, such as in their classes or residence facilities, to accomplish their purposes. Such an environmental configuration may challenge student affairs professionals to program for student needs in a more natural, family-like atmosphere than might be possible in a more fragmented climate. The primary accountability standard on such a campus is likely to be on global environmental effects where evidence of student learning and development is valued.

Understanding division culture is equally as important as understanding institutional culture. The standards and mores of operation may be deeply embedded in the division culture, and violating them may resemble treading on a taboo. New staff need to know how business is conducted (and not conducted) in hidden as well as visible ways. In fact, including explicit instruction on hidden rules of the workplace would be very helpful to new staff. They need to know how formal and informal communication occurs within the division, protocols for contacts with one's own and with other supervisors, how information is shared (especially confidential or sensitive information), the role of and standard forms of personal interaction with nonprofessional staff, how new ideas are handled, taboos, and generally accepted notions of how one gets ahead in the division. New staff often want to know how they can change things if they see a better way of doing business and they need instruction before the fact to avoid having otherwise good ideas quashed simply because a proposal came from a new staff member who failed to understand cultural pathways and potholes. For instance, is it better to present ideas by writing a proposal (either detailed or broad conceptual) and submitting it for consideration, or to present them orally to colleagues and others higher in the administrative structure and then direct their steps depending on the reactions received? How important is it to get support from faculty members before undertaking an endeavor?

Expectations for Professional and Personal Performance

Orientation to new roles and duties needs to make clear what is expected of the position and, equally important, what performance standards will be used to evaluate success on the job. These expectations and performance standards should be established during the position analysis phase that precedes recruitment and selection. Both the new staff member and the supervisor of the position need to be very clear about them, for they directly control whether the new staff member will succeed and whether the divisional and institutional interests will be served. Unless these familiarization objectives are accomplished at least by the end of the orientation period, it is very difficult for supervisors to assist a staff member who is not performing up to standard, especially if the staff member argues that performance standards were never made clear. In fact, if the standards were not made clear at the beginning of duties, it is entirely reasonable for the staff member to disclaim full responsibility for ineffective performance.

Expectations of new staff should include clarification of personal, as well as professional, goals. Though some may argue whether institutions have an obligation to assist employees to achieve personal goals, most contemporary organizational and managerial authorities assert that such inclusiveness in the routine business of the organization clearly is in the best interests of the organization. A fully energized, goal-directed, well-trained, and personally fulfilled staff member simply is a more valuable employee than one who feels it necessary to seek all personal satisfaction outside the place of work. Furthermore, a developmentally and socially flourishing person is more likely to be educationally effective with students and colleagues than one who sees work as totally separate from other aspects of life. Wholesomeness is a necessary, even if not a totally sufficient, condition for promoting student learning and development. Thus, orientation of new staff should include acknowledgment and reinforcement of the importance of achieving personal, as well as professional, goals in the position.

Relationships Between Faculty, Staff, and Students

Finally, orientation of new staff needs to include what is expected of them in their relationships with faculty, other staff, and students. Are staff expected to work collaboratively with faculty and other staff? If yes, which ones? The new staff member needs to know the rationale for separatism, if it exists. In some environments, students are treated as partners in learning; are staff expected to create these interactive relationships? Are there social taboos on campus? If staff are expected to attend certain social events and not others, they need to shape their behaviors to avoid making serious mistakes. On some campuses, communication patterns are more hierarchical than collegial. Occasionally, a hidden rule of the workplace is that junior members of the staff should not leave phone messages asking senior members to call them back but rather to say that the junior member will call again later. Successful staff are not likely to obtrusively challenge taboo-like cultural artifacts, and neither should they be made vulnerable to unintentional invasions of some culturally consecrated territory. They need to know in advance what the terrain looks like, where the crevices are, where the well-roamed paths lie.

Orientation Approach

There is no one best way to accomplish the objectives of orientation of new staff to their positions. In fact, unique forms and styles within a division of student affairs may be effective. Certainly, both informal and formal approaches can be employed effectively. The keys may be intentionality, clarity, and completeness. Such precepts suggest that supervisors take direct action to orient staff to their positions, inform them accurately about the organizational and cultural milieu of the environment, and unveil all relevant concerns about successful performance on the job.

Recommendations for Practice

Evidence presented in this chapter justifies several recommendations for practice regarding the orientation of staff to new positions.

First, all staff who are assuming new positions, whether from inside or outside the institution, should be oriented intentionally, explicitly, and thoroughly. This recommendation suggests a degree of formality in the process at least to the extent that supervisors in the division are informed of the essential topics that should be addressed during the orientation process and that there is a mandate for thorough orientations to be conducted for each new staff member. Orienting staff to new positions is too important to the success of both the individual and the institution to leave it to chance or to assume that it will be done by well-meaning supervisors or colleagues.

Second, the content of orientation of staff to new positions should address all matters of concern to staff success, not simply the routine matters pertaining to benefits and procedures. Expectations for staff member performance, crucial for later supervision, staff development, and performance appraisal, must be clarified and detailed for thorough understanding. In addition, aspects of the divisional and institutional culture that establish important mores and folkways, especially pertaining to interpersonal relationships and to institutional reward structures, must be open to discussion and analysis. We strongly recommend (as is required in CAS standards) that each unit (or perhaps the whole division) have a written statement of ethical standards to which the division leadership pledges to adhere. This statement should be presented and discussed thoroughly with each new staff member as he or she enters the institution.

Third, a commitment should be made to conduct explicit orientation of mid-level administrators without fail. Often it is assumed that these persons already know what they need to know to perform their new duties well; the new administrator may contribute to this view by trying to project self-confidence and competence to her or his new colleagues. But the performance of mid-level administrators is so crucial to the overall success in staffing practices in student affairs that nothing should be assumed about their skills or their understanding of their positions. It is important, however, that the orientations for this level of staff be designed to meet individual needs; except for information about institutional benefit plans, general policies, and social introductions, orientation for mid-level managers should look considerably different from that organized for entry-level staff.

We further suggest that the minimum content for orientation of staff to new positions for both entry-level and mid-level managerial staff be consistent with the content areas shown in Table 6.1.

Summary

Orientation of staff to new positions occurs generally in partnership between the unit in which the new staff member will work, the division of student affairs, and the institution. Each part of this partnership has a vital role to play in well-conducted orientation activities. The institution generally handles briefings on policies, procedures, and benefits. Institutional reward systems may be included in this part, although this generally requires interpretation within the student affairs context because this information is usually presented from the point of view of faculty. The division of student affairs generally handles activities that establish how individuals and administrative units work together and how administrative units contribute to the larger purposes of the division and the institution. The unit in which the new staff is assigned generally handles the specific duties to be completed, expectations for staff performance, supervisory climate and guidelines, opportunities for staff development, information about the campus cultures, and evaluation guidelines.

An undeniable fact emerges from this analysis. Far too little is known about new-staff orientation in the field of student affairs. Little information about the topic is available in literature of the field. One suspects that orientation is taken for granted by vice presidents and deans: "Well, yes, we expect our department heads and supervisors to orient new staff members" is a sentiment likely to be heard in conversations with these leaders. No doubt they mean it, but the evidence suggests that the job is not getting done well enough on many campuses. The need for more research and more thoughtful commentary from scholars and leaders of the field is indicated.

Table 6.1. Minimum Content Requirements for New Position Orientation.

Entry-level Staff	Mid-level Manager Staff
Details about staff benefit programs and options available	Details about staff benefit programs and options available
Detailed explanation of position responsibilities[a]	Detailed discussion of short- and long-term directions of the unit[a]
Discussion about educational and operational philosophies that permeate the unit and other units employees will often interact with	Discussion about educational and operational philosophies of the institution and the division
Overview of divisional or unit goals or both[a]	Overview of division goals and past unit goals[a]
Discussion about how individual's position fits into the unit's plans[a]	Discussion about how individual's unit fits into the division plans[a]
Instruction about the interface of the unit with other units of the division and institution[a]	Instruction about interunit and division-institution interaction[a]
Instruction about office and division culture, mores, and folkways	Instruction about institutional and divisional culture, mores, and folkways
Instruction about faculty, staff, and student cultures and crucial relationships among them	Instruction about faculty, staff, and student cultures and crucial relationships among them
Discussion about performance expectations from supervisor[a]	Discussion about performance expectations from supervisor[a]
Instruction about how to complete required reports and forms, including deadlines and reporting protocols[a]	Discussion about crucial needs of the unit[a]
Discussion about decisionmaking in the unit[a]	Discussion about decisionmaking throughout the division
Discussion about interpersonal relationships within the unit[a]	Discussion about interpersonal relationships within the institution[a]

Entry-level Staff	Mid-level Manager Staff
Discussion about unit, division, and institutional reward systems[a]	Discussion about division and institutional reward systems[a]
Identification of past problems or issues and history of any interpersonal conflicts encountered by previous position holder[a]	Identification of past problems or issues, history of interpersonal conflicts within or between units or individuals, explanation of measures taken to deal with the situation(s)[a]
Discussion of ethical standards staff are expected to observe[a]	Discussion of ethical standards staff are expected to observe[a]

[a] Topic should be addressed during orientation for new position holder if he or she is already employed at the institution.

Chapter Seven

Supervising and Managing Staff

Often when persons in higher education hear *supervision,* they envision an entry-level staff member trying to learn the ropes or someone being called on the carpet. In other words, they think of staff members as needing supervision when they are new and inexperienced and do not know what they are supposed to do, or when they have done something wrong or improper. This view holds that staff do not need supervision if they are well qualified for the demands of their position, understand their responsibilities and the workings of the institution, and fulfill expectations and meet deadlines. To provide someone who is doing a good job with supervision could be interpreted as an insult or put-down, or at best a waste of valuable time. Supervision, by such thinking, is equated with incompetence or malfeasance.

Such a jaundiced view of supervision is rooted in several built-in contradictions evident in many higher education institutions. To paraphrase Bunker and Wijnberg (1988), who wrote about supervision in social service agencies, supervisors and frontline service providers and educators receive different internal and external rewards for what they do. Administrative supervisors are praised and rewarded for maintaining order, being predictable, assuring accountability, promoting fiscal prudence and economy, and supporting the values of the institution's leadership. Service providers and educators, however, gain professional-organizational approval and recognition from peers (and to some degree from students) for meeting professional standards, the quality of the programs and services provided, cooperation with peers, and capacity to represent the interests of their clientele, which may at times conflict with the interests of powers within the community. The idea of supervising professionals also seems incompatible with the ideals of collegial governance and consensus decision making.

In this chapter we discuss why adequate supervision has been difficult to conceptualize in higher education and summarize the somewhat limited range of research and literature about supervision in higher education, especially within student affairs. Because supervision is seen as the linchpin of the staffing model and because we were unable to find cogent conceptionalizations of supervision appropriate for student affairs practice in the literature, we present a theoretical model called *synergistic supervision*. Finally, we offer suggestions on ways practitioners can use synergistic supervision concepts and processes to improve everyday practice.

Professionals in Bureaucracies

There appear to be inherent conflicts caused by being a professional in a bureaucratic organization. Scott (1969) identified four areas of conflicts: resistance to bureaucratic rules, rejection of bureaucratic standards, conditional loyalty to the organization, and resistance to supervision.

To be a professional means owning extensive knowledge and skills that allow operating at a sophisticated level and an ideology that defines the purpose of one's work. Many bureaucratic rules are by design simplistic and conceptualized as applying to everyone in the organization, but professionals' work is complex, requiring multiple interrelated decisions that vary from situation to situation. Professionals, by definition, possess the knowledge and experience that qualifies them to use a wide latitude of decision making, not simple obedience to an organizational rule or policy.

Resistance to bureaucratic standards often centers around the definition of professional practice. "If student affairs divisions see their goal as making an important contribution to the education of students and if the institutional authorities see it as [principally] exercising control over student behavior and providing ancillary support services, then conflict is bound to ensue . . ." (Winston and Dagley, 1985, p. 58). Conditional loyalty to the institution also presents a problem from a bureaucratic perspective. Student affairs professionals who have completed a reputable graduate preparation program that emphasizes adherence to professional standards and the values of the profession develop a professional self-identity that is independent of an employing institution. Some practitioners may become more concerned with getting and maintaining a reputation among peers (often nationally) than with pleasing institutional superiors.

Finally, resistance to bureaucratic supervision presents a problem. For professionals, it is generally assumed that the supervisor possesses greater (or at least commensurate) experience and knowledge in the area than the person being supervised. At the upper levels, this assumption may not be satisfied. If the chief student affairs administrator reports to the president or other executive officer, that person is not likely to possess an extensive background in student affairs and may not view it as a professional area that requires specialized knowledge and skills. (If the chief student affairs administrator does not have appropriate academic preparation and extensive professional work experience, then the resistance may be moved farther down the organizational structure.) As Blimling (1993a) noted, many college presidents have difficulty conceptualizing student affairs as a profession because they view it as similar to academic affairs. From their perspective one usually rises to positions of leadership in academic affairs through a succession of increasingly responsible positions (department chair to college dean to academic vice president, for example). There generally is no formal academic preparation required for these positions. Faculty-administrators typically possess a terminal degree in any given academic discipline and distinguish themselves as teachers and perhaps researchers, which leads to their election or appointment as department or division heads. Administrative skills and knowledge are acquired on the job and through imitation of predecessors, and possibly sharpened in workshops and summer institutes. (Why, then, should not a respected, level-headed professor who establishes rapport with students easily be named to head the student affairs division?) Within this context, student affairs professionals are sometimes instructed to do things that are contrary to accepted professional standards or incongruent with the profession's basic values. In such cases, resistance to supervision is to be expected (and perhaps to be applauded).

Perspectives from Literature

If there were a direct relationship between the level of concern for a particular practice in student affairs and the amount of literature on the subject published in the field's journals, it would be clear and convincing evidence that supervision is a neglected domain. Very little literature is published on this vital topic, especially with sufficient detail to guide practitioners to better performance in supervision. The most thoughtful recent contributions to supervision literature are provided by Schuh and Carlisle (1991) and Dalton (1988, 1996).

What we would classify as supervision, Dalton (1996, p. 498) calls "talent development." The important activities associated with this process include assessment of employees' skills and knowledge, design of specific learning and performance objectives, focus on improvement in performance, recognizing and rewarding achievement, training staff for leadership, and measuring learning and development outcomes.

Dalton (1988) identifies the legal implications and constraints of employment and supervision but offers sound advice regarding several essential practices, including the importance of accurate job descriptions; careful search, hiring, and orientation procedures; work hours; health and safety issues; and the importance of interactive communications among personnel. His experience, knowledge, and insight on the subject are revealed by his straightforward advice to never underestimate a personnel problem. Anyone who has ever held supervisory responsibilities knows the wisdom of this comment. In his more recent work he offers practical suggestions on means of getting the most out of one's staff.

Dalton (1996) also identifies six trouble spots that supervisors often encounter: underestimating the importance or potency of personal issues as they affect performance, rewarding the wrong behavior, pursuing tasks without vision, pursuing the vision without working out the details with subordinates, failing to see leadership as service, and ignoring one's own advice—that is, failing to model what one advocates.

Schuh and Carlisle (1991) provide more detailed guidance about supervision and evaluation. While focusing on the relationship more than on specific acts, they define supervision as the process of one staff member providing opportunities, structure, and support to another. They underscore the importance of motivation issues, including conditioning theory, expectancy theory, and motivator-hygiene theory; supervisory styles, including one-dimensional supervision, two-dimensional leadership, and facilitating development; and elements of supervisory success, including managerial philosophy, staff needs, and values. Schuh and Carlisle also focus on career development and mentoring issues whereby readers are especially admonished to be sensitive to gender, race, and ethical issues.

Mills (1993) emphasizes the importance of clear communication and assignment of responsibilities for middle managers, who are often called on to act in emergencies without benefit of consultation with the chief student affairs administrator. As he points out, "Middle managers may have both responsibility and authority in some areas, but they are also charged with implementing decisions from a higher level" (p. 127). The quality and nature of the supervision they receive is, therefore, crucial for middle managers.

These managers deserve close consultation and support from their supervisors as they discharge their duties. There is reluctance, however, on the part of some staff at this level to request supervision because they are afraid that it may be perceived as incompetence or a means of transferring unpleasant tasks to the boss.

Delegation is one of the most important skills middle managers must acquire and is an essential aspect of staff supervision. Mills (1993) offers three principles central to effective supervision by middle managers: responsibility and authority should be delegated together, along with clear boundaries; staff should have delegated to them only matters they are developmentally ready to handle; and supervisors should keep abreast of, but not micromanage, items that have been delegated.

These are important contributions to the literature on supervision, and their perspectives are generally supported in the views taken from our research. Some of the ideas need to be explored further, however. Nothing was found in the literature that comes close to presenting what might be called a model of effective supervision.

Perspectives from Research

Supervision has proved an elusive subject to pursue through research. We found that to be true in both our survey research and in the case studies.

Survey Findings

It is difficult to determine the current state of affairs concerning supervision based on the survey data we gathered and reported in Chapter Four. Apparently, most practitioners view themselves as providing supervision to their staff every two to four weeks; however, almost one-fourth indicated that they provide supervision once or twice a year or less. When asked about the supervision they receive themselves, respondents on average reported receiving supervision about half as often as supervisors reported providing it. There is obviously a difference in perception here. (Staff and supervisors who completed surveys, however, were not matched.)

Based on the information provided by the staff who received supervision, the only consistent subjects included in supervision are short-range work assignments or projects and "new knowledge and information." This conception of supervision is very narrow and does not, in our opinion, constitute adequate support for staff. Overall, however, staff report being satisfied with the supervision they receive, perhaps because they are unaware of how much richer and more helpful supervision could be.

Case Studies

At the eight campuses we visited to conduct case studies, there was universal acknowledgment that supervision is a vitally important institutional function. Beyond that affirmation, however, there is little commonality across campuses and no systematic approach to supervision on any campus. Practices vary widely, perhaps, for important reasons; for example, one should not approach supervision in a two-person office in the same way as where there are a score of staff at varying levels of experience and responsibility.

On most campuses, training in supervision is rudimentary or nonexistent. At the one campus that has extensive training, there was some apprehension expressed by some mid-level staff about the effectiveness of the supervision provided. For the most part, the quality and frequency of supervision seem to be more a reflection of the values and skills of the individual mid-level administrators than institutional or divisional policy or goals.

Supervision was generally conceptualized as either a coordinating function—distributing work load and making sure nothing falls through the cracks—or as a supportive and educational service provided to inexperienced personnel. There seems to be little recognition that supervision could and should also focus on improving organizational effectiveness in a more fundamental way.

Based on the case studies, it is not possible to determine the effectiveness of supervisory practices. On each campus there seem to be bright spots and areas of little or no activity.

Supervision Defined

Supervision in higher education is a management function intended to promote the achievement of institutional goals and to enhance the personal and professional capabilities of staff. Supervision interprets the institutional mission and focuses human and fiscal resources on the promotion of individual and organizational competence.

Supervision is one of the most complex activities that student affairs professionals are called upon to perform. To do it properly and adequately requires broad knowledge of the activities that are part of the functional area or areas for which one has responsibility, a detailed knowledge of the institution and both its formal and informal operational processes, a caring attitude, and well-developed interpersonal relationship skills. Good supervisors are called upon to use the full range of knowledge and skills they have acquired through years of professional practice. Supervision frequently is intellectually challenging and emotionally demanding.

Functional Components of Supervision

Bunker and Wijnberg (1988) identify six interrelated functions involved in supervision of social work professionals that also seem applicable to student affairs professionals: articulating the unit's mission and needs, monitoring and managing the climate of the unit and institution, fostering individual practitioner development, developing teamwork capabilities and work-group resources, coordinating work activities (interunit liaison and conflict management), and promoting active problem solving.

Articulating the Unit's Mission and Needs

As the characteristics of student bodies shift and their problems and issues change, it is essential that units within the student affairs division stay abreast of those changes and adapt programs and services to meet students' new needs. This requires the supervisor to remain abreast of the current literature and to initiate processes that will ensure that the unit is sensitive to changes in its clientele. Because the student affairs division is a system of interrelated purposes and activities, supervisors also have a responsibility to keep other parts of the division informed about that unit's experiences and to sensitize the entire institution to the changes. Supervisors who actively inform others in the institution about their units and their issues and concerns also build credibility with the unit's staff. In other words, good supervisors must be effective spokespersons for their units—both within the division and with larger publics.

Care must be exercised, however, in how the information about the unit's activities and its clientele's concerns are articulated. Communication should be done in ways that give frontline staff credit for their contributions and recognize their accomplishments. Otherwise, staff may come to view this activity as personal aggrandizement on the part of the supervisor, which may have a deleterious effect on the unit's morale and effectiveness.

Monitoring and Managing the Climate

All organizations create unique work climates. Some climates support or encourage goal accomplishment, congenial interpersonal relationships, and esprit d'corps. Others dampen or constrain staff members' motivation and commitment to the organization and its mission. Although the prevailing organizational climate tends to be self-reinforcing and somewhat impervious to change, it "can be altered when concerted efforts are made by key climate-setting actors to redefine the affective context of work activities" (Bunker and Wijnberg, 1988, p. 84). In most organizations, supervisors are such key persons who can be influential either in transmitting and reinforcing the prevailing climate or in acting as a buffer between a unit's staff and the larger organization. Even though it is not possible to completely insulate a unit's staff from the negative press of the larger institutional climate, it is generally possible to create subenvironments where staff feel secure, appreciated, and affirmed, even if somewhat isolated.

Studies by organizational psychologists (such as Campbell and others, 1970) have identified four dimensions that vary across organizations and seem particularly influential in creating work environments that motivate staff to give their best efforts and to feel good about themselves as members of the institution. Clarity of the task structure is one of the factors related to arousal of achievement motivation. When tasks and goals are ambiguous and there is a high degree of external control, most workers feel little motivation to go beyond minimum requirements and also may feel considerable frustration because of perceived conflicting demands and expectations. The degree of challenge and decision-making responsibility allowed is another important factor that influences the motivation to achieve. When staff members are given permission to exercise judgment and the freedom to structure their own responses to problems, they generally exhibit more energy and commitment to satisfactory performance of the unit. The third factor, rewards, differentiates organizational climates. The degree to which the organization emphasizes rewards rather than punishments "evokes either defensive anxiety in the presence of punitive threats or the expectation of having one's self and contribution confirmed through positive recognition and reinforcement" (Bunker and Wijnberg, 1988, p. 85). The level of social inclusion and harmony perceived by staff is another important organizational climate variable. If staff members experience social support from the supervisor and others in the unit, they are more likely to develop the attitudes and behaviors that foster cooperation. But if they experience an atmosphere characterized by frequent conflict and acrimonious interactions, they are likely to react defensively, which makes cooperative efforts difficult if not impossible.

Miller (1990) offers six guidelines that supervisors can follow to create and maintain an environment that fosters the maintenance of professional competence and positively affects the unit's performance:

- Develop participative processes for selecting important goals within the unit so that the members can have ownership, which will create a congruence between personal and organizational goals.
- Create an image of vitality, excitement, and achievement of results that helps the organization attract, develop, and retain vital people.
- Seek ways to institutionalize caring and nurturing support of staff's career aspirations, which includes providing opportunities to broaden skills and experiences through varied work assignments and support for continued formal education and continuing professional development.
- Develop environments that support the individual in being sufficiently secure to risk experimentation, to try approaches different from the past, and to push at the frontiers of application of new concepts and technologies to the needs of clients.
- Make vitality and effectiveness of the unit goals on par with goals related to the delivery of programs and services.
- Pay careful attention to matching people with assignments so that their skills are used, but not in such a repetitive manner that it stifles the growth of new capabilities or eliminates the variety necessary to avoid obsolescence and burnout, and support renewal.

Even though supervisors cannot completely control the climate within their units, they need to remain sensitive to how staff members perceive the work environment. When conditions become unfavorable, supervisors should address the issues. If an atmosphere of openness and candor has been established, then supervisors usually can facilitate the unit's self-diagnosis of the concerns. If such a climate does not already exist, then an outside consultant may be needed to assist the unit in identifying the issues associated with the adverse work environment and developing strategies to address them.

Fostering Individual Development

If an organization is to receive the benefit of the full capabilities and talents of its employees, it must devise ways to assist individuals to mature as human beings and as professionals. If the workplace

is seen as providing opportunities to satisfy developmental needs—
such as receiving recognition for contributions, having opportunities to work on interesting and challenging problems or projects,
and having opportunities to develop new professional and personal
competencies—then individuals are much more likely to exceed
minimum expectations and to make significant contributions to the
institution. Fostering development requires the supervisor to know
what is going on in the lives of those they supervise and to make
reasonable accommodation to support staff members in addressing
developmental and other personal issues. To do this requires a
knowledge of adult development theory, rapport with staff, open
two-way communication, and a caring attitude. The supervisor
should establish a relationship with staff that communicates that he
or she is an ally for career advancement. (These topics will be
addressed in greater depth in subsequent chapters.)

Developing Teamwork Capabilities and Group Resources
Generally in student affairs, unit performance is not merely the
sum of individual efforts. The quality and efficiency of a functional
area, "as well as maintenance of morale and motivation, are functions of intragroup relations and the stage of group development. . . . The . . . supervisor is, therefore, concerned with the
development of the unit as a work group capable of acting
together to accomplish shared objectives" (Bunker and Wijnberg,
1988, p. 91). Student affairs as a professional field, then, is ill-suited
for Lone Ranger types.

Important purposes of team building are addressed by Reilly
and Jones (1974) and include promoting a better understanding
of each member's role in the work group, developing a better
understanding of the team's role in the larger organization,
increasing communication among team members about issues
affecting performance and efficiency, finding effective means of
handling tasks and interpersonal conflicts within the team, becoming better able to use conflict constructively, promoting collaboration and lessening competition among members, and enhancing
interdependence among group members.

According to Reilly and Jones, the extent to which teams create high-level performance depends on the degree to which mem-

bership is attractive to individuals (cohesiveness), the degree of interdependence in performing tasks or providing services, and the degree to which group norms and goals are congruent with the purposes of the unit or institution.

A word of caution is required about team building and teamwork. The concept is almost sacrosanct in student affairs circles; everyone claims to be in favor of it. There are several conditions, however, that must be satisfied for teamwork to play a constructive role in a unit's operations. First, the tasks to be performed must lend themselves to the involvement of multiple staff members. It makes no sense to build a team to do work that could be accomplished by an individual. Second, team building must be work-goal related. Even though good morale and healthy interpersonal relationships (perhaps even friendships) can result from the team building process, that should not be the primary reason for undertaking it. Team building and maintenance is not a feel-good prescription. There are less time-consuming and less expensive ways to address interpersonal relationship issues. Third, there must be opportunities for members of the team to make significant, independent decisions that do not require the approval of the supervisor. Supervisors must be willing and able to share decision-making authority for teamwork to be meaningful. If supervisors attempt to convince staff members that they have the authority to make decisions when they really do not, the likely outcome will be feelings of resentment, betrayal, and lowered morale, which generally will have the effect of lessening the unit's productivity. Fourth, good teamwork does not mean there is an absence of conflict. Wise supervisors and team leaders make conscious efforts to employ staff who complement, not duplicate, their leadership styles and personalities. It is tempting to seek like-minded professionals with the same style when selecting new staff members because it tends to produce a more harmonious organization. It is indeed essential that staff members and supervisors share similar perceptions of each other's roles and have similar goals and objectives for the unit. Hersey and Blanchard (1977, p. 152) maintain "that organizations need an 'open' dialogue where there is a certain amount of conflict, confrontation, and differing points of view to encourage new ideas and patterns of behavior. . . ."

Coordinating Work Activities

Supervisors are called on to continuously balance four competing demands that influence how work is to be done: professional norms and standards, individual abilities and attitudes, formal job designs used in selection and appraisal, and service strategies and practice models designed to fit the distribution of student needs and institutional values (Bunker and Wijnberg, 1988).

An example may serve to illustrate interrelated relationships and needed adjustments. Suppose one is the supervisor of a student activities unit at a small public college. There are a director, two entry-level professionals, and two secretaries in the unit. In coordinating the multiple activities for which the unit is responsible, the director as supervisor is called upon to adjust the demands of quality professional practice (perhaps as outlined in the CAS standards and other documents) and the abilities, skills, and attitudes of the staff members. If one of the staff members (call him Albert) is a recent graduate of a master's-level professional preparation program, the supervisor, when assigning responsibilities, must take into account Albert's lack of experience in this institution and his youth in the field. Likewise, the job description used in the selection process that resulted in Albert's hiring was relatively fixed. What exactly Albert is asked to do as the year begins should be balanced by his changing skills and knowledge of the institution as the year goes on. Albert may well be expected to assume greater responsibilities at the end of the year than he was at the beginning. Also, job descriptions should reflect how the unit is organized and its goals in terms of student outcomes.

Where student affairs units have several positions with similar educational requirements, some have adopted a policy of periodically redesigning position responsibilities. For instance, in a dean of students' office, there may be three assistant deans whose areas of responsibilities include student discipline, Greek life, minority student services, international student services, and support of student government. When the assistant dean responsible for Greek life and student government resigns to take a new position, the dean and assistant deans may meet to discuss a redistribution of assignments. If an organizational redesign results, the new position advertisement may seek someone to work with student discipline and student government, as the other responsibilities are being redistributed to the remaining assistant deans. Such an arrangement allows the remaining staff to gain wider experience in students affairs and to introduce some novelty to their work life though new responsibilities and exposure to different facets of the student population.

Promoting Active Problem Solving

Work in complex organizations, as most colleges and universities are, almost by definition requires supervisors to cope with multiple frustrations on a daily basis. Besides the problems caused by students' lack of cooperation, youthful excesses, malicious behavior, and failure to follow instructions, supervisors often are required to deal with unreasonable procedural demands, insufficient resources, inadequate facilities, uncooperative colleagues, and lack of appreciation of the role of student affairs. Because of the inherent difficulties of doing their jobs, some student affairs practitioners have adapted to the system so well that they have reduced their aspirations and "have become resigned to their conditions or have become cynical, bitter, and quick to blame" (Bunker and Wijnberg, 1988, p. 111).

Mobile practitioners frequently flee these adversarial work situations, leaving behind coworkers who feel that they cannot escape but who often psychologically disengage from the organization as a means of coping. Others maintain their ideals and continue the struggle year after year to better the lives and educational experiences of students. Still others observe the rituals of job performance but do not make a true investment of themselves in either the process or its outcomes. A few engage in efforts to change conditions by borrowing ideas from other campuses or by seeking to bring together like-minded colleagues who attempt to implement theory-based interventions.

It is vital that supervisors convey a sense of confidence and optimism about making small, incremental changes in the organization that will improve the lives of both students and staff. Bunker and Wijnberg (1988, p. 112) comment: "A succession of small successes is the only way to restore hope that organizational follies can be corrected and that workers need not resign themselves to impotent and passive acceptance of whatever exists or is decreed." For supervisors, problem solving is both an attitude and a process; it has both political and technical aspects. Effective problem solving in organizations requires more than just defining problems and devising strategies to solve them. The effective supervisor must also be skillful in generating alternatives and weighting selection criteria, as well as in advocacy, "in engineering of assent, and in designing participative processes" (p. 113). Solutions to problems, no matter how innovative or potentially effective, seldom get implemented unless coalitions of influential players in the organizations can be formed.

Supervision: Another Perspective

Schuh and Carlisle (1991) point out that *supervisor* in the business world generally refers only to first-line managers who work with classified, union, or production personnel. Within this context, to supervise implies that the worker must be scrutinized, evaluated, motivated, or taught what to do (Phillips, 1985). Within the context of student affairs practice, however, a radically different perspective on supervision is proposed. Supervision is viewed as essentially a helping process, which is designed to support staff as they seek to promote the goals of the organizations and to advance their professional development. Staff in student affairs have a right to expect competent supervision from their employers throughout their careers. This concept of supervision envisions staff members and supervisors collaborating to accomplish the organization's goals and to help the staff member mature both as a person and as a professional practitioner.

Approaches to Supervision

The general approaches to supervision of professionals in higher education may be categorized as authoritarian, laissez faire, companionable, or synergistic (adapted from Winston, Ullom, and Werring, 1984).

Authoritarian supervision is based on the belief that staff members require continuous attention because they are often undependable or immature—basically, because people will attempt to work as little as possible unless someone monitors them carefully. Because staff members cannot be trusted to fulfill their responsibilities conscientiously or because they lack the necessary skills or maturity to handle difficult tasks, the supervisor must check up on them frequently. Conflicts between the unit and the organization are handled by the supervisor, who either defends the unit (if it is in the right) or brings the staff in line with the organization's goals or rules. The supervisor is ultimately responsible for staff members' performance; consequently, close observation is an essential part of the supervisor's responsibilities.

Laissez faire supervision is based on the desire to allow staff members the freedom to use their talents and skills in accomplishing job responsibilities. This philosophy of practice often is articulated as: "hire good people and then get out of their way." This approach requires supervisors to set the direction for the staff and then allow them to work out the best ways to accomplish the established goals individually. Supervision is offered if they run into trouble. As a result, staff members view supervision as an admission of failure—that is, as something to submit to when they encounter a situation they are unable to handle on their own. Conflicts between the supervisor's unit and other parts of the institutions are dealt with by allowing staff to work out their own solutions; if they fail, the supervisor steps in and takes over. Because seeking advice or asking direction is an admission of failure, supervisors are called in by staff generally only when things have progressed to a serious state or have gotten completely out of hand. Supervision in this approach is synonymous with crisis intervention or "cleaning up the mess."

Companionable supervision is based principally on a friendship-like relationship. Above all else, supervisors seek to be liked and to create harmonious relationships among staff members; they concentrate on being buddies with the staff they supervise and avoid confronting staff members about poor job performance or mistakes in judgment as long as possible. Unpleasant situations or problems are ignored in the hope that staff members will be able to work things out, thereby avoiding unpleasantness and confrontation. Supervisors give staff members a great deal of personal support as an indirect means of helping them deal with problems. Companionable supervisors usually provide staff members considerable personal attention and opportunities for social interaction. Organizational conflicts are dealt with by the supervisor supporting or defending staff against outside attack; it is essential that staff members never doubt their supervisor's support. Work life, however, is much like a roller coaster ride of pleasant highs and painful lows. Once crises pass, supervisors work hard to repair the damage to the relationship.

Synergistic supervision is a cooperative effort between the supervisor and staff members that allows the effect of their joint efforts to be greater than the sum of their individual contributions. Supervision in this approach has a dual focus: accomplishment of the organization's goals and support of staff in accomplishment of their personal and professional development goals. This approach to supervision emphasizes the identification of potential problems early; the supervisor and staff member then jointly develop strategies to prevent or ameliorate problem situations. Supervision is dedicated to assisting all staff members to enhance their knowledge and skills, which can lead to advancement within the organization and profession. Conflicts between the supervisor's unit and other parts of the institution are dealt with as situations that require joint problem solving; as a team, the unit's staff devises strategies to either resolve the conflicts or to minimize their negative effects on accomplishment of the unit's goals. Supervision is a continuous, ongoing process. Supervision sessions have a predictable structure, which includes explicit attention to both the supervisor's and staff member's job-related and personal concerns.

Synergistic Supervision

Most student affairs practitioners (both vice presidents and other staff) in our survey endorsed synergistic supervision as being most descriptive of how they approach this important management task (see Chapter Four). We believe it has the greatest utility for working with student affairs practitioners. The phrase *synergistic supervision* emphasizes this conceptualization of supervision and how it differs from other approaches. Its cooperative nature allows joint effects to exceed the combination of individual efforts, which can be expressed in a mathematical metaphor: $1 + 1 = 3$.

Important characteristics of synergistic supervision include: dual focus on accomplishment of the organization's goals and support of staff in accomplishment of their personal and professional development goals, joint effort, two-way communication, a focus on competence, growth orientation, proactivity, goal-based, systematic and ongoing processes, and holism.

Dual Focus

Synergistic supervision as a management function attends to the accomplishment of the institution's and unit's goals—as well as fulfillment of the organizational maintenance functions assigned the unit—and also to the personal and professional welfare of the staff. As DeCoster and Brown (1991, p. 569) note, "The ideal framework for professional development is built by interlocking individual and organizational goals." Likewise, organizational effectiveness is maximized when staff members "perceive their own goals as being satisfied by the accomplishment of organizational goals" (Hersey and Blanchard, 1977, p. 124), which McGregor's (1966) management theory calls integration of goals.

For synergistic supervision to work, staff members need to feel that they have a significant influence on selecting and defining goals and in devising strategies to accomplish them. If they perceive goals as being imposed on them, they are unlikely to make personal investments in the goals' achievement.

Most units have certain responsibilities or duties (for instance, on-call duty, supervision or observation of large student gatherings, or making ID cards) that are not negotiable and that may be viewed by the staff as onerous. The unit is unlikely to have the option of deciding whether or not to assume these duties. Such situations can be made more palatable, however, if the staff is involved in deciding how responsibilities are assigned or in scheduling duty periods. If the staff perceive fairness and equity in the process and work load, they are much more likely to perform conscientiously. As Terry and Franklin (1982) found, when staff participate in decision making, there is an increased likelihood that the decisions will have greater accuracy and wider acceptance, which has the by-products of better communication, more cooperation, and higher commitment.

The other focus of synergistic supervision is the personal and professional growth of staff. Staff are much more likely to show loyalty to the supervisor and the institution and unit when they perceive that the supervisor is sincerely interested in them as individuals and is able and willing to assist them in accomplishing personal and professional objectives. In order for a synergistic supervision approach to be realized, the supervisor and each staff member need to establish a relationship based on trust, respect, openness, and mutuality. Unlike the companionable approach to supervision that emphasizes the establishment and maintenance of a friendship-type relationship as the principal means of supervision, synergistic supervision requires a cordial, mutually respectful relationship (not necessarily friendship) as a necessary, but not sufficient, condition for successful supervision.

Joint Effort

A defining characteristic of synergistic supervision is the principle that supervision is not something done to staff but rather a cooperative activity in which each party has an important contribution to make. (It is this combination of energy that makes the approach *synergistic.*)

For supervision to be successful from institutional and staff perspectives, both parties must be willing to invest time and energy in the process. Lacking such commitment, there is little hope that synergistic supervision can be put into place. When goals are clearly identified and plans for accomplishing goals are worked out jointly between the supervisor and the staff member, then success or failure also falls on both sets of shoulders.

Two-Way Communication

Two-way communication is essential for effective supervision. Synergistic supervision is dependent on a high level of trust between staff members and their supervisors, so staff members must be willing to allow supervisors to learn about them personally and the details of their daily work life without being defensive. Staff members also must feel free to give their supervisors honest, direct feedback. Supervisors must check frequently on whether or not they are setting up situations in which it is comfortable for staff to give them feedback, especially negative feedback.

Focus on Competence

Supervision concentrates on four areas of staff competence: knowledge and information, work-related skills, personal and professional development skills, and attitudes.

* *Knowledge and information.* To be effective, staff members must understand how college students develop and must have accurate information about laws and other legal parameters of practice, standards of professional practice, ethical standards, and institutional rules and policies, services, programs, and other institutional resources.

* *Work-related skills.* Staff need a wide range of skills (for example, interpersonal communication, goal setting, public relations, leadership, confrontation, conflict resolution, computer usage, bookkeeping, and clerical skills) to be effective. Even though staff may have received training and were once proficient with a skill, they often need refreshers if they do not regularly use a particular ability. It is often difficult for practitioners to remain current in theory and practice in skill areas because the periodical professional literature does not address these topics frequently. Synergistic supervision concentrates on identifying current levels of skills and devising methods through which staff can acquire new skills or refine already developed skills. (Strategies for addressing these areas are addressed in Chapter Eight.)

* *Personal and professional skills.* To be effective as persons and professionals, staff members need another wide range of skills (for instance, time management, personal management such as diet or exercise, retirement planning, anger control, career planning, or stress management). Being an effective staff member means making serious efforts to acquire new skills; likewise, to be effective professionals, staff members need to keep their job-specific skills current. (Strategies for addressing these areas are also addressed in Chapter Eight.)

* *Attitudes.* Working in student affairs is seldom a mechanical or solitary process; it usually involves working with other people.

Consequently, the attitudes staff members display are often as important as what they actually do. Whether a staff member approaches tasks with an attitude of enthusiasm or sarcasm often determines his or her ultimate success. Attitudes are, therefore, an important subject of supervision.

As Mouton and Blake (1984, p. 8) note, "Administrators . . . usually pause to consider the quality of employees' attitudes only when they have become so negative or deviant as to result in confused, divisive, unacceptable, or even illegal behavior." For many student affairs administrators, there is reticence to address staff members' attitudes for fear of invading their privacy or unconstitutionally interfering with the exercise of basic American freedoms. "In democratic societies, for example, no responsible . . . [public sector administrator] would prescribe attitudes towards politics, religion, or issues of private morality. Nor is it relevant to view such attitudes as aspects of on-the-job efficiency or as career advancement criteria" (p. 8). In private institutions, the extent and degree of institutional inspection and prescription in these areas should be clearly communicated to prospective employees and provided to staff in writing at the time of their employment.

Certain attitudes, however, do affect performance and satisfaction and are, therefore, legitimate areas of concern for supervisors. "Positive attitudes can strongly motivate an individual to apply knowledge or skills to constructive purposes, while negative attitudes can hinder the appropriate use of the knowledge and skills. Aiding individuals to test their attitudes against criteria, to become better aware of how their attitudes influence their thought and behavior, [and] to perceive a range of available attitudes" (Mouton and Blake, pp. 8–9) are important responsibilities of a synergistic supervisor. Another important reason that supervisors should address attitudes is because staff tend to congregate with others who share the same attitudes. "This social cohesion reinforces the retention of those shared attitudes, as each person knows that others feel the same way" (p. 93), thereby making attitudes even more powerful forces for constructive or disruptive action within a unit.

Growth Orientation

As mentioned earlier, synergistic supervision attends to both personal and professional areas of practitioners' lives. Of particular importance is career development. Supervisors should provide assistance, if desired, to staff as they pursue work that is meaningful and personally satisfying. Schein (1978) introduced the concept of career anchors to help clarify a person's occupational self-concept. The concept is composed of three elements: self-perceived talents and abilities, which are based on actual successes in various work settings; self-perceived motives and needs, which are based on opportunities for testing oneself in real situations and receiving feedback; and self-perceived attitudes and values, which are based on actual encounters between the staff member and the values of the institution and work setting. If a supervisor can understand a staff member's career anchors, it may be much easier to help that person progress up the career ladder and find work assignments that are congruent with his or her interests and abilities.

Schein (1978) identified six career anchors that seem to apply to most student affairs professionals as well as to the male graduates of the Massachusetts Institute of Technology that he studied:

- *Technical and functional competence.* The self-image of people who have this anchor is tied to their feelings of competence in the particular areas they are in, and consequently they are not interested in management (for instance as a VPSA), though they will accept management responsibilities within their technical or functional area of competence. For them the area of work is what turns them on, and they indicate that career growth for them means continued advancement within that area only. In student affairs, examples of positions that may be held by people with this anchor include housing directors, registrars, and financial aid directors.

- *Managerial competence.* The self-image of people in this group involves management per se as the ultimate goal. Specific technical or functional jobs are seen only as necessary interim stages on the way to the higher, general administrative levels. They see the necessity of becoming competent in one or more functional areas, but no one area captures their commitment. Instead, they perceive their competence to lie in the combination of analytical competence (the ability to identify, analyze, and solve problems under conditions of incomplete information and uncertainty); interpersonal competence (the ability to influence, supervise, lead, manipulate, and control people at all levels of the organization toward more effective achievement of organizational goals; and emotional competence (the capacity to be stimulated by emotional and interpersonal crises rather than exhausted or debilitated by them, the capacity to bear high levels of responsibility without becoming paralyzed, and the ability to exercise power without guilt or shame). Staff who aspire to be vice presidents or presidents may hold this career anchor.

• *Security and stability.* People anchored in security tend to do what is required of them by their employers to maintain job security, a decent income, and a stable future in the form of a good retirement program, benefits, and the like. By implication, such people will, more than others, accept an organizational definition of their careers and have to trust the organization to do the right thing by them. Whatever private aspirations or competences they may believe themselves to have, they must rely on the organization to recognize such needs and competences and to do the best by them that is possible. Staff who are place-bound in areas with few colleges and universities may come to hold this career anchor.

• *Creativity.* These people seem to have an overarching need to build or create something that is entirely their own product. Self-extension through the creation of a product or process is the key to these people's career anchor. In student affairs, there are staff who are very good at creating innovative programs that require originality, ingenuity, charisma, and organizational skills but who lose interest once the programs are up and running successfully.

• *Basic identity.* People with this career anchor tend to see their title, uniform, and other trappings of office as a fundamental basis for their self-definition. Such people seek occupational situations that clearly define their roles externally through highly visible means of status or through symbols that have relatively little to do with the work they perform. Identification with prestigious offices or institutions often serves this function.

• *Service to others.* Some occupations such as counseling, social work, and some aspects of medicine, teaching, and the ministry allow persons to express basic needs, talents, and values to work with others in a helping role; the interpersonal competence and helping are ends in themselves rather than means to an end. Some of the allied professionals in a student affairs division in areas such as student health or counseling may hold this career anchor.

Just as successful student affairs practitioners base their work with students on an understanding of developmental theory, successful supervisors need an understanding of adult development theory as they work with their staffs. It is essential that supervisors be aware of the kinds of developmental changes that are going on in the lives of the staff they supervise, as well as in their own lives. Table 7.1 summarizes some of the developmental tasks that people face through the life cycle in relation to their work and career. Drawn from the literature and our own experience, here the tasks have been made somewhat more specific to careers in student affairs. Not all practitioners, of course, face these issues in the same way; circumstance, personality, and earlier life choices play significant roles in determining a person's psychosocial development.

Hodgkinson (1974) and Sprunger and Bergquist (1978) emphasize the importance of understanding the adult development issues that staff face to provide effective supervision and motivation. For example, Sprunger and Bergquist (p. 209) relate developmental theory to supervision of young professionals age twenty-two to about age thirty. They assert that at this stage the young professional is "usually motivated by intangibles, like the interest and praise of his [her] mentor or another respected superior, as well as low-key and friendly competition with other young administrators. But probably the most important motivation is that there be consistency between the values and goals espoused by the mentor and his [her] actual behavior."

In the next stage of development (roughly age thirty to age thirty-nine), other motivations seem to be more salient: "clear

Table 7.1. Life Cycle Tasks and Work in Student Affairs.

Approximate Age	General Issues	Life Tasks To Be Faced	Career or Professional Tasks
24–30	Making *provisional* commitments to a range of adult roles	Test career choices	Find entry-level position in student affairs
	Developing a sense of self, thereby achieving a capacity for intimacy with spouse or partner and close circle of friends	Establish "home" separate from family of origin	Try application of knowledge and skills acquired in graduate school (read and watch others to learn about student affairs work if no professional preparation)
	Becoming more discriminating in one's relationships	Seek a spouse or partner	
	Solidifying lifestyle choices	Learn to get along with (perhaps live with) significant other, spouse, or partner	
		Solidify a lifestyle	Accept partial responsibility
		Further develop sense of integrity by humanizing values, showing social responsibility and congruence between values and behavior	Accept subordinate role and learn how to get along with peers and supervisor
			Develop initiative and realistic level of aggressiveness within the norms of the institutional culture
		Start to have children (for some)	Develop sense of professional confidence
		Women explore (make) choices about whether to pursue career, family, or career and family	Deal with feelings of success or failure in first job
			Find a sponsor (maybe a mentor)

Approximate Age	General Issues	Life Tasks To Be Faced	Career or Professional Tasks
			Reasses decision to enter student affairs profession in terms of talents, values, and career opportunities and constraints
			Build network of colleagues outside the employing institution
			Attend professional conferences and present show-and-tell programs
			Consider and make decision about doctoral study
			Make move from entry-level position
30–45	Becoming one's own person—widening, deepening, and stabilizing one's commitments	Put down roots	Decide whether to make sacrifices in order to "make it" in a career or to settle for security
	Coming to terms with the fact that time is limited and finite	Come to terms with one's marriage or other relationship (substituting a realistic assessment for the idealized vision of one's 20s)	Decide whether to become a specialist in a functional area or to pursue a general administrative position in student affairs (such as VP)
	Growing out of one's illusions or unrealistic expectations	Manage conflict between family and career	
	Making decisions about completion of the family	Child rearing (for some)	

Table 7.1. *(continued).*

Approximate Age	General Issues	Life Tasks To Be Faced	Career or Professional Tasks
	Coming to terms with aging by recognizing first signs of bodily decline Beginning to recognize one's own mortality	Begin to evaluate the efficacy of one's "dream"	Establish a clear identity within the profession and within an institutional category (such as community college; research university; private liberal arts college) Develop long-range career plans in terms of ambitions, types of progress sought, targets against which to measure progress Become fully aware of career anchors
40–55	Making extended reassessment of one's dream Redefining family relationships (children leaving home; reestablish relationship with spouse or partner or divorce) Establishing a more stable integration and life structure of prior role models or conformity pressures Reopening oneself to the world	Gain sense of autonomy and voluntary commitment—a sense that one is making one's own choices Accept uniqueness of one's life Deal with empty-nest syndrome—helping spouse to adjust to loss of parental role and transition to some other role Cope with dependence or death of one's parents	Establish niche in professional association(s) in which one can make contributions Make decision about seeking senior administrative positions (such as VP) Recommit to student affairs career, move into academic administration, or leave the field Become a mentor

Approximate Age	General Issues	Life Tasks To Be Faced	Career or Professional Tasks
	after a period of being closed	Make greater civic contributions	Cope with fear of loss of competence and competition from younger people "on the way up"
50–65	Dealing with concern about "running out of time" Mellowing, warming up, and valuing spouse or partner, children, and friends Reviewing one's life work and contributions to the world Growing concern with broader issues of society and community, loss of specialization and growth of wisdom Anticipating retirement and different lifestyle Adjusting to declining health and strength	Ensure that one stays in contact with one's friends, because of loss of interest in making new contacts and friendships Establish adult relationships with one's children Learn to be a grandparent Make concrete plans for retirement, including different living arrangements and reduced income Find new sources of satisfaction in hobbies, family, social and community activities, and so on	Learn how to handle high-level political situations both inside and outside the institution Learn how to handle higher levels of responsibility and power without becoming paralyzed or emotionally upset Prepare to disengage from career

Note: Table based on Schein (1978, pp. 29–46) and supplemented by Chickering & Havighurst (1981), Levinson & Levinson (1996), Levinson, Darrow, Klein, Levinson, & McKee (1978), Bergquist, Greenberg, & Klaum (1993), Carpenter (1991).

definition of job responsibilities, peer affiliation and support, and job stability but not confinement. Salary levels may be important . . . [more so than in the earlier stage because] direct gratification can be delayed only so long" (p. 210).

Synergistic supervision is a growth-oriented activity. Because the primary focus of synergistic supervision is not to correct problems or discipline staff, the activity can produce important personal benefits for the staff and should make the work place stimulating and personally rewarding. Staff members, however, are always accountable for their actions (or inactions). From time to time, supervisors will need to address inadequacies and take steps to help the staff member improve her or his performance. To the extent possible, synergistic supervision seeks to make dealing with staff shortcomings a positive learning experience rather than a punitive one.

Synergistic supervision promotes a positive work environment. Where this approach to supervision prevails, the distinctions between levels of staff are minimized and interpersonal relationships are rewarding. In other words, this approach to supervision makes working more enjoyable and personally satisfying. It also makes the building and maintenance of teams more likely.

Proactivity

Synergistic supervision focuses on identifying potential problems early. Rather than reacting to problem situations after they have gotten so difficult that they cannot be denied or ignored, synergistic supervision emphasizes early identification and development of strategies by the supervisor and staff member *jointly* to prevent or lessen their effects. Supervision should attend to the minor irritations of student or organizational life before they become full-blown problems, and should aggressively and proactively evaluate needs and wants of the clientele and develop interventions to address them. To ask for assistance or advice from a supervisor is not a sign of weakness in the synergistic perspective.

For a staff member to present problems to a supervisor does not mean that the problems are being transferred to the supervisor for solution. Nor does it imply that the supervisor will or should encroach on the staff member's autonomy to attack issues and problems. Supervisory sessions should be times that permit staff members to inform the supervisor of the issues they face, to receive reactions to various alternative means of addressing them, and to get feedback about how various constituencies may react. By doing this, staff members will become less likely to act on incomplete information, make decisions in isolation, or stumble into organizational quicksand. Supervisory sessions are also times that permit the supervisor to offer staff members suggestions about other ways to approach situations, to inform them about issues on the institutional horizon that may affect their areas of responsibility, or to alert them to practices or activities that may cause problems in the future. For the staff, supervisory sessions should be used to inform supervisors about mistakes or incidents that have taken place and that may need to be addressed at higher levels of the institution. As a veteran student affairs administrators often told his staff, "If you make a mistake or even do something stupid, I can accept that and am willing to help you work things out; I, however, will not forgive failures to keep me informed. I don't like surprises!"

Goal-Based

For synergistic supervision to be effective, both supervisors and their staffs need to have a clear understanding about the expectations each has of the other. One effective way to manage this is through the development of goals and statements of expectations that are periodically reviewed and evaluated for accomplishment.

For professional staff, we recommend a biannual session during which each supervisor and each of the supervised staff members meet and establish goals (and evaluate—and adjust when necessary—previously established goals) for the next six months, next year, and next five years. Supervisors should identify areas of need in the unit that are appropriate for the staff member to address and perceived areas of personal and professional development needed by the staff member. The staff member should provide the supervisor with information about her or his short-term and long-range personal and professional goals and a list of goals she or he plans to accomplish in the next six months, next year, and next five years. Following a discussion and perhaps negotiation, the supervisor should provide the staff member with a memo of expectations that incorporates the agreed-upon goals and expectations. Individual goal-setting sessions ideally would be preceded by group goal-setting activities in which the whole staff would participate in developing goals and means of accomplishing them. If an institution has an ongoing strategic planning process in place, this process could fit within that structure.

We suggest that supervisors and staff meet bimonthly specifically for the purpose of monitoring progress and making adjustments. Because circumstances change, it may be necessary and desirable to discard some goals as no longer feasible or of lesser importance than others and to add new goals to meet changing demands. Because of the hectic pace of life in student affairs, it may be necessary to schedule these meetings far in advance and to jealously protect them from interference from daily demands. We recommend that this process operate on a different schedule from that used for performance appraisals, although the degree to which staff have been successful in accomplishing goals is important to consider in performance appraisals.

Systematic and Ongoing Processes

An essential feature of synergistic supervisory sessions is that they are not a response to crises but a routine part of professional life. We strongly recommend that periodic individual and group supervisory sessions be held—perhaps weekly for new staff to monthly for more experienced staff. Supervisory sessions should have a predictable content and format and should include a discussion and evaluation of activities since the last session, reports about actual or projected trouble spots, and a discussion of planned activities. Supervisors should be careful to acknowledge both good and problematic performances and accomplishments. On a predetermined schedule as discussed above, short-term and long-term goals and expectations should be examined.

Group supervision sessions may be useful if there are several staff members being supervised who have comparable job responsibilities. In order for group supervision to be effective, however, the staff members must first coalesce into a cohesive group. Group supervision requires that the group become involved in its members' supervision. If the supervisor is unwilling to relinquish a major part of his or her authority to the group, group supervision may not be successful.

Group supervision should not be confused with staff meetings, where people come together to share information about upcoming events, request support from other staff members for campus activities, and work out schedules and times for other meetings. Such meetings are important for coordinating activities and work assignments but generally do not fall within our definition of supervision.

In our case studies (see Chapter Three), a good example of group supervision was found at Florida State University. There the vice president meets with his senior administrators, who are divided into three teams of department heads. They work as a team on problems or issues each is facing. It is to these groups that the vice president brings emerging university issues for discussion and development of response proposals. Jon Dalton, the vice president, functions as the nominal team leader, but encourages team members to interact directly with each other. He believes that such an approach promotes cooperation across departments and taps more resources for problem solving.

If the synergistic approach to supervision is to be successful, it must be a continuous process. For supervisors and staff to communicate effectively and to take shared responsibility, there must be ongoing, systematic, regular attention to the supervision process.

Holism

A holistic approach is fundamental to synergistic supervision. It is impossible to separate people and their attitudes and beliefs from their professional positions. Who one *is* determines to a large extent the kind of job one is able to do. Synergistic supervision concentrates on helping staff become more effective in their jobs and personal lives, and supports them in their quest for career advancement. To be truly effective, a person must have goals to which they regularly attend. Staff, consequently, have a right to expect support in accomplishing those goals just as they do in fulfilling their job responsibilities.

Recommendations for Improving Supervision

Even though we argue that synergistic supervision is appropriate for student affairs professionals at all levels, this does not mean that each individual needs or will profit from identical treatment. This certainly would fly in the face of our commonsense experience, which is that entry-level and seasoned professionals do not need the same kinds of supervision. Supervision must be tailored to the individual and the context. As Hersey and Blanchard (1977) argue in their theory of effective leadership, the level of direction required is dependent on the supervisee's skills and knowledge of the tasks to be performed, experience in dealing with a given situation, level of personal maturity, and developmental stage. Everyone—from beginning activities adviser to vice president—is entitled to ongoing, systematic supervision, but not of the same content or kind.

Supervising the Experienced, Competent Professional

All staff members, no matter the length of their tenure in the field or expertise, deserve regular, thoughtful supervision. The kind of supervision provided these staff members, however, is considerably different from that provided new professionals or staff new to their positions or the institution. These staff members, for example, generally do not need assistance in determining what tasks need to be performed, instruction about commonly accepted practices, or explanation of how the informal administrative structure functions. The kinds of supervision experienced, competent, and well-motivated professionals need include:

- Frank appraisals of the contributions of their units' productivity and relative contributions to the division's goals or strategic plans
- A nonjudgmental sounding board for ideas or strategies for dealing with troublesome issues or personnel
- Candid feedback about how they as individuals and their unit are perceived within the institution
- Concern and active participation in the establishment and evaluation of personal performance objectives

- Someone to keep difficult issues on the table that the seasoned professional may wish to avoid in the hopes that they will go away
- Advanced warnings about impending changes (even if only rumors are available)
- Occasionally an understanding ear for discussion of personal or family problems
- Honest assessment and suggestions for improvement that can contribute to the staff members' career advancement
- Praise and encouragement when responsibilities are well-met and goals are achieved. As Eble (1978, p. 81) cautions, however, "avoid effusive and indiscriminate praise. Knowing and caring about what someone does may be the highest form of motivation."

As Clement and Rickard (1992) found in their study of leadership in student affairs, the most effective leaders serve to empower the staff members they supervise. Sandeen (1991, p. 22) notes about the relationship between the president and the vice president for student affairs: "The most effective . . . [vice presidents] do not want their presidents looking over their shoulders, becoming involved in the day-to-day administration of the student affairs division. They do want and need presidents who understand them, what they are working to accomplish, and what they need to be successful." The same can be said for senior student affairs staff members' expectations of their supervisors. Sandeen (1991, p. 22) also notes that "If presidents are unsupportive, inconsistent, or unpredictable, the student affairs leader will achieve very little success." The same results will be produced by an unsupportive or inattentive supervisor in student affairs.

Supervising the Ineffective Middle Manager

When staff are well prepared for the demands their positions place on them and are motivated to achieve and advance professionally, the climate for supervision is usually congenial and highly productive. On the other hand, if staff members have lost enthusiasm for their work and have reached a career plateau beyond which they either no longer aspire or are prevented from advancing toward, supervision is much more difficult. At many institutions there may be staff who have risen to middle-manager positions as department directors and who are entrenched in the institution but are no longer effective. They may not be able to, or want to, make significant changes in their operations. While these people may once have been highly productive and valued employees, they begin to simply go through the motions to meet expectations and are careful to adhere to institutional policy and procedures religiously. They perform well enough that it is difficult to build a well-documented case for dismissal based on lack of performance, but they lack the creativity, energy, and enthusiasm needed to energize their departments or to try new approaches themselves. Often, talented, aspiring new professionals recruited into these departments quickly become discouraged and seek more professionally supportive positions elsewhere.

As William Tate, the late legendary dean of men at the University of Georgia, often said when describing academically unmotivated students, "Working with a boy that won't try is like going bird hunting and having to carry the dog." Attempting to supervise staff who lack motivation to advance the institution and the work of student affairs is equally frustrating. Many of the leaders interviewed by Clement and Rickard (1992) for their study of leadership in student affairs commented that motivation to achieve was a characteristic that they sought when hiring new staff because they had found it very difficult to deal with unmotivated persons.

There are no easy answers to these kinds of personnel issues. Synergistic supervision rests on the assumption that the staff being supervised yearn to serve students, want to enhance their own development and learning, and are professionally motivated.

The supervisor should address these issues with staff members to make sure their perceptions of their situation and those of the supervisor are similar. When motivation to improve is not present in the staff member, the supervisor must resort to other tactics such as the following:

- Engage the staff member in genuine dialogue about perceived behavioral and attitudinal deficiencies.
- Determine from the staff member ideas for self-rejuvenation and, within reason, agree to work toward their accomplishment.
- Make a plan that is mutually agreed upon to ensure changes in the staff member's performance.

- Monitor the implementation of the plan regularly—at least once per month and perhaps more often.
- Offer short-term job rotation options to the staff member.
- Conduct group job enrichment planning sessions about how to improve the effectiveness of the unit in which the staff member is employed or is assigned to lead.
- Reassign the staff member to a challenging, short-term project with a clear understanding that the performance on the new assignment will be used to determine long-term job security.
- Make sure that the institutional performance appraisal system does not reward behavior or attitudes that are nonproductive.

Recommendations for Practice

We have three recommendations for improving supervision in student affairs. First, supervision is often treated as higher education's dirty little secret; everyone participates—sometimes poorly and sometimes well—but no one wants to talk about it openly. The first step toward improving supervision is to deal with it explicitly and openly. It should not be treated as a mystery, but the components should be a matter for ongoing dialogue between supervisors and their staffs. Staff should be given genuine opportunities to be specific about what they want and need from their supervisors; in turn, supervisors should be explicit in their expectations concerning the staff member's performance.

Second, supervision needs to be systematic if it is to realize its full potential of enhancing staff performance. Whereas informal supervision is essential to effective practice (corrections or praise given immediately after the event have greater impact than at any other time), to be effective (that is, to significantly improve individual functioning and organizational effectiveness) supervision must become integrated into ongoing practice. If supervisory sessions are perceived as an additional duty, then they will frequently get pushed to the side in the heat of day-to-day emergencies and other legitimate concerns.

Finally, a collection of ideas garnered from work on the synergistic supervision model and from the literature are presented in Table 7.2 in the form of supervisor dos and don'ts. They are self-explanatory and in many cases represent commonsense advice for practitioners from entry level to chief student affairs administrator.

Table 7.2. Recommendations for Improving Supervision.

Do	Don't
Openly discuss the goals and process of supervision with each staff member	Treat supervision as a routine administrative task
Include advancement of staff member's personal and professional goals in the supervisory process	Establish supervisory structure without genuine input from staff member
Show concern and interest in staff member's personal concerns	Attempt to become a staff member's therapist
Work at establishing friendly relationships with staff	Allow romantic or "special" caring to develop with persons supervised
Treat staff members equitably	Show or *appear to show* favor to some staff members
Confront problems and issues when first realized	Confuse the value of the person with his or her behaviors
Support the decisions of superiors with subordinate staff and students	Hide disagreement from supervisor during decision-making process
Publicly admit when wrong or mistaken	Criticize (correct) staff members publicly
Deal with staff members face to face	Discuss a staff member's problem behavior with another subordinate or coequal staff member
Keep confidences	Hesitate to consult with supervisors or other professionals
Be direct, open, and honest	Try to send indirect message or message through a third party to a staff member about his or her conduct
Keep records of supervisory contacts	Rely on memory for details of supervisory sessions

Do	*Don't*
Establish specific performance objectives or program outcomes periodically (at least biannually)	Fail to follow up on accomplishment of objectives periodically
Recognize and reward achievement	Assume that a "good job" is the norm and does not require acknowledgment
Make realistic assignments based on a knowledge of the staff member's experience and skill level, personal maturity, and current life situation	Assume that everyone on a staff or in an office should do the same thing at the same time
Make explicit connection between supervision and staff development activities	Assume that staff members can always identify the areas in which they most need to develop skills or acquire knowledge
Listen and learn from staff supervised	Assume final knowledge about supervision or about a supervisory relationship

Summary

Supervision is the linchpin of the staffing model presented here. Good supervision serves both to promote the accomplishment of institutional goals and to advance the personal and professional development of staff. In a well-functioning, integrated student affairs division, supervision is directly related to determining the content and scope of staff development programs and activities and is closely tied to the performance appraisal process. Through the supervisory process, new skills and knowledge needed by staff are identified and can be addressed. Likewise, good supervisors possess intimate knowledge of the work performance of the staff they supervise and regularly provide them with feedback and constructive suggestions for improving performance.

There are six broad, functional components of supervision. These include articulating the unit's mission and needs, monitoring and managing the climate of the unit and the institution, fostering individual practitioner development, developing teamwork capabilities and work group resources, coordinating work activities, and promoting active problem solving.

We call our approach to supervision *synergistic* to distinguish it from prescriptive approaches used in industrial settings and to emphasize the cooperative nature of the supervisory process (thus, $1 + 1 = 3$). This approach to supervision focuses both on the accomplishment of organizational goals and the support of staff's pursuit of personal and professional development. It stresses joint efforts by the staff and their supervisors, requires two-way communication, focuses on competencies, is growth-oriented, is proactive, is based on goals, requires a systematic ongoing process, and is conceptually holistic in its approach.

Chapter Eight

⎮ Staff Development

Staff development is the principal staffing mechanism for personnel, program, and organization improvement in student affairs. Staff development often is referred to by other terms, such as inservice education and continuing professional education, but by any name it represents intentional efforts by supervisors and administrative leaders of student affairs to improve staff members' effectiveness, leading to improved organization effectiveness. Staff development cannot be seen as a totally separate staffing practice. It is especially intertwined with supervision and performance appraisal, where objectives for personnel, program, and institutional improvement also are integral. But in this chapter we focus on the conceptually distinctive aspects of the practice, discuss them related to research and literature, and offer guidance about the effectiveness of staff development approaches used in the field.

Perhaps nowhere in staffing practices is the application of student affairs values more evident than in staff development activities. This is not surprising, of course, because the commitments and the approaches to continuing education of staff are precisely parallel to the commitments and approaches for educating students. Both are conceptually focused on development as the primary outcome of education, and both recognize the central nature of the profession's covenant with human dignity, equality, and community and enduring values.

Overall developmental patterns of staff are discussed in Chapter Seven as a guiding framework for supervision. These patterns of growth are to some extent naturally occurring phenomena, but, as illuminated in the earlier chapter, they provide crucial perspectives for a synergistic supervisor who often is explicitly concerned with maximizing goal achievement for both staff members and the organization. Thus, the synergistic supervisor is developmental in orientation. How this orientation is put into practice through intentional staff development is the subject of this chapter.

The financial environment of higher education is another important contextual matter for staff development. As will be shown, not all staff development activities are expensive, but some costs are almost always associated with intentional education of staff, and recent economic conditions have curtailed some investments in this important staffing practice.

As with other staffing practices, several problems limit the effectiveness of current staff development activities:

- Not all are well connected to other staffing practices such as supervision and performance appraisal.
- Systematic determination or assessment of staff needs is often lacking in staff development practices.
- Staff development may not remedy certain staff deficiencies that seem to remain regardless of opportunity for remediation or the frequency of addressing them.
- Staff development activities may not sufficiently address the needs of the institution.

This chapter describes the persistent issues in staff development and then presents the details of what is known about current practices from our studies of literature and from our research. Use of the model of staffing for staff development is detailed, followed by several recommendations for practice. Some conclusions about our studies of staff development summarize the chapter.

Persistent Issues in Staff Development

Staff development is almost universally accepted as a major staffing practice. It is often conducted well; there are clear benefits to well-managed staff development activities and almost everyone is involved to some degree. Problems arise from conceptual or systemic weaknesses, mismatches between what is needed by staff and what is provided departmentally or institutionally, and a lack of proven effectiveness in some cases.

A significant issue in staff development is the lack of integration or connectedness with other staffing practices. There is no doubt of the perceived importance of staff development by student affairs leaders. Furthermore, there is acknowledgment among leaders, at least at the case sites studied, that staff development is related to supervision and to performance evaluation. Still, anything more than an intellectual connection among all staffing practices is not strongly supported by evidence on the subject. It is difficult to see how many sponsored staff development activities are related to either supervision or to performance appraisal.

Related to this issue is the problem of a lack of systematic determination or assessment of staff needs. While we may assume certain needs, such as a need to address currency of new knowledge among all staff, it seems self-evident that divisions should employ scientific methods for learning about staff needs more than the ad hoc committees that seem to be the preferred method for determining institutionally sponsored activities. This problem is exacerbated by the tenuous connection between supervision, staff development, and performance appraisal. Supervision and performance appraisal, usually based on a commitment to individual and institutional improvement, should provide the systematic method for discovering needs and prescribing remedies.

Certain staff deficiencies seem to persist regardless of opportunities for remediation or the frequency of addressing them. This issue is related to the problem of involvement versus effect. Participation does not automatically translate into learning. While involvement is a necessary prerequisite to learning, it is no guarantee. Many, perhaps most, student affairs staff participate in some staff development activities each year, but what is learned by these staff members is unknown. The fact is that certain staff deficiencies often remain year after year. Whether this is a failure by either the staff member or the supervisor to address the problem or a failure by the staff member to learn from opportunities provided is unknown. The issue also is related to whether the staff member and supervisor make the right choice about staff member participation in events and opportunities. When many activities are available and staff are given more or less free choice to decide which opportunities are right for them, they may not make the decision based on an intention to change themselves. It is possible that some staff members know they can satisfy their supervisors by participating in something labeled staff development without deliberate premeditation on their own deficiencies.

Additionally, institutions have evolving staff development needs based upon their unfolding plans, and these seem rarely to be addressed in staff development activities. Plans often require staff development, yet little evidence was discovered in our studies that these matters are widely anticipated or dealt with in an orderly manner. Teaching staff about a new policy or procedure may be considered a staff development activity, but sometimes carrying out new plans calls for a very different set of skills than currently possessed within the institution. New requirements for the widespread use of technology is one example.

As important as staff development is to individuals and to the organizational units of student affairs, development activities are not always well received or well done. Privately, many staff know that staff development is important but dislike participating in planned events on campus. Indeed, some planned activities are downright boring and unhelpful, and if learning does result from them, it is mere luck.

Perspectives about staff development from literature and research reveal these shortcomings but also point to excellent practices. The literature review and overview of our research findings that follow paint a reasonably full picture of the history and current condition of staff development practices.

Perspectives from Literature

Arguing that staff development should be a major function of student affairs and more than a mere service to staff members, Stamatakos and Oliaro (1972, p. 269) lamented the "paucity of professional literature on the subject." They suggested, somewhat cynically, that the reasons for this absence of literature might be that the practices are so successful that none is needed, that they are being carried out under some other name, or (their preferred argument) that they are relatively unimportant in the day-to-day administrative priorities. They listed only five references, four of them general criticisms of the field of student affairs and not papers specifically devoted to staff development practices. The one source cited that did deal with staff development directly was Truitt and Gross's (1970) seminal paper on the subject that outlines principal purposes for staff development still relevant today:

- An in-service education program should be based on objectives that give direction to the overall student personnel program and provide a basis for evaluation.
- Each in-service education program must be planned, initiated, and perpetuated in view of individual staff and institutional goals and needs.
- In-service education should be geared to varying levels of professional preparation and experience of individual staff members.
- In-service education programs should involve maximum participation of the total staff in the planning and ongoing activities.
- Study topics and activities for in-service education programs should reflect both immediate and long-standing issues that face the staff, institutions, and student personnel work as a profession.
- In-service education programs should utilize the knowledge and skill of the program participants as well as that of consultants and other resource personnel.
- Opportunity should be made to allow the application of new knowledge and increased understanding of theory and technique, which are gained through in-service education activities, to the program and services of the institution.
- In-service education programs should be continuously planned, conducted, and maintained during a regularly designated time in the normal work schedule of the staff.
- In-service education programs should be continuously evaluated with the program participants playing a major role in the evaluation.
- Responsibility for initiating, implementing, and directing an in-service education program should rest with one individual, preferably the chief student personnel officer (pp. 215–217).

One of the earliest studies of staff development activities was conducted by Miller (1975). His comprehensive survey of student affairs practitioners resulted, in part, in a rank-order preference by staff of types of continuing education programming. From most to least preferred were "(1) participation away from campus at professional development workshops offered by professional associations and others; (2) bringing in outside experts as resource consultants for on-campus in-service education programs; (3) do-it-yourself on-campus in-service education programs; (4) attendance at national, regional, or state professional association conventions; and (5) attending academic courses offered by graduate education programs" (p. 261). Miller also found that only 20 percent of the institutions reporting had a formalized (presumably written) policy statement about staff development.

Since the mid-1970s, however, considerable literature has been published about staff development in student affairs. Over the past twenty years, dozens of journal articles and book chapters have appeared in the literature and most of them are useful in one way or another. Many articles address specific suggestions for staff development practices, generally telling the story of what worked at a particular place and time, while others offer broad-gauge conceptual advice on the subject, generally grounded in the experiences of practitioners or scholars. Most are not research based, though some are, and the results typically show mixed reactions to felt need and actual practice. Rarely do authors offer new ideas, particularly conceptual ideas, but there are exceptions to this generalization and their contributions to the literature are especially useful.

Comprehensive Reviews of Literature

Overviews of the subject of staff development are very worthwhile to practitioners and scholars alike, as they touch on many aspects of the practice. The most extensive of these overviews is that of DeCoster and Brown (1991), in which a coherent and comprehensive presentation of multiple perspectives on the subject can be found. Dalton (1989) offers a briefer but still useful overview, as does Baier (1985), who includes several specific suggestions for staff development practices. Further, Stimpson (1993) includes some useful advice in his paper dealing also with initial employment practices. An extremely useful piece from the field of adult and continuing education is that of Baskett and Marsick (1992), which shows the relevance of the scholarship of the field of continuing education to student affairs, especially by detailing the role of self-assessment in staff development. Delworth (1978) offers multiple views of the training function for student affairs. Of these overviews, by far the most extensive reference list of staff development practices is offered by DeCoster and Brown (1991).

Beginning with a philosophical foundation, DeCoster and Brown contend that all staff development activities must be concerned with and conducted in the contexts of both human development and organization development. They agree with Creamer and Shelton (1988), who conducted a literature review of both preservice and in-service education in student affairs, that the literature reveals two distinct perspectives for any conceptual framework for staff development: staff effectiveness (or human development) and institutional effectiveness (or organization development). DeCoster and Brown argue, however, that no distinctions should be made in practice between the two and that they should be well integrated for staff development activities to be most effective.

DeCoster and Brown's synthesis of literature on staff development also suggests that a "curriculum" emerges around six goals: (a) facilitating interaction with colleagues and associates, (b) developing functional skills and specific competencies, (c) promoting self-understanding and self-actualization, (d) [exposing staff] to innovative programs, (e) providing opportunities for professional renewal, and (f) conveying theoretical and philosophical knowledge (1991, p. 568).

These goals generally are achieved, according to DeCoster and Brown, by the application of selected methods or approaches, including academic course work; national, regional, and state convention attendance; on-campus programs utilizing either internal or external consultants; off-campus workshops, seminars, and institutes; staff orientation and social functions; organizational newsletters and other written communications, organizational staff meetings, special research and program grants, and committee and task force participation; ongoing supervision, performance evaluation, mentoring and general relationships with colleagues; and administrative fellowships and internships (pp. 568–569). Arguing that staff development processes should not be separated from the day-to-day activities of professionals, a view supported by Woodard and Komives (1990), DeCoster and Brown further synthesize these approaches into five general strategies that closely parallel performance expectations on the job: individual motivation and self-assessment, supervision and performance evaluation, mentoring relationships, structured learning opportunities, and professional participation, service, and contributions. Finally, DeCoster and Brown show that effective staff development is related to various contexts within higher education and discuss at length the connections between the issues and staff development. These contexts include issues in higher education such as improvement of teaching and learning, reform of the general education curriculum, outcomes assessment, values education, dealing with diversity, community, commitment, and internationalizing the campus, relations between academic and student affairs, personal and professional circumstances, and institutional commitment and resources.

Dalton (1989) contends that staff development is an integral part of personnel management, serves as a motivator for high performance by promoting individual growth and development on the job, provides a bridge between graduate education and professional practice, provides basic competences for staff hired without formal education or professional knowledge of the field, and provides a source for professional renewal for staff who have been on the job for some time. He then translates these reasons for staff development into three broad purposes—benefiting students, improving individual staff members, and improving the organization—but prefers a narrow definition of staff development "to be specific about goals and objectives and to identify essential program content more easily" (p. 535). Dalton's definition of staff development is "the intentional and systematic effort to enhance the knowledge and skills of staff members" (p. 535), explicitly excluding some common activities such as socials and award and recognition ceremonies as not dealing specifically with knowledge and skills. This definition appears to limit staff development to one side of the individual-institution equation posited by DeCoster and Brown (1991) and supported by Creamer and Shelton (1988). It also seems to exclude one of his own general purposes: to benefit students. Further, Dalton differs with DeCoster and Brown in his synthesis of literature regarding what might be used to form a core curriculum for staff development. Dalton believes that published literature can be characterized in five themes: mission and philosophy, communication skills, management and leadership skills, professional ethics, and current professional issues. He also encourages the use of other resources to promote staff development, including academic courses, institutional in-service programs for employees, attendance at local, state, and national professional organizations, and involvement in job rotation, job enrichment, mentoring, and self-directed training.

Other Views from Literature

Merkle and Artman (1983) offer their definition of staff development, and it resembles DeCoster and Brown's: "a planned experience designed to change behavior and result in professional and/or personal growth and improved organizational effectiveness" (p. 55). This definition is preferred by Baier (1985), who sees multiple advantages to staff development including to "help improve staff morale, stimulate creative problem solving, increase staff productivity and efficiency, facilitate goal setting, improve staff skills, increase staff awareness of the importance of keeping current and up-to-date, and raise skill levels" (p. 221). Baier describes several vehicles for staff development, some common and probably widespread in practice, and others used less commonly but having great potential. Some of the more common vehicles suggested include a staff newsletter, new-staff orientation activities, coffee hours, and workshops and seminars. Less common activities include a mini-university program, also described by Beeler (1977a), composed normally of short skill development courses, student affairs program grants generally directed toward program enhancement, self-instruction training modules, research and literature reports, temporary staff assignments, interdepartmental staff exchanges, mentoring, and piggyback activities that take advantage of other programs being offered by the institution to the benefit of student affairs staff. Lawing, Moore, and Groseth (1982) address the special problem of using staff development for retention of staff and for assisting them to advance to the highest levels of administrative service if desired.

Stimpson (1993) makes a special point of suggesting that the relationship with one's supervisor provides perhaps the best opportunity for staff development. The supervisor knows the job and its requirements better than anyone else and is able to provide training or education by taking advantage of the moment when the staff member is most ready to learn. Regardless of the circumstances or contexts of staff development activities, Stimpson argues that certain steps always should be taken to ensure desired outcomes: provide focused purpose and clear objectives, use relevant educational materials, evaluate the program, provide trainer support and supervision, and connect staff development with performance evaluation.

Baskett and Marsick (1992) edited a very useful sourcebook on continuing professional education based largely on results of a conference of leading researchers and continuing professional education practitioners. While the entire book contains state-of-the-art examples of staff development from a variety of fields, the chapters by Baskett and Marsick and by Klevans, Smutz, Shuman, and Bershad (1992) contain especially relevant discussions. Baskett and Marsick focus on contemporary views about staff development or continuing professional education and explore the importance of "ways of knowing" language. They assert that ways of knowing is a dynamic phrase referring to a form of learning that "involves a continuous cycle of moving to greater certainty on a variety of issues, actions, and agendas" (p. 2). Certainly the language is consistent with much of the developmental literature in student affairs. They also clarify who is a professional and what is meant by learning. Drawing from Jarvis (1983), they craft a definition around the idea that a professional is one who is in constant search for a mastery of the type of learning needed to offer an effective service to clients. They proceed to further define learning as "a personal, emotional, and cognitive act, the results of which are unique to the individual" and as dealing primarily with "the way in which people construct meaning in their personal and shared organizational lives" (p. 3). Baskett and Marsick also discuss where learning occurs, the social contexts for learning, differences between practical and formal knowledge, the sources of knowledge, resources for learning, and cycles of learning.

This discussion sets the stage for detailing of the utility of self-assessment as an effective process in discovering what one needs to know and for learning it. This explanation is offered by Klevans, Smutz, Shuman, and Bershad (1992) and employs specific examples, such as from the field of architecture, where the system would work. The discussion is provocative for the field of student affairs, suggesting the potential for the use of a similar process for continuing professional education and for staff development in student affairs. The process seems comparable to the self-assessment and self-regulation processes used by CAS in the application of standards of practice and is thus familiar to most professionals in the field. In fact, the process was considered by the Interassociation Committee for Continuing Professional Education, a committee jointly sponsored by ACPA and NASPA, which made recommendations to both associations for how the process might be used on a widespread basis (Creamer, 1995). These proposals were not adopted, however, though the Professional Development Council of ACPA continues to consider them in its planned continuing professional education.

Focusing on the specialized training function of staff development, Delworth (1978) and her colleagues describe concepts and processes associated with the function, approaches to the development of interpersonal skills, use of self-paced and videotaped materials, use of manuals, role of supervision, and the role of evaluation. Though somewhat dated, the source does provide a general overview of the training function and guidance to other worthwhile sources.

Models for Staff Development

Models for staff development—comprehensive, divisionwide conceptual plans—are relatively uncommon in the literature. Though it is debatable what constitutes a model in the literature versus a description of customary organizational activities, in this instance the reference is to a postulated way of thinking about aspects of professional practice that relate to individual or institutional improvement. For example, Truitt and Gross (1966) offer insightful commentary about the purposes of staff development, useful practices are described by Merkle and Artman (1983), Beeler (1977a; 1977b), and Robinson and Delbridge-Parker, (1991), and needs of staff are chronicled by Rhatigan and Crawford (1978) and Cox and Ivy (1984). But such papers do not meet the standard for a model of practice. They tend to highlight a particular aspect of staff development rather than to present ideas about how all potential aspects of a comprehensive program might fit together. Certainly, they do not clarify both individual and organizational perspectives.

By the definition of model followed here, some proposed models in the literature take either the individual or organizational perspective and, thus, limit their usefulness to practitioners. One example of this is provided by Creamer (1988), who argues that in-service education should be structured to capitalize on the individual motivation of professionals. He foresaw the application of a broad curriculum of knowledge and skills addressed through a system grounded in the expression of individual professional needs, institutional support for individual initiatives, and the use of institutionally sanctioned strategies or methods. This combination, Creamer argued, would lead to individual need gratification and continuous growth and development on the job. Such a model includes the benefit of recognizing the application of the ethical principle of autonomy as described by Krager (1985): "The premise of professional development goes beyond directed training. It uses the challenge of new opportunity. Staff members should be given flexibility in negotiating, designing, and selecting new duties and activities. Expression of differing opinions and approaches to professional growth can be encouraged as well as individual style and innovation. Both the challenge and the freedom offered must be tempered by staff readiness" (p. 39). The Creamer model, however, does not focus on organizational improvement, a limitation noted by Young (1988), who critiqued the model.

Young (1987) proffers his own model of professional education for student affairs that includes three primary dimensions: professional development stages, types of interpersonal contact, and modes of education. Young's conceptualization suggests that staff development needs can be understood by using this model and that specific activities of staff development can be determined and tailored to recognize the current developmental stage of practitioners (whether the practitioners are operating in formative, application, or additive stages), the target of staff interactions (whether focused on students, students and staff, or staff only), and the primary method used by the staff member (whether inquiry, application or performance, or instruction). Arguably, this model errs on the side of being so sweeping in its concepts as to limit its utility, but it does acknowledge realities of wide-ranging duties and functions and staff and ever-changing developmental status of staff. Both conditions suggest that staff development activities used with some staff may not be appropriate for others and that activities used during one period of a staff member's professional life may not be effective in the current period.

Burke and Randall (1994) offer a model of staff development that addresses both individual and organization perspectives. Based upon a career development system of the Coca Cola Corporation, they offer a matrix plan in which purposes of staff development are depicted on one axis (career opportunities, matching-selection, performance review, career development sessions, and career development reviews) and roles of staff members, supervisors, and executive student affairs officers on the other axis. This model "presents an ongoing sequence of staff development for an entire division of student affairs" (p. 77), according to its authors. The model is intended to address several perplexing problems in student affairs divisions, including encouraging promotion from within the organization, developing talent within the division in advance of staffing needs, placing appropriate responsibility for staff development on supervisors, and assigning the primary responsibility for development on individual staff members. Burke and Randall also outline the underlying assumptions of their proposed model, including staff development as a divisional priority, student affairs philosophies as institutionally defined, institutional loyalty as a desirable goal, multiple career goals as achievable below the level of executive student affairs officer, helping relationships between staff persons and supervisors as being a must, staff members as interested in career development, successful staff development programs as voluntary and based on staff needs, interinstitutional mobility as being encouraged and facilitated, position qualifications as based more on skills, abilities, and divisional talent needs rather than years of experience in a particular job category, and the role of the student affairs generalist as being encouraged through ongoing training and job diversification (p. 79). The Burke and Randall model appears to emphasize professional development over personal development and sharpens the role of supervisor in the overall scheme while providing "a continuous opportunity for self-assessment, skill development, and exploration of career opportunities" (p. 79).

Research on Staff Development

Most literature on staff development is not research based; the literature that is tends to be descriptive in nature, employing survey methods. Such is the case with Miller (1975), who describes the nature of on-campus and off-campus in-service programming and staff members' preferences between them; Rhatigan and Crawford (1978), who discovered that student affairs staff prefer discussion formats for staff development over other approaches and that they least prefer reading activities; and Upcraft (1971), who revealed little effect of formal education on the performance of executive-level student affairs administrators. An expanded approach was taken by Barnes and O'Donnell (1985), who first analyzed survey data from a single institution case study of a mid-size university on the West Coast, then constructed and administered a survey to executive student affairs officers at thirty institutions in NASPA Regions IV, V, and VI.

The case study employed a fifty-item self-report questionnaire. Seventy-two staff members in the division of student affairs at the mid-sized West Coast university responded to items pertaining to articulation of divisional philosophy, service goals, and performance objectives; staff assessment of performance evaluation practices within the division; staff views of career advancement opportunities; and staff views of professional development opportunities. The case study analysis "revealed organizational dissonance, vertical communication problems, haphazard employee evaluation procedures, ambiguous promotional paths, and traces of employee cynicism" (p. 10). Some astonishing findings came from this phase of the Barnes and O'Donnell study. For example, while most staff were "satisfied" with current performance evaluation methods, "97 percent believed their supervisors needed training in how to evaluate staff performance" (p. 6), "over 60 percent of the respondents reported that administrators needed training in defining measurable objectives, allocating staff resources efficiently, and implementing procedures which established time lines and progress toward job-related objectives" (p. 6), "the greatest training need identified for administrators was in giving constructive feedback to those being supervised" (p. 6), "staff most frequently reported that they were expected to determine their own strategies for skill improvement at their personal expense" (p. 7), and "employees with the greatest length of service were the most pessimistic regarding opportunities for advancement" (p. 10).

In contrast to these findings, Barnes and O'Donnell discovered in the second phase of their study that the thirty vice presidents who completed a ninety-eight item questionnaire constructed from the single-institution case study reported "a high degree of unanimity in their divisional philosophies and management practices" (p. 10). The vice presidents reported that they had clear statements of mission, purpose, philosophy, goals, and objectives for the division and for each department and that they had written performance objectives for staff. They also reported theory-based management styles, policies that supported career advancement, and extensive opportunities for staff development.

This study suggests that perceptions of staffing practices held by staff members may be very different from perceptions of the same practices held by vice presidents.

Perspectives from Research

The centrality of staff development to overall staffing practices is clearly evident in our surveys, case studies, and literature review. Much is known about this staffing activity, as is reflected in the profession's literature on the subject. A wide variety of staff development activities can be found on most campuses, and the activities generally are supported by institutional funds and by supervisors. The following generalizations capture the essential findings about staff development from our studies.

1. Staff development activities are sponsored universally in divisions of student affairs.

No surprise about this. Based on everything we know about student affairs operations, staff development is near the heart of the most basic commitments of the division. This commitment seems to be a covenant between the division and its staff. It clearly reflects the values of the profession as discussed in Chapter One and demonstrates the centrality of the importance of people in an organization.

All data available to us suggest that participation in staff development is a norm of student affairs operations. Our case studies were especially revealing in this regard in that without exception, staff development was seen as vital to successful staffing practices in the institutions. Staff development also appeared to be the most operative and interest-bearing of all staffing practices; that is, leaders at the institutions are actively and intentionally carrying out many activities based on their beliefs and policies, could articulate their chosen strategies in detail, and could point to improvements in staff performance as a result of the activities offered.

In some cases, especially at Johnson County Community College and Broward Community College, staff development arises from explicit policy. In both of these cases, a line item of the total institutional budget is devoted to the practice. The result is multiple opportunities for staff development and widespread participation in the opportunities provided.

Opportunities for staff development were found at the institutions studied that range from highly structured and extensively planned programs to casual and fortuitous events. Examples of the former include formal professional conferences staged by the student affairs staff at Florida State University and at the University of Maryland-College Park. The Florida State University program is an annual event called the Institute on College Student Values where the overall theme remains the same each year; at the University of Maryland-College Park the event is called the Maryland Student Affairs Conference and a new topic is chosen each year. The latter is a drive-in conference, the former a multiday event. Both provide ample opportunities for learning by the respective student affairs staffs who attend, but they also provide rich opportunities for leadership by on-campus professionals, as the tasks for staging the events are rotated annually among campus staff, usually department heads. Both events attract participation from student affairs professionals from other campuses. In contrast to formality, at these same institutions "seizing critical moments" is frequently cited as a potent method of learning. One staff member said, "We get asked a lot of difficult questions which leads to some good professional discussions."

2. Social events, invited speakers, and short departmental workshops are the preferred vehicles for sponsored staff development activities.

This is clearly evident in the survey data presented in Chapter Three, which indicate that division-level workshops and long departmental workshops are sponsored much less frequently. Case data support the generalization but give a fuller account of the variety of activities used on many campuses, including invited speakers, divisional and departmental meetings, retreats, awards ceremonies, and social events.

Naturally, the number and style of these events vary by institution, but all are prominent in the planning for staff development. Use of off-campus events such as attending professional conferences is also employed on each campus studied, but the level of participation in these events varies widely depending upon campus resources and the philosophy of division leaders. Some events were identified that seem to be restricted to a particular institution. The University of North Carolina-Wilmington, for example, employs a "professional development contract" that allows for consultation with supervisors to negotiate a plan for improvement based on individual interests and institutional needs. Another example restricted to only a few of the schools studied is at the University of Richmond, where individual staff are expected to make brief presentations during regular staff meetings about important topics such as readings from professional journals. Other institutions employ this tactic also, such as the University of Maryland-College Park, but it was not found universally on the campuses studied. One department head at James Madison University insisted that conference attendance alone is no guarantee of learning; he wants to see a plan prior to attendance and to see results, perhaps through an on-campus presentation, upon return from the conference.

None of these tactics for staff development are especially innovative or unusual. In fact, the opposite is true: these campuses employ everyday-type activities to help staff improve themselves. It is noteworthy, however, that these institutions do so much in the area of staff development. Observed activities on the campuses matched the rhetoric of the division leaders. Every executive leader of the respective student affairs divisions said that great emphasis is given to staff development, and the evidence gathered on site confirmed the claims.

3. *Individual initiative accounts for a significant portion of the staff development that occurs in divisions of student affairs.*

Initiative for staff development is a two-way street, and staff members themselves have a professional obligation to stay current with their skills and knowledge; very often they exercise this responsibility by initiating self-improvement activities. Table 4.7 shows the variety of these initiatives but one can easily imagine that self-initiated activities are not limited to those shown in the table. Reading professional literature, holding conversations with colleagues about important topics, seeking advice from a supervisor, consulting with an expert on a topic of concern, and engaging in personal or departmental research projects are examples of self-directed and likely very productive activities.

Staff may also take the initiative to broaden their experience by volunteering to assist another unit with a project. Often it is possible to negotiate release time with a supervisor to devote to a project or activity in another functional area. For those who wish to improve their research and professional writing skills, they can initiate contact with experienced faculty members and offer to assist with their projects or to develop and implement a joint project.

4. *Many colleges do not have specific line items in their division budgets for staff development.*

This is somewhat surprising, though it perhaps can be explained by the fact that many institutions maintain the budget for staff development at locations other than the division of student affairs. There may be a specific line item in the office of human resources, for example, that is used to support staff development activities throughout the institution. Even so, it seems odd that a major unit so committed to staff development would not maintain significant control or management over the needed resources to carry it out. Research universities are more likely than not to have specifically targeted budget items for staff development, but even this type of institution often does not. Only about 40 percent of comprehensive universities report maintaining such a budget line in the division of student affairs. It is quite uncommon for liberal arts institutions and community colleges to maintain such a line in their divisional budget.

5. *Most divisions of student affairs do not have written policies about staff development.*

Again, this is surprising. Some do, of course, and in fact some of our cases have very specific policies that shape almost everything they do in staff development. Interestingly, the institutions in our case studies with the strongest written policies regarding staff development are the community colleges, only 19 percent of which in our surveys reported that they maintain specific line item budgets for the activity.

Given the powerful association between the values of the profession and the near universal commitment to staff development, perhaps it is felt on many campuses that written policies are unnecessary. But a lack of them can be interpreted to mean that only soft support is available, and only when the institution has spare change. We strongly recommend the promulgation of written policies regarding the student affairs division's commitment to staff development that are carefully negotiated and widely endorsed within the larger institution.

6. *Divisions exercise a variety of methods to carry out staff development activities; the most common approach is the divisionwide committee.*

There are benefits and pitfalls to using this approach. A clear advantage is that it involves as many staff as possible in their own developmental activities. The major disadvantage is that committees are notoriously awkward in planning and executing important responsibilities and, depending upon their leadership, may be ineffective in serving the entire division staff. Further, this approach tends to homogenize activities and plans for middle-of-the-road needs of staff. When this is the case, the single strategy that supposedly fits all actually misses the needs of most staff.

It is likely, however, that the use of divisionwide committees occurs in concert with other strategies. Specifically, the structure that puts the department leadership in a central role for planning and executing staff development makes sense for a number of reasons, including the fact that the leadership involves supervisors who ultimately will conduct formal performance appraisals for staff and who hold explicit responsibility for staff improvement.

Using the Staffing Model in Staff Development

Institutionally sponsored efforts to help staff members improve themselves likely will be shaped, if not totally determined, by certain cultural features of the division and institution. The type and level of skill needed within a student affairs operation may depend upon the work ethos and the expectations established by the administrative culture, for example, and thus determine the course of staff development initiatives. Naturally, staff members may initiate and sustain self-improvement activities on their own. Many do; often it is expected by the institutional culture. What the institution initiates and pays for, however, has a direct connection to these cultural dimensions of the administration.

Any effective program of staff development must include certain components. These components are inherent in the staffing model presented in Chapter Two and are elaborated upon here. Stated simply, effective staff development must attend to staff and organization improvement, derive from a developmental plan, include attention to both process and product, be anchored in day-to-day work, be multifaceted and ever changing, and recognize maturation and growth in staff.

Dual Purposes: Staff and Organization Development

The purposes of staff development practices have a dual focus, that is, they must attend to individual staff and to organization development simultaneously. These are not incompatible goals any more than are the similar dual goals of the synergistic supervisor, although they do embody competing interests that often must be accommodated in environments with limited resources. For staff development to be successful, however, both goals must be achieved—that is, they must be mutually supportive—and this commitment will require creativity and flexibility in plans for staff development.

Developmental Plan

Like other developmental activities directed toward change or growth, the processes of staff development must be intentional, active, and potent. A particular emphasis on intentionality that yields a developmental plan is indicated. The plan for individual growth should reflect current personal and professional status regarding attributes needed to perform assigned duties, short- and long-term goals, and alternative methods for achieving the goals. There should be a plan for organization improvement as well. This plan should reflect the manner in which the staff members' contributions to programs and services of the unit are tied to enhanced institutional effectiveness. Thus, both individual and organizational needs are included in the plan for development.

Process and Product

Staff development aims for improvements in staff and organizational effectiveness, the products of the practice; but it also is a process, a way of doing business, that affects interpretations of job requirements, relationships with colleagues, and perspectives on the methods of education. Staff development occurs in a social context and emphasizes team work. Rarely is an individual in student affairs expected to perform duties in isolation from others. Indeed, no one expects the division of student affairs to achieve its purposes apart from other staff of the college or university. Certain purposes of the institution, especially objectives related to student learning and personal development, require full cooperation of all members of the organization. Such teamwork is built on a foundation of collaboration, the joining of effort by many people toward a common goal or purpose. Staff development is a process that demonstrates the commonness of purpose of all staff and the crucial nature of individual knowledge and skills to perform assigned duties in relation to the achievement of these larger goals. Staff development serves also to model the methods of education. Those methods that are effective to enhance knowledge and skill of staff also will work to promote student learning and personal development. One should not expect to be successful in the improvement of staff using methods with less potency than those employed to teach students.

Anchored in Day-to-Day Work

As a process, staff development is ongoing and anchored in day-to-day work. Thus, it is visible in all personnel functions of the division. No other staffing function is unrelated to staff development. This connection is especially apparent in the relationship of supervision to performance evaluation. Staff development is the bridge between the two functions, overlapping with both. Good supervision involves the identification of needed improvement in staff, as does performance evaluation. Remedies always include prescriptions for improvement through planned staff development activities. It also may be said that determination of needed staff development is lent credibility in the context of supervision and performance evaluation. Still, some determinations for needed improvements occur in the context of institutional requirements. As requirements of the institution change, such as when market forces cause restructuring of educational services, staff members may be expected to learn new skills and to assume new duties. Discrepancies between requirements of the institution and the capabilities of current staff are relieved through intentional staff development activities.

Multifaceted, Ever Changing

Staff development is multifaceted, targeted to many different people in a variety of role functions, and must be ever changing. As guarantor of change through educational activities, staff development must employ methods with proven effect. Event attendance, for example, is insufficient in most cases to ensure change in either attitude, beliefs, or behavior, especially if the event is unrelated to the specific context of an individual's job. Activities requiring thoughtful interaction and reflection couched in a context of requirements of the job are far more likely to result in desired effects on behavior.

Recognizes Maturation and Growth

Similarly, staff development must recognize variations in the maturity and growth of individuals and the organization. Some staff may be only beginning their professional lives; others have served the profession and the institution for many years. Some have received formal education to prepare them for their professional work; others have not. Functional roles of staff in a complex student affairs division are diverse, and each may require special attention when enhancing staff competence. Staff occasionally change roles within one institution or move to another and require "retooling" for the new responsibilities. Such circumstances may require tailoring of staff development opportunities if they are to be effective; however, as if these conditions do not offer sufficient complications to the process of staff development, each staff member constantly is maturing as a function of developmental processes and encountering evolving needs for further learning and growth as time goes by. Staff development activities, therefore, must reflect multiple individual and organizational conditions if they are to be effective.

When fully integrated with other staffing functions in the manner suggested here, staff development represents a key dimension in the achievement of excellence in student affairs. These practices are in fact the educational manifestation of the profession's values. They embody the basic philosophies and beliefs and provide a stage for their implementation.

Recommendations for Practice

We recognize the centrality of staff development activities in sustaining quality staffing practices, and we acknowledge that many divisions of student affairs and their institutions support extensive opportunities for staff members. Obviously such commitment should continue, but several matters should be addressed to ensure the most beneficial results for individuals and for institutions.

First, divisions of student affairs should always have a written set of policies that govern staff development activities. These should be the result of widespread and continuous involvement of student affairs staff members and should make clear the balance of responsibilities of individuals, administrative units, and the total institution in conducting the overall program. Such policies should clarify expectations for continued professional education of each member of the staff and specify the general options available for self-improvement. They also should make clear the connection between continuous professional development and institutional rewards such as salary adjustments and promotions. Finally, these policies should ensure adequate institutional funding for staff development activities.

Second, staff development initiatives should be tied to supervisor-staff member assessments of needed improvement. There should be clear connections between observed or demonstrated need for improvement and activities supported or provided. Though it is justified to permit participation in learning events that have to do with one's special interests and talents, it is never sufficient to endorse it at the expense of engagement in areas identified by supervisors as needing improvement. Supervisors must help identify development needs of their staffs, and such assessments should become a matter of record that is formally monitored over time. Thus, sponsored staff development activities should be purposefully determined based on careful assessment of staff member needs, effectively conducted using accepted methods of teaching and learning, and administratively managed and monitored to ensure constant development toward mutually determined professional and personal goals.

It is important to ensure the full integration of staff development, supervision, and performance appraisal. The substance of individual staff development, at least that which is explicitly supported by the administrative unit or division of student affairs, is to a considerable extent determined by the results or outcomes of supervision and performance appraisal processes. Care should be taken to make these three staffing practices as seamless as possible.

Third, staff development programs should augment individually determined goals for development. This aspect of a comprehensive program is necessary to achieve two purposes: rewarding individual initiative to encourage optimal development and maximum contribution to the institution, and including individual initiative to recognize the variable needs for development among diverse staff of varying age, experience, and prior skills.

Fourth, staff development programs should employ variety in methods of delivery. Nothing fancy, novel, or unique is necessary, but serious involvement in multiple activities should be. Participation in professional meetings, workshops, and conferences is fundamental and should be available to all staff, but opportunities to demonstrate leadership in conducting such activities should also be required. Participation in social events is important but never sufficient for professional growth. Serious reflection time with one's supervisor about personal and professional development should be mandatory. An individually tailored plan, agreed to by staff member and supervisor, is essential. In the end, staff development is about teaching and learning. The most advanced methods of teaching and the most serious expectations for learning are both foreseen in this approach.

Summary

Staff development is widely endorsed as an essential aspect of staffing practice throughout student affairs. Almost all student affairs divisions support some kind of staff development activities each year.

The literature of the field and the research on the subject show the centrality and to some extent the vitality of staff development in student affairs. Institutions and divisions of student affairs endorse staff development initiatives and offer some institutional resources to support them.

Staff development has a dual purpose: to enhance both individual and institutional capabilities. Like other learning activities, staff development should proceed from a plan that is derived by careful assessment of individual and organization needs. It should embrace both process and content objectives and should be anchored in day-to-day work. Staff development programs must be flexible and responsive and attend to unique needs and varying levels of maturity and development of staff members.

The typical approach to organization is to form a division committee or joint division and department committee to survey staff members about their interests and staff development needs. An important part of staff development is believed to be attendance at off-campus conventions and workshops. Most institutions provide at least some financial support for staff members to attend such events. There is little evidence, however, that either on- or off-campus activities have any direct relationship to the institution's needs or to individuals' developmental needs.

The model of staffing advocated in this book holds that staff development should have a direct and obvious connection to both supervision and performance appraisal. Only then can staff development truly address both institutional and individual staff needs.

Chapter Nine

Performance Appraisal

Performance appraisal is an organizational system comprising deliberate processes for determining staff accomplishments to improve staff effectiveness. It is closely tied to supervision and staff development within the overall staffing scheme of the student affairs division, but may be considered discrete from other staffing functions in the sense that performance appraisal includes an official and authoritative judgment about staff behaviors on the job that usually is directly connected to the institution's reward structure. Changes to staff compensation, job duties, opportunities for promotion, or even the level of satisfaction of staff in their assignments is linked to official decisions about performance.

The problems of creating and sustaining an effective performance appraisal system within student affairs are profound. Despite the presence of virtually universal policies that require performance appraisal following either governing body or institutional policies, most systems in colleges and universities are flawed and ineffective. Student affairs divisions likewise are committed to some institutionally based performance appraisal system—and sometimes have interdependent systems of their own—that are equally flawed and ineffective. It is ironic that everyone seems to know that an effective performance appraisal system is crucial to a high-quality division of student affairs, but few have found the means, or in many cases even the will, to create and nurture a system that works well.

Perhaps the nature of the appraisal of staff performance is seen as anathematic to the historic values of the profession. If so, there is little reason for it. After all, we conduct assessments of student performances regularly. Is evaluation of staff performance so far removed from assessment that it creates an internal and deeply felt conflict in student affairs professionals? This is speculation, of course, but as we have seen in other discussions of staffing practices, the strongly held values of the profession seem always to have a pervasive influence on how we conduct ourselves when dealing with our colleagues.

Fortunately, the available literature on this subject is revealing about the difficulties of conducting effective performance appraisal. This chapter details much of it and places it in the context of other relevant literature from outside the field. Our own research also addresses the issues. In addition, we synthesize the available evidence to point to the most penetrating insights into the practices in student affairs divisions. As with other discussions about staffing practices, we focus on application of the staffing model proposed in Chapter Two and conclude with some recommendations for practice.

Persistent Issues in Performance Appraisal in Student Affairs

Staff working in student affairs tell many stories, mostly negative, about their experiences with performance appraisal. These stories, coupled with other evidence presented in this chapter, suggest serious problems within the professional practice of student affairs. Here is a sampling of recent experiences of current practitioners told verbatim to the authors. No claim is made here that these stories represent the most important issues in performance appraisal and they certainly are not comprehensive. They are, however, real stories from real staff members in our field, and they point to some serious problems with existing systems of performance appraisal.

> My first performance appraisal occurred after five months on the job (it was scheduled to occur at the three-month mark) and was conducted by my supervisor who previously was assigned to do about half of my current job. I received no training and supervision for my new duties. She dwelled on my shortcomings and took particular glee in citing the "fact" that I had not established a good relationship with a particular member of the staff (meaning that it was not the same kind of relationship she had established with him) as an example of my "weaknesses."

While serving as director of residence life at a religiously affiliated college, I was involved with a team of colleagues from across the institution in a review and revision of the college's performance appraisal process. The final product was a new form to record the results of appraisals, and everyone agreed that the primary purpose of the appraisal process was to benefit staff members, especially in terms of their professional development. About six months later, I was fired; that is, terminated effective at the end of the academic year. At no time prior to this action had I received anything but positive evaluations from my supervisors, and at no time prior to or after notification was I given the benefit of the "developmental" procedures called for in the new process.

My job description called for me to summarize part-time staff members' evaluations in a report to the dean. Occasionally, these summaries portrayed the part-time person in an unfavorable light. The dean informed me that I should include nothing in these reports to reflect negatively on the part-time staff to avoid "problems" and "lawsuits." I felt dishonest, and felt that such a perspective diminished the value of the entire process.

I was the most recent hire in a division of student affairs. I was at a small, private college that was enrollment driven. The admissions numbers did not come in as expected so there was talk at the college of the need to cut budgets and possibly personnel. In my weekly meeting with my supervisor (dean of students/CSAA) he pulled out a piece of paper with the names of the staff (clerical and professional) listed by years/time at the institution. My name was at the bottom. He intimated that if he was asked to identify personnel cuts that this was the way he would proceed; that is, starting at the bottom until he reached the budget number (salaries) he was given to cut. He did not come out and say I would be let go or explain his rationale for his method. He did-n't have the b——— to do that. He just showed me this piece of paper. No thought about evaluation of staff or programs. The budget was met by other means and no staff were cut, but this is not my idea of the way to proceed in this situation.

I worked in residence life in a small, private liberal arts college where horror stories abound about performance appraisal. The year before I came to the position, the story is that staff found their evaluation forms in their mail boxes with a note, "Just ask if you have any questions." This year, the process was not much better. I learned one morning that my one-on-one appraisal meeting was to be held that afternoon. On the way to lunch, I stopped by my office and found my evaluation form duly completed. At our meeting in the afternoon, my supervisor asked whether I had received my form and proceeded to mention two or three very general things about my hall. I suppose that this process is an improvement over last year, but it was very unsatisfying to me. I did not find the process helpful or motivating.

I knew that I should have been concerned about my appraisal when I heard that my supervisor claimed that an evaluation was not a good one unless tears were shed. The two of us literally spent five hours (in two sittings) going over our evaluations of one another. I did not realize until much later that at no point did we discuss my performance in specific areas of responsibility (such as supervision, advising, judicial). Instead, he provided a very thorough assessment of my personality. I learned a lot about myself, naturally, but nothing that helped assess my skills in the job I was hired to do. My evaluation of him, however, was the worst part. He effectively managed to turn my criticisms of him back to my own misguided expectations of a supervisor. Some points he managed to undermine altogether. It was a very surreal experience.

I conducted a recent performance appraisal with a staff member who thought that she was a wonderful performer, but with whom I had concerns. Besides completing the form which the personnel office required, I decided to write out word for word what I was going to say to her because in our previous conversations about her performance she was exhibiting "selective listening." I was concerned that this would be a surprise to her (though I had attempted to communicate my concerns previously). I also was concerned that she would find the reading of my comments too structured and impersonal, yet I wanted to be thoughtful about exactly what to say. Though she began to cry during the reading of it she complimented me on the time I took to write out my comments and asked for a copy. She said it meant a lot to her (I not only mentioned my concerns but also reiterated how valuable she was to our group).

There are important messages in these stories; they leave the indelible impression that performance appraisals in the profession often are conducted badly, under professionally unhealthy conditions, and that they create deleterious effects on staff. Not all individual appraisals are conducted badly, of course, any more than all systems are poorly constructed and managed. The final story among those above reflects a wholesome and effective appraisal tactic. The others do not, however, and one must sadly conclude that the proportion of good to bad experiences in these stories may mirror reality in the larger profession.

There are interesting paradoxes in the evidence available about performance appraisal in student affairs, and these matters should be investigated in future studies. For example, apparently many staff members are not appraised formally and regularly; yet most staff report that they are reasonably satisfied with their appraisals and with the processes used. Is it plausible that many staff in student affairs have no experience with effective performance appraisal systems and do not know how to evaluate the system in use at their institutions? Is it plausible that staff members really do not want to be appraised against performance criteria and therefore raise few questions about ineffective systems in use?

Performance appraisal systems in student affairs are generally simplistic and ineffective. They are, without doubt, the weak link in student affairs staffing practices. Serious investigations of these conditions are warranted and constructive remedies are indicated. There seems to be an institutional schizophrenia about performance appraisal in most colleges and universities. At the institutional level, virtually all colleges and universities know that performance appraisal is essential; yet few seem to have perfected the process for doing it constructively. At the individual level, everyone wants to be evaluated fairly; yet many seem to mistrust the system in use. Clearly there is widespread resistance to existing performance evaluation systems. Some of the discussion in this chapter may show why these conditions exist.

Perspectives from Literature

Compared to literature dealing with performance appraisal of teaching faculty, little parallel literature is available to guide the development of performance appraisal systems in student affairs. Drawing heavily from views about sound business management practices and his own sense of the vital relationship between performance appraisal and staff development in student affairs, Brown (1988) provides the most comprehensive statement about performance appraisal in the field. Sims and Foxley (1980), McIntyre (1974), Schuh and Carlisle (1991), and Nordvall (1977) also write directly about the subject; overall, however, one comes to the impression that professionals in student affairs do not care to write about the subject of performance appraisal any more than they care to plan and carry out performance appraisal systems. Much of the literature on the topic written by professionals in the field tends to be approached in other staffing contexts, such as selecting and training of staff (Stimpson, 1993), supervision (Mills, 1993), and mentoring (Batchelor, 1993).

Literature concerning performance appraisal for faculty in higher education is abundant and has been the subject of careful analysis (Blackburn and Pitney, 1988). Some literature is available about performance appraisal of academic administrators, such as some work by Seldin (1988). By contrast, no such analysis of literature about the appraisal of performance of student affairs educators exists. Wexler (1995) provides a discriminating review on the subject for two-year student affairs personnel, but reports little evidence directly derived from literature in student affairs about the role of trust, the major subject of his study, in performance evaluations. Similarly, evidence about the evaluation of teachers in schools is far more abundant than that about school counselors. Stronge and Helm (1992), for example, found more than 2,000 documents on the subject of teacher evaluation chronicled by ERIC in a nine-year period between 1982 and 1991, but only about 200 similar documents for school counselors in the same period.

Literature from Outside the Field

Performance appraisal is a common topic in business management literature, and while it may not precisely translate to appraisal practices in student affairs in higher education it is clearly relevant. Two recent treatments of the subject are cited here for illustration. First, Daughtrey and Ricks (1989), writing about contemporary supervision, give considerable attention to performance appraisal, calling it a process "of measuring and reporting employee behavior and accomplishments for a given period of time for the purpose of improving job performance" (p. 248). They place supervisors in the central role for conducting these processes and show that employee evaluation and development are the two major purposes of the activity. Common activities associated with performance appraisal, in their view, include setting performance standards, articulating these standards to employees, observing employees doing their work, collecting data about employee performance, facilitating employee self-appraisal of their work, conducting formal appraisal of employee performance, evaluating employee performance, and providing feedback to employees. Daughtrey and Ricks also recognize some of the more common errors made by evaluators, such as allowing personal bias (perhaps about race, gender, or ethnicity) to influence their judgments, applying a "halo effect" to ratings (assuming that a person strong in one area is strong in all areas or vice versa), rating everyone as average to avoid making discriminating judgments, being either too harsh or too lenient in decisions about employees, giving high ratings to people one likes and low ratings to people one dislikes, and allowing the recency of events (remembering what happening recently, but forgetting what happened weeks or months ago) to influence final judgment about staff. Typical appraisal formats discussed by Daughtrey and Ricks include comparative formats, such as ranking and paired comparisons; absolute formats such as narrative, critical incidents, graphic rating scales, weighted checklists, and behaviorally anchored rating scales; and outcome-based formats such as standards of performance and management by objectives.

Their discussion about rewarding performance shows some clear differences between many for-profit environments and those of higher education; they list extensive company-based rewards that ordinarily are not available to supervisors in higher education. Some of these include bonuses, company cars, gifts, and profit sharing. Rewards listed that are associated with the relationship between employee and supervisor, such as autonomy, trust, feedback, and developmental support, and those intrinsic to the job, such as challenge, responsibility, and variety, do have relevance in higher education.

Similarly, Mosley, Megginson, and Pietri (1993), writing about empowering and developing people through supervisory management, discuss several topics closely associated with performance appraisal. They define the process in simple terms: "Performance appraisal is the process used to determine to what extent an employee is performing a job in the way it was intended to be done" (p. 364). In their view, there are multiple purposes for performance appraisal, including providing a basis for administrative actions such as salary adjustments, determining whether certain goals have been achieved such as for affirmative action, ascertaining employee training and development needs, and improving the relationship between supervisor and employee. They discuss employee self-rating, subordinate ratings, and peer ratings, but emphasize that most performance appraisal is carried out by immediate supervisors. Methods of appraisal emphasized by Mosley, Megginson, and Pietri include rating scales and employee comparison techniques.

Certain other sources from the field of management are cited frequently by most authors writing on the subject of performance appraisal. Three of these deserve special note.

First, Baird, Beatty, and Schneier (1982) provide a sourcebook about performance appraisal and "how it is used to manage and improve individual and organizational performance" (p. ix). Their down-to-earth and very practical treatment of the subject includes careful discussion about basic issues including what performance appraisal is, how to define criteria that provide accurate measures of performance, how the performance system must be connected to the larger organization, who trains raters, who does ratings, legal requirements for performance appraisal, and using performance appraisal as a tool for human resource development. Further, Baird, Beatty, and Schneier display questionnaires, outline role-playing possibilities for training, provide case studies of performance appraisal, and even provide overhead transparency masters for training and for workshops. Two of these authors, Schneier and Beatty (1978), also have compiled a resource of readings taken from other sources that, in part, deal with performance appraisal. Two readings, one by Cummings and Schwab (1973) pertaining to methods of appraisal and one by Kearney (1976) addressing the value of behaviorally based performance appraisal systems, are especially germane to this review.

Second, Henderson (1980) explores the subject as a theory-to-practice issue and provides detailed discussions about central issues, including goals of performance appraisal and how they help the organization achieve its mission, processes underpinning performance appraisal systems, personnel involved in performance appraisal, and implementing a comprehensive system of performance appraisal.

Third, the work of DeVries, Morrison, Shullman, and Gerlach (1981) is often cited by authors. They provide a review of literature on the subject current to the date of their publication that is structured around past practices and purposes; current practices, core measurement processes, contextual factors and who participates, comparisons of performance appraisal systems, and implementation issues in performance appraisal; and future issues related to theoretical advances and environmental forces.

Literature from Student Affairs

Literature about student affairs is not clear on the extent to which performance appraisal is a systematic and ongoing activity at the institutional level. Though dated, Meabon, Sims, Suddick, and Alley (1978) found in a national survey that fewer than 50 percent of the student affairs officers conduct periodic performance reviews of their staffs. However, the need for performance appraisal is clearly established (Brown, 1988; McIntyre, 1974; Nordvall, 1977; Stimpson, 1993; Upcraft, 1988) and considerable guidance about how to conduct such appraisals also is available (Fortunato and Waddell, 1981; Sims and Foxley, 1980). What is missing in the literature is evidence of actual practices in the field.

Brown (1988) provides a careful and comprehensive treatment of performance appraisal practices that should be supported in student affairs. Calling the process "assessing and recording staff performance for the purpose of making judgments about staff that lead to decisions," Brown argues that the major purpose of the process is staff development. He also insists that performance appraisal must be seen as a system and that the system must be designed to achieve its major purposes.

> If the system is used for staff development purposes, for example, it must provide useful feedback to staff members on directions for professional growth, and it must be viewed as a helpful, nonthreatening process. A system to determine training needs should provide indicators of deficiencies and distinguish environmental constraints from weaknesses in skills. Promotion decisions require indicators that help predict a staff member's performance in a job that involves greater responsibility, as well as indicators of current performance. Using performance appraisals to make salary or other reward decisions demands a process that is accurate, that

provides a wide range of performance indicators, and that has credibility among the staff [p. 7].

Brown also details certain key characteristics of an adequate performance appraisal system in student affairs that could be used as a heuristic guide for designing and implementing such a system:

1. A student affairs staff and management team coordinates development of the system and monitors its effectiveness.
2. A purpose statement links the appraisal system to the student affairs unit's mission and to its organizational style.
3. A behavioral job description derived from an adequate job analysis serves as the basis for setting goals with each staff member.
4. Job standards provide guidelines for determining adequacy of performance.
5. Top management, middle management, and staff support the system.
6. Appraisal tools and procedures are accurate, reliable, and credible.
7. The appraisal process focuses on behavior rather than on personality traits or attitudes.
8. Training programs exist both for staff involved in conducting appraisals and for those being appraised.
9. Management and staff engage in an ongoing process of setting goals and providing feedback rather than depending only on end-of-the-year review sessions.
10. The interview process focuses on problem solving and staff development.
11. The pervasive orientation is that performance appraisal is an educational and developmental process [p. 7].

Brown discusses a variety of rating scales in a way similar to other authors on the subject, but he shows a clear preference for the behaviorally anchored rating scale (BARS). He maintains that such scales can and should be developed by following four steps: gather critical incidents of exceptional, good, average, and poor performance; categorize incidents into performance dimensions; check the reliability of the categories with other competent judges and with studies of job performance dimensions; and assign numerical weights to the job behaviors. This approach to performance evaluation is discussed in greater detail by Kearney (1976), who describes certain distinguishing characteristics of BARS. Among these are emphasis on development goals of staff, focus on specific jobs (rather than on global performance expectations), identification of definite, observable, and measurable behaviors, and differentiation between behavior, performance, and effectiveness.

Throughout Brown's thorough and comprehensive treatment of performance appraisal in student affairs, emphasis is given to the point of view that the activity should be designed, monitored, and evaluated as an organizational system, not just as a loose connection of necessary organizational functions. He notes that constant care of the system is necessary for it to remain viable as circumstances within the organization change, and emphasizes without fail that the overriding purpose of the system should be to help in the further development of staff.

Methods of Performance Appraisal

Methods of performance appraisal in higher education are well reviewed by Fortunato and Waddell (1991) and Braskamp and Ory (1994), writing about faculty performance evaluations; by Fortunato and Elliott (1988), writing about guidelines for developing policy on performance appraisal; and by Sims and Foxley (1980), writing about student affairs staff performance appraisal. Braskamp and Ory (1994) provide a very thorough review and analysis of a process they call faculty assessment that includes setting expectations, collecting and organizing evidence, and using evidence. They also portray this process as a developmental activity where the appraiser metaphorically sits beside the faculty member to gain full perspective on the work of faculty.

According to Sims and Foxley, who relied heavily upon the work of Cummings and Schwab (1978), methods of appraising student affairs professionals can be classified according to their general approach: comparative methods, absolute standards, management by objectives, and direct indexes. Each method may include some variations in the general approach. For example, comparative methods include straight ranking (rank-ordering all staff from the most to the least effective), alternative ranking (a variation on straight ranking that involves alternatively choosing the most effective and the least effective staff members on a list, moving their names to another list, and returning to the ever smaller list to repeat the process until a ranking is achieved of all staff from the most to the least effective), paired comparisons (a procedure that compares each staff member to every other staff member one at a time leading to a final ranking that is determined by the number of times a particular staff member is chosen over other staff members), and forced distribution (a process that requires the evaluator to assign a certain proportion of all staff to a classification such as "top 10 percent," "above average 20 percent," and "bottom 10 percent").

Absolute standards methods include critical incidents (a qualitative method of evaluation where critical requirements of the job are identified and the evaluator is asked to rate each staff member on each category, or where the supervisor writes about performance incidents when they occur to accumulate evidence of a pattern of performance; see Fortunato and Waddell, 1981, for details), weighted checklists (a qualitative process of consensually weighting a list of staff performance statements that is then given to the evaluator without the weights noted who then checks whether the staff member engages in each of the statements), forced choice (a qualitative process that requires the evaluator to choose the most descriptive statement for each staff member from a list of items, some that discriminate between successful and unsuccessful performance and others that discriminate between desirable and undesirable staff traits, grouped into clusters or categories), conventional rating (a quantitative process of rating each staff member—for example, excellent, average, poor—on a form containing staff member traits), and behaviorally anchored rating scales (BARS, a quantitative version of the critical incident methods that contains scales anchored in descriptors of actual job behavior and precise levels of performance that are agreed upon by a panel).

Management by objectives (MBO) methods are based on an evaluation of the extent of goal achievement for each staff member agreed upon between supervisor and staff member at the outset of each evaluation period.

Direct index methods normally rely upon measurement of outputs from each staff member and are rarely used in student affairs.

Both Fortunato and Waddell (1981) and Sims and Foxley (1980) discuss selective pitfalls of performance appraisal that resemble the discussion of Daughtrey and Ricks (1989). They emphasize problems associated with errors of the halo effect, prejudice and leniency, and central tendency. Central to performance appraisal are concepts of being clear about what the job is (Lenney, Mitchell, and Browning, 1983) and what constitutes different levels of performance. According to Kirkpatrick (1993), these concepts should be negotiated between supervisor and staff member at the outset. Kirkpatrick is especially clear on the need for standards of performance in this matter and claims that there are eight characteristics of well-structured standards: they are based on the job, not the person in the job; they are achievable; they are understood; they are agreed on; they are as specific and measurable as possible; they are time oriented; they are written; and they are subject to change (pp. 161–164).

Consequences of Performance Appraisal

Despite far-ranging and virtuous advice from many authors from multiple disciplines, performance appraisals seemingly do not always have the intended results. In their careful study of performance appraisal research for faculty, Blackburn and Pitney (1988) draw several conclusions that justify the exercise of extreme caution for planners of such systems in student affairs operations. Here are selected conclusions from their study of literature about performance appraisal systems for faculty in higher education that appear to have direct relevancy to student affairs:

> The literature shows that most current systems of performance appraisal or evaluation do not lead to improved performance. It does show, however, that performance appraisals can be dysfunctional, lead to reduced productivity, and create morale problems. The outcomes of performance appraisal have a significant, often negative, impact on the climate of the organization and the commitment of its employees [p. 21].

Rater and ratee characteristics, the measurement vehicle, and the context in which the rating is done are all important factors related to the validity of performance evaluation [p. 21].

Of the several conditions shown to facilitate performance evaluation systems, employee participation in the design and implementation of the appraisal system is one of the most important [p. 21].

Performance-based reward systems usually produce the behavior that is desired and rewarded, but they often produce other unwanted outcomes, such as an excessive focus on individual rather than collective performance, emphasis on short-term versus long-term results, and greater concern for extrinsic rather than intrinsic rewards [p. 22].

Unless performance-based reward systems are carefully structured, the quantity of activity rather than the quality of the outcome will take precedence [p. 22].

In his literature review, Wexler (1995) drew similar conclusions to those of Blackburn and Pitney, emphasizing especially the finding that performance appraisal in higher education typically has not achieved its objectives and, in fact, may have resulted in adverse consequences to staff motivation and productivity. He pointed especially, however, to one condition—trust between staff member and appraiser—that may lead to perceptions of fairness and ultimately to better accuracy in performance appraisals. This observation is consistent with Fulk, Brief, and Barr (1985), who suggest that trust of supervisor may be more important than other process characteristics of the performance appraisal operation. Both of these views lend support to the idea of involving all staff in planning and executing performance appraisal systems.

Some interesting problems are revealed in studies of merit pay systems. Meyer (1975, p. 41), for example, reports data from Rochester University showing that "to the extent that pay is attached directly to the performance of the task, intrinsic interest in the task itself decreases." Thus, a major purpose of performance appraisal systems, to seek improvement on the job, may actually result in less concern for the duties of the position if staff are paid on a merit basis. Equally perplexing is another situation cited by Meyer showing that research supports the conclusion that merit pay plans are likely to threaten the self-esteem of the majority of staff. If the system makes staff feel less worthy within the institutional context, there seems little hope that improvement will result in their work. Meyer, Kay, and French (1965) earlier found some consequences of performance appraisal that are equally disturbing. Among these findings are that criticism has a negative effect on achievement of goals, and praise has little effect one way or the other on performance. These circumstances can only leave an appraiser in a quandary about how to handle the responsibilities of judging staff performance. Some positive findings included in Meyer, Kay, and French's study are these: performance improves when specific goals are established; coaching should be a day-to-day, not a once-a-year, activity; and mutual goal setting, not criticism, improves performance. Such findings offer guidance to appraisers and may provide partial solutions to the otherwise conflicting results from even well-intended appraisal processes.

Perspectives from Research

Several generalizations can be drawn from our research into performance appraisal. Most carry negative connotations relative to the espoused goals for the staffing function: staff and organization improvement. Performance appraisal systems apparently exist universally in higher education, but they are widely believed to be deficient or ineffective in some ways. The systems are applied perfunctorily in most, but not all, institutions.

1. *The purposes of performance appraisal in student affairs are indeterminate and only modestly related to staff improvement.*

Our evidence shows almost no support for a conclusion that student affairs divisions use performance appraisal for institutional improvement and only modest support for the notion that it is used for staff improvement. The appraisal functions are quite simply carried out routinely or mechanically and often have no effect on the staff or the institution. Compared to other purposes, appraisers most often use their judgments to establish new goals for staff and to set salary adjustments, but even these purposes are not uniformly applied, even from year to year within the same institution.

Our case study data found only a modest relationship between performance appraisal and staff compensation. Florida State University, for example, reported no direct connection between performance appraisals and salary adjustments. In that case, outside forces, such as the Florida legislature, may determine salary adjustments at least at an institutional level. Shortage of money for salary adjustments often was revealed in the context of discussing performance reviews, suggesting that the process of formal review is hardly worth the effort when salary adjustments come in the 2–3 percent range, as was cited at Samford University. A connection between performance evaluation and salary adjustment was found at the University of North Carolina-Wilmington, however; one department rates staff members on a scale weighted for the nature of responsibilities assigned (such as in a behaviorally anchored scale) and then judged by the evaluator according to how well standards for the responsibility were met. The level of performance on each responsibility is multiplied by the weight of the responsibility, yielding an overall rating score that is used to determine the level of salary adjustment provided. But at most institutions the relationship between performance appraisal and salary seems indeterminate, to whatever extent it is thought by staff to exist. Staff members sense, even if they cannot be certain, that their performance appraisal results in some way affect their salary adjustments, at least over time.

2. *Most performance appraisal systems in student affairs employ simple rating forms completed by supervisors on an annual basis, but some examples of complex and effective performance appraisal systems exist.*

The most common system of performance appraisal is principally a form of comparative annual rating of staff by supervisors. Supervisors use their observations, evaluations of the effectiveness of programs assigned to staff, and data provided about goal achievement as their primary basis for judgments about staff performance. Personal performance reviews with staff are sometimes used to culminate the overall appraisal process, but the climax may be the simple act of completing a form that is preserved in personnel files that may, or may not, be used again.

Our case studies did reveal some effective systems of performance appraisal, but even at those sites efforts were under way to change the systems, as they were generally perceived to be inadequate in some ways. The most fully integrated system of performance appraisal was found at James Madison University, where thorough personnel evaluation is expected of every supervisor and the activities of performance evaluation are well connected to all other staffing practices. JMU is committed to a developmental orientation in all staffing practices; thus performance evaluation occurs routinely (in conjunction with other ongoing processes, such as dialogues between supervisor and staff member about important, fortuitous issues); formatively, so as to result in no surprises at the formal end-of-year reporting; and consistently with other evaluation activities required of all units in student affairs, such as program self-studies that appear to be happening all the time in one unit or another. Even though a new institutionally based and merit-based system is being implemented that is generally believed to be an improvement in performance evaluation, the current system is widely supported by staff and supervisors. The JMU system appears overly time-consuming, and it might properly be judged so except that the system is totally embedded within other ongoing supervisory functions and thus is treated routinely by both supervisor and staff member.

Other colleges' systems that work well include that of Johnson County Community College, where a multifaceted system is in place that requires three forms of data on each staff member each year: a fall formative report, student evaluation data about program effectiveness in the unit to which the staff member is assigned, and a spring report that focuses on the level of goal achievement. The college also provides formal training for evaluation functions. Still, the overall sentiment of staff is that the system works "reasonably well . . . most of the time"—reasonably well because most staff believe that everyone is involved, but only most of the time because they believe the effectiveness of the system is not guaranteed and needs refinement.

The University of Richmond holds a good example of parallel systems operating within one institution. One system is operated formally by the institution, and the other is devised and carried out by some of the functional areas of the division of student affairs. The institutional system involves completing a form on each staff member and turning it in to the human resources department. It is not clear what happens to the form once it is filed. The functional area system consists of a variety of approaches based on periodic feedback of a formative nature to staff members by their supervisors. Some of these variations are more formal than others, but as one staff member put it, "This is a small college. There isn't any place to hide."

The University of Maryland-College Park is an excellent example of the presence of multiple views on the effectiveness of performance appraisal. Most staff believe it is the least well accomplished of all staffing practices at the institution, yet most feel well evaluated themselves. In some departments, the approach to staff appraisal varies with each staff member (depending on such issues as size of office and length of time in the position); appraisal, whatever the form, is conducted routinely throughout the year. Some departments use carefully crafted worksheets completed by both staff member and supervisor as a preconference activity that is discussed at the supervisor's supervisor level before the actual evaluation conference. There are no surprises in this system, and both supervisor and staff member report feeling very involved in the final judgments about performance. Still, the university is working on a new system to be managed at an institutional level. No one is completely satisfied with the present system, though this dissatisfaction seems driven mostly by units of the university other than those in student affairs.

Some of the performance appraisal systems studied rely largely on goal achievement as the primary indicator of effectiveness. Not surprisingly, in these cases the effectiveness of the functional area units determine to a reasonable extent the judgments about performance of the members of the unit, especially the department heads. Such was the case at Florida State University, where each department head is required to establish and submit goals for the year and to submit an annual report at the end of the academic year that includes an evaluation of the extent to which the goals of the unit were accomplished.

3. *Most student affairs professionals at all levels are appraised once per year, but many receive no regular reviews by their supervisors.*

Survey results presented in Chapter Four show that about 55 percent of deans, directors, coordinators, and nonadministrative personnel receive an annual performance appraisal. About 30 percent of respondents received no appraisal in the past year. The remaining 10–15 percent of respondents received more than one performance appraisal during the past year.

These findings stand in contrast to those from case studies where all divisions of student affairs conduct performance appraisals of some sort according to some plan. Only one college, however, consistently revealed strong support for its current system; significantly, this institution was planning to change the system at the time of the campus visit. Having a system does not, of course, guarantee that every staff member is well appraised, and this may account for the differences between case study and survey data.

4. *Many performance appraisal systems in student affairs are widely recognized as the weak link of staffing practices, and the institutional systems generally are perceived to be deficient.*

The weak-link conclusion is supported best by case study data. This judgment was heard frequently during the on-site visits. All institutions reported formal processes of some kind normally related to institutionwide policy or practice, but the perceived effectiveness of the systems of personnel evaluation ranged from "all personnel are evaluated each year with no exceptions" to "performance evaluation is an annual chore associated with completing forms that no one pays any attention to." In most cases studied, there was a uniform opinion among the staff interviewed that performance appraisal functions at their campus are the weak link in the staffing practices chain. Even where the processes were thought to be functioning adequately, efforts were underway to improve them, as they were generally believed to be deficient in some manner.

5. *The most effective performance appraisal systems in student affairs are informal.*

Our data suggest that performance appraisal systems generally are ineffective, yet most staff seem satisfied with their appraisals. It is possible that staff do not have an appropriate basis for comparison and therefore see the current system in a favorable light. It also is possible, and this is the explanation we adopt, that many systems are more effective than they appear in objective data because they are carried out informally. Thus when questions are asked about discrete aspects of the system, a misleading impression may be given. Staff may receive infrequent formal performance reviews, for example, but feel that their ongoing experiences with their supervisors in which informal appraisals are made and discussed more than adequately deal with the matter. A possibility may be offered where this approach is likely the only one that would work well. Consider a two-person staff, one officially the supervisor of the other. Both have worked effectively together for many years and have frequent, daily interactions. Performance appraisal occurs in this situation every day and it is a two-way street; each is appraising the other. A more formal system might interfere with their work and almost certainly would result in diminishing the quality of their relationship.

When this perspective is combined with the idea clearly supported in the literature that appraiser attributes are perhaps the single most important aspect of the overall system, the conclusion is that informal, routine interactions between supervisor and staff based upon a meaningful and personalized relationship may be a very effective approach to performance appraisals for all staff.

6. Most student affairs professionals are satisfied with their positions.

This contentment seems important to any judgment about the overall effectiveness of performance appraisal systems (and other staffing functions). Student affairs staff generally like their work and are satisfied with their positions. Working directly with students reportedly provides the greatest single source of gratification for staff; however, one suspects that this general happiness with their work is based upon many aspects of the work, including relations with supervisors and other staff and the fact that performance appraisal work well enough to not endanger their general contentedness.

Using the Staffing Model in Performance Appraisal

Performance appraisal can be conducted effectively in such a manner to achieve the dual purposes of staff and organization development. To create and sustain such a system, however, requires the full consideration of many ambient institutional factors. The system must accomplish both the evaluation and the development of staff, be sensitive to institutional productivity standards and rewards, be based upon standards grounded in the context of the work to be performed, be fully participatory and interactive, be clear, open, and fair, include ongoing review of positions and individual performance, encourage leadership behavior in appraisers, and use workable formats that avoid all systematic biases.

Effective performance evaluation systems are very complex and very sensitive and they must be designed with great care. Their effectiveness is related in part to tying the system to a source high enough in the institution to guarantee sufficient authority, credibility, and resources to make it work. An effective performance evaluation system is pervasive within the institution; thus the systems are extraordinarily complex. Concurrently, they are exceedingly sensitive. When conducted well, the system will reveal strengths and weaknesses in both the organization, such as may be revealed through ongoing position analysis, and in the staff, whose futures may very well be tied to the inherent judgments about performance and subsequent rewards.

Dual Purposes: Evaluate and Develop Staff

Performance appraisal has two overall purposes: to evaluate staff relative to job requirements and to develop staff for improved performance. Performance appraisal, therefore, is related on the one hand to institutional needs and on the other hand to staff needs, abilities, motivation, and expectancies. This dual function is not new. We saw it in discussions about supervision and staff development where the dual responsibility was to individuals and the institution. In this case, the dual—or, actually, multiple—functions of performance appraisal ask that the system judge performance against some established standards and expectations and to accomplish the task with such skill that the judgment information can be used to benefit the staff member. The overriding purpose of performance appraisal is to help staff to improve and, thus, to improve organizational effectiveness. The truth is, however, that it is very difficult to make critical judgments about performance and to offer developmental support to staff within the same system. As was shown in the literature review, the outcomes of performance reviews often are negative regardless of the nature of appraiser judgment. The fact remains, however, that the overarching purpose of performance appraisal is to evaluate staff for the explicit purpose of staff and organization improvement.

Organizational System: Productivity and Rewards

Performance appraisal systems are related to the institution's productivity requirements. It is clear to any executive-level administrator that institutional productivity is related directly to the productivity of the staff; thus appraisal systems are expected to reveal underproductive units and to serve as a response system to focus attention on the problem. One of the most crucial response systems is the institution's reward structure. Hypothetically, productive staff as revealed through the performance appraisal system are rewarded, often by upward salary adjustments, while underproductive staff are recompensed in other ways. A major problem results, as also was shown in the literature review, in that expectancies of staff often differ from findings of careful performance appraisal and the result may lower staff motivation and performance. Even when reviewed positively for performance, staff reactions are not always in expected directions.

Contextual Standards

The contextual nature of staff performance appraisal must be emphasized. Judgments about staff performance cannot be made independent of the organization and its culture. The authorization of a particular job within an organization is based on findings from a carefully conducted job analysis, exhibiting evidence that the completion of the job is essential to the achievement of organizational mission. (See Chapter Five for detailed discussion of this process.) The parameters of the job are determined from this analysis, and position descriptions are prepared to ensure that persons hired understand the organizational needs to be met through the position. Thus, in periodic judgments about actual performance by individuals hired to carry out the functions of a particular job, a pervasive view must be taken that includes ongoing analysis of the requirements of the position, the constraints placed on performance in the job by the institution, and the adequacy of the behaviors of the staff member employed to carry out the required functions.

A further contextual perspective on performance appraisal is the recognition that limitations on performance may reside in the environment of the organization as well as in the capacities of the staff member. A staff member expected by position description to advise student groups such as fraternities or sororities, for example, may have little control over certain behaviors of students or their motivations. Therefore, it must be recognized that appraisals of staff performance are mediated by the organizational climate and that these conditions should always be taken into account by appraisers.

Attributes of individual staff members provide a further context for performance appraisal. Needs of staff may vary legitimately during appraisal periods, such as the desire for further job-related education or training. Motivations of staff also may vary reasonably as a consequence of life circumstances or in the circumstances of others on whom they depend to carry out the duties of the position. Over time, expectancies also may vary based upon realistic assessments of feasible results of their work given evidence of repeated efforts in the past; thus effort may be affected by historical records of results. Each of these individual factors are domains for consideration when judging staff performance and for suggesting needed changes. It is entirely reasonable to expect changes in staff behavior when deficiencies in performance are determined; however, staff behavior alone may not represent the totality of possible causes for the deficiency.

Participatory and Interactive Appraisal

The performance appraisal system must be participatory and interactive. Such systems are more than the sum of their collective processes. Given the extraordinary investment of both the institution and its people in the results of performance appraisal, it is imperative that the systems be designed in concert with all stakeholders and that they be open to constant interaction with these same stakeholders. Plans made jointly by staff and administrators have a far better chance of working as intended than plans made in isolation by either party. Such a process requires large investments of time, energy, talent, and psyche, but the payoff is ownership by all parties. For ownership to persist, the systems themselves must undergo regular if not constant evaluation. Thus the interactive component of performance appraisal systems is vital for their effectiveness, especially in the long term.

System Attributes: Clarity, Openness, and Fairness

It is virtually self-evident that the performance appraisal system must possess the attributes of clarity, openness, and fairness. It should be noted that these attributes are firmly related to the historic values of the profession. These are system qualities generally expected by student affairs professionals, as they so closely represent professionals' most basic beliefs about education, and they are the qualities most often challenged in actual practice within performance appraisal systems. Despite the self-evident nature of these attributes, they are difficult to create and sustain in complex systems. The standard of clarity, for example, suggests that both staff member and appraiser know fully and definitely the requirements of the position, how well it has been conducted in the past, the extent of environmental and personal constraints on job performance, and the devices that will be used to arrive at a judgment about individual performance. Suppose, however, that circumstances within the institution changed drastically since the last formal appraisal and that expectations for the position were modified as a matter of course in day-to-day activities. A colleague may have left unexpectedly during the past year and, because of fiscal constraints, the duties of the vacated position were reassigned to remaining personnel. Suppose further that conditions external to the institution also changed suddenly, resulting in a change of internal priorities. Clarity about how to appraise staff may be lost in these circumstances and, with no intended malice, the appraiser may not be able to conduct a formal review that meets the preconditions of clarity and may give the impression of not being open (because the rules changed along the way) nor fair (because the final rules may appear to have been made up on the spot).

Ongoing Review of Position and Performance

Much of the difficulty in achieving conditions of clarity, openness, and fairness can be overcome if the systems are ongoing. An effective performance appraisal system will conduct ongoing evaluations of both the position and the person occupying it. Under conditions of ongoing position analysis and performance appraisal, there are few surprises, and changes to the environment are quickly incorporated into the official appraisal system. Such requirements are time-consuming for all concerned with appraisal, but the advantage is that they keep this most sensitive institutional system truly functional in a manner that serves the interests of all.

Appraiser's Leadership Attributes

A key requirement for an effective performance appraisal system is the consideration that supervisor or appraiser behavior may be more important than the vehicles or formats used in the system. Appraisers, acting as leaders within the institution and for their staff, are far more likely to experience successful results from the appraisal system than will appraisers who behave as nonleaders, even though they are technically proficient in the task of appraisal. Leaders possess authority for their judgments not available to nonleaders based upon a record of effectiveness within the organization and ascribed respect. These conditions allow leaders to model desired behavior and to prescribe behavior sought from staff with the advantage of organizational prestige and power.

Workable Formats That Avoid Systematic Biases

Finally, effective system requirements for performance appraisal must include workable formats that avoid systematic biases. Effectiveness of performance appraisal is not closely related to the use of a particular device or format. Most any device or format may work, though some offer more promise. Use of behaviorally anchored rating scales (BARS), for example, shows special promise, but the approach is extremely difficult to implement fully. Conversely, use of simple checklists of performance criteria with intended institutionwide application to be completed at a prescribed time during the year and then sent to a personnel office for filing is almost certainly doomed to failure. Not only does this approach fail to produce useful information for individual or organizational improvement, it almost certainly will produce hostility and alienation toward the system of performance appraisal. Under these conditions, everyone—supervisor and staff member alike—resists the practice altogether.

A related system requirement is to avoid methodical biases in the use of any format. Several of these biases are well reviewed in the literature. Among the more notorious biases include practices such as giving preferential treatment to some but not all staff, rating all staff the same, being overly lenient or overly harsh toward some or all staff, and practicing conscious or unconscious racial or gender prejudice. Adopting a format that includes the standards of clarity, openness, and fairness and that involves more than one appraiser may help control some of these biases.

These complex, sensitive, and high-stakes systems require serious and constant attention by top-level institutional management. Simplistic approaches to performance appraisal will not work to achieve the goals of staff and organization improvement.

Recommendations for Practice

Like other staffing practices, there are no magic bullets for creating and sustaining an effective performance appraisal system. Many systems work well if they are properly designed and nurtured. Proper design means creating a system that fits the culture of the institution and attends to all other aspects of the practice as suggested in the staffing model. Thus the final system must attend to staff evaluation and improvement; ensure unit and institutional productivity; provide appropriate rewards for achievement; involve all stakeholders in the process; be open, clear, and fair; provide for ongoing review of performance and of position descriptions; include leader behavior in appraiser roles; and avoid systematic biases.

A key ingredient in an effective performance appraisal system is will. Leaders in student affairs must commit themselves to the practice and to doing it well. Performance appraisal must be taken seriously. This means in part that ample time is devoted to the practice. No compromises in will, time, or effort should be tolerated.

Make sure that the appraisal system fits the culture of the division and that it is complementary to the institutional appraisal system. Make sure also that the system is responsive to both individual and organization improvement.

An effective performance appraisal system is one that incorporates valuation processes routinely and regularly. Effective performance appraisal does not occur once each year; it occurs all the time, with multiple marker events throughout the year. There should be no surprises in performance appraisal at the official end of the year; staff and supervisors should have communicated clearly on many occasions about judgments of staff member accomplishment. Performance appraisal is not simply an event, it is a process that must be nurtured constantly.

Be sure that the system is completely integrated with other staffing practices, especially with supervision and staff development. These components ideally should be seamless; each part should be concerned with the other two in every action taken.

All experienced practitioners in student affairs know that things change within the environment—needs emerge, new demands are placed on the institution and the division, resource limitations or expansions occur, new leaders arrive, new ideas are discovered, uncontrollable events occur—and they necessitate continuous adjustments in performance appraisal practices. Constant adjustments in the working arrangements between supervisor and staff member may be necessary, and the system must allow for them. Performance appraisal must be real! It cannot be based on last year's agreements if this year's conditions differ significantly.

Recognize that both individuals and the environment create opportunities and inhibitors regarding performance. When staff members do not live up to last year's expectations, be sure to account for whether circumstances within the environment may have inhibited their opportunities for achievement.

Guard against systematic biases in the appraisal system. This is an issue of fairness, as has been noted; certain systemic biases are insidious and will destroy the best of systems if tolerated. There must be active diligence in this regard. Publishing the criteria used in staff evaluations and conducting periodic public discussion about them may help a unit keep its guard up against such occurrences.

Cultivate genuineness in the adopted performance appraisal system. Certain aspects of an effective system must be formal, but informal practices should be allowed and encouraged. Be sure the informal and the formal practices complement one another.

Summary

Performance appraisal generally has two broad goals: to evaluate a staff member's performance according to the position description, and to assist staff members in improving themselves and their ability to accomplish the work assigned to them. A related goal is to help determine staff member compensation or salary adjustment.

With little directly relevant literature available, especially research-based literature dealing with student affairs in higher education, the current condition of this staffing practice is unclear. Available evidence suggests that few institutions and divisions of student affairs carry out appraisals well, and certainly not in a methodical, systemic manner. Some evidence suggests that staff feel reasonably well-evaluated; therefore, the formal operating systems of performance appraisal may not be the best indicator of how well it is handled.

Without doubt, many staff members believe their institution's performance appraisal system is not working well. Most recognize the necessity of personnel appraisal or evaluation systems, but question their effectiveness. Even when appraisal is done well, resulting benefits are uncertain. Indeed, the consequences of performance appraisals often are negative relative to some very important goals for appraisal, such as motivating staff toward improvement. Even when appraisers are well trained, they may not be comfortable with it or feel adequate to carry out the duty.

Improvement in performance appraisal systems is possible, but it requires an abundance of will, talent, and time to create and nurture an effective system. Several suggestions for achieving this result are offered in this chapter, but there are no simple solutions; great care and even greater effort is required.

Chapter Ten

Staffing Practices That Ensure Quality in Student Affairs

Staffing practices in student affairs are best understood contextually. In earlier chapters we demonstrate that neither recruitment and selection, nor orientation, nor supervision, nor staff development, nor performance appraisal of staff operate alone within divisions of student affairs. These contexts include the unit, division, and institutional cultures; the history, purpose, and geographical location of the institution; the legal, political, social, and economic environmental conditions in which higher education operates within the United States; and the values of the profession. Each context, or all of them acting together, help to shape contemporary staffing practices in student affairs.

This book is devoted to a comprehensive discussion of contemporary staffing practices in student affairs taking into account each of these important contexts. In concluding it we want to carefully illuminate these practices, because we believe that the quality of the staff who carry out the mission of student affairs is a key factor in the quality of educational programs and services provided in America's colleges and universities. Correspondingly, we strongly believe that the quality of staff is directly connected to the quality of the divisional and institutional staffing practices.

We began our study of the subject wanting to know more about staffing practices in student affairs and, with that knowledge, to offer ideas for improving them. We chose to study the status quo through a variety of methods. First, we reviewed the available literature. About some staffing practices it was revealing, showing previous attention by scholars and practitioners in the field. Such was the case, for example, with recruitment practices and staff development practices. Other areas had no such revealing treatment, but in all cases we attempted to review and analyze the literature for relevant and helpful suggestions for improving overall staffing practices.

Our second method was to conduct a large-scale survey of practitioners. We used lengthy questionnaires to collect information from a randomly selected group of institutions and invited staff from multiple functional areas of student affairs to respond. These data added to our insights and showed especially the kinds of well-established practices currently in use. We obtained a reasonable insight into current policies and use of resources in support of staffing practices, for example, but our information was limited by the nature of surveys themselves, including a less-than-hoped-for return rate.

Finally, we used case studies to provide firsthand observations and reports from practitioners. We conducted eight of these studies, two each at research universities, comprehensive state universities, small liberal arts colleges, and two-year community colleges. This allowed us to converse with people conversant with our interests and concerns, and we learned much about how staffing practices are conducted at some very successful institutions. We chose the case sites based on generally held beliefs that their student affairs operations are of high quality.

Staffing and Quality

Our interest in conducting this study and presenting our conclusions and ideas for improvement of staffing practices were motivated by concerns for quality in student affairs. We believe one of the best assurances of quality in student affairs is to guarantee the quality of staff members, which is accomplished by a combination of tactics including hiring the right people and then carefully and deliberately nurturing them through the division's staffing practices.

We recognize that quality is an elusive asset and that there are many legitimate views about what it is and how it is determined. Generally, however, quality at the institutional level is measured by how well goals are achieved. Goals vary depending upon the purposes of the institution, but authorities generally agree on three aspects of institutional quality: it can only be determined when the goals sought are absolutely clear, measuring it can be done in many ways depending on what is sought, and measurement should employ many types of data.

Quality of student affairs, likewise, normally is judged by how well the combination of educational and service activities contributes to certain educational outcomes in students and the functioning of the institution. Service to students has always been a firm commitment of the profession and has gone hand-in-hand with an equally firm commitment to developing the "whole person." Indeed, student affairs professionals believed for many years that individualizing and personalizing educational services were the primary reasons for the existence of the profession. In recent years these commitments have been clarified around an array of developmental aims of education, but historically the most persistent and ever present distinguishing characteristic of the field has been its values. These elemental commitments to human dignity, equality, and community, as discussed in Chapter One, may be the most crucial standards for quality in the field.

Additionally, professional associations help to establish standards of quality. They promulgate statements of ethical standards, for example, and in student affairs they support certain standards of practice (Council for the Advancement of Standards in Higher Education [CAS], 1986) that are intended to help functional units of student affairs to guide themselves to greater effectiveness. Historically, professional associations have used accrediting and credentialing practices to help ensure quality at an institutional level. For the most part, these practices have had little influence in student affairs per se. They are more common in counseling services, but because of the great diversity of activities incorporated into student affairs divisions, they have never taken root in the field. (See Creamer and Woodard, 1992, for a complete discussion of this issue.) More recently, the National Association of Student Personnel Administrators (NASPA) and the American College Personnel Association (ACPA) have taken tentative steps to address issues of quality. One such venture led to the promulgation of a quality assurance model (Creamer and others, 1992) that details the issue and promotes certain association responses to promote the assurance of quality within institutions. (See Appendix C for a report by a study group on quality assurance.) The most recent professional activity in this regard has been an effort to refocus the profession on its historic purposes for student learning and personal development through the Student Learning Imperative (Schroeder, 1996) initiative by and NASPA's 1996 convention theme on student learning.

Irrevocable connections between the quality of staffing practices and of overall student affairs programs and services have been highlighted throughout this book. In the beginning of our study, we held certain hypotheses about the relationship between staffing practices and quality of higher education. Most were sustained by our findings and are stated here as context or perspective for our enumeration of staffing principles that we recommend for professional practice.

Hypothesized Relationship Between Staffing and Program Quality

Our assertions about the connections between staffing practices and quality performance include the following:

- The quality of educational programs and services provided by a student affairs division depends on the knowledge, skills, commitment, and professionalism of the staff who create and deliver them.
- A division's staffing practices directly affect the quality of the work performed and the satisfaction, emotional well-being, and personal and professional growth of all involved in the enterprise.
- Staffing practices are embedded in the institutional and division cultures and must be understood within that context.
- Institutional and division culture is formed and transformed by the contributions of the people who make up the organization.
- Staff members working cooperatively toward common goals increase the probability of producing excellence within an organization.
- Organizations that value their members and demonstrate concern for their personal and professional welfare increase the probability of producing excellence.

- Student affairs divisions that select employees based on the criteria of candidates' levels of knowledge, skills, experience, and fit with the institution have the most effective and productive staffs.
- Student affairs divisions that explicitly value continued professional development and encourage and reward staff members who actively pursue new learning opportunities will remain vital even in the midst of environmental turbulence, including resource shortfalls.
- Student affairs divisions that conscientiously integrate the selection, orientation, supervision, staff development, and performance appraisal functions are most likely to have strong, productive staffs for sustained periods of time.
- Persons assuming new positions who are thoroughly and completely briefed about the expectations of the position, institutional policies and operating procedures, the formal and informal structures of the institution, and the resources available will be more productive than those required to discover these things for themselves.
- Student affairs divisions that systematically and thoroughly provide individualized, caring supervision to all staff will be rewarded by greater productivity, loyalty, and esprit d'corps.
- Student affairs divisions that have periodic, thorough, sensitively administered, and goal-related performance appraisals that focus on improving staff accomplishments will increase effectiveness and efficiency.

These beliefs illustrate the manner in which staffing practices in student affairs are related to some of the most important concerns of higher education and how culture and behavior interact to affect outcomes. Great care must be exercised to ensure the integrity of these interlocking connections if higher education is to achieve its most treasured quality-related goals.

We undertook the task of exploring certain aspects of these vital links by examining the nature of current knowledge and practice of staffing practices in student affairs and report details of our findings in previous chapters. In this concluding chapter, we wish to summarize these findings and state them in the form of principles for practice. We believe that the overall quality of staffing practices will be enhanced significantly if these principles are adhered to in routine activities. Their application will, we believe, ensure the integrity of the postulated quality links.

Principles of Staffing Practice

Based on evidence from our studies, certain principles of staffing practice may be asserted. Each is enumerated here and annotated briefly as a way of summarizing previous documentation.

Recruitment and Selection

Selecting the right person for each position is the first consideration in successful student affairs staffing practices and transcends all other staffing concerns.

Fit between the person and the institutional environment is crucial to success in the position. Placing highly talented people in an environment where they do not fit usually produces unhappiness and poor performance.

Formal credentials and experience should be considered in choosing the most suitable person for the position. One should keep in mind that a rigorous professional preparation program often equips its graduates well for undertaking new tasks in creative and innovative ways.

Care should be exercised not to confuse experience with qualifications when making hiring decisions. Frequently, applicants are eliminated from consideration for a position because they have not performed the duties specified in the job description before. Without denying the worth of experience, talented, well-educated but less experienced professionals frequently can quickly acquire new skills and move programs and services to new levels of effectiveness, whereas less talented but more experienced practitioners can adequately meet current job expectations but will be unable to go beyond present requirements to meet changing conditions. The best candidate is usually the best-qualified professional, not necessarily the most experienced one.

The recruitment and selection process matters; it should be conducted with careful premeditation and meticulous attention to detail.

Conduct a thorough position analysis. Determine exactly what needs to be done considering the existing staff (or sought-after staff if there are multiple vacancies). Frequently it is in the organization's and individuals' best interest to consider reassigning responsibilities among existing staff before writing a job description for the new position. Determine the essential knowledge, skills, personal attributes, credentials, and previous experience required for a person to excel in the position.

Establish a clear purpose or set of performance expectations for the position.

Empower and clearly charge a search committee to identify the best person for the position. In charging the committee, explicit limits of authority and decision making should be clearly set forth. Once these limits are established, it is usually wise to protect the committee from all outside influences as they perform their assigned duties.

Establish written ethical and procedural guidelines that meet legal standards for the recruitment and selection process.

Observe all institutional and division policies in conducting the search, screening the candidates, interviewing finalists, and making final recommendations to a hiring authority. Generally, improvisation during the selection process leads to unforeseen trouble.

At institutions that do not adequately represent people of color, ethnic minorities, and women, devise plans that will rectify the situation.

Orientation

Orientation of new staff should be handled deliberately, systematically, and thoroughly.

New staff orientation begins during the recruitment and selection process and continues throughout the early stages on the job.

Ensure complete familiarization with educational and operational philosophy, the institutional and divisional culture, expectations for successful performance on the job, and normative expectations about relationships among faculty, staff, and students.

Whether formal or informal approaches are used, all student affairs divisions should have a detailed outline of topics to be covered and subjects to be discussed with each new position holder. This applies as well when an internal candidate is selected to fill a new position. (Certain areas such as staff benefits and introduction to the student clientele may be unnecessary for staff already familiar with the institution's characteristics.)

Supervision

Supervision is a vital staffing practice, second only to selection of new staff in determining a division's effectiveness. It is the linchpin that holds the staffing process together.

The purpose and process of supervision should be clearly communicated to each staff member. Supervision should address both the organization's expectations of the staff member and the staff member's personal and professional growth. Adequate supervision focuses both on assisting staff members to realize their personal and career aspirations and on helping them make the maximum contribution possible to the organization's mission.

Supervision should be based on goals or objectives and the careful monitoring of activities related to accomplishment of those goals. The content and process of supervision is dependent on the level of knowledge and experience the staff member has in fulfilling the assigned responsibilities. For example, seasoned professionals do not need to be told what to do but may need another experienced professional to act as a sounding board for ideas and as a conduit of information, official or unofficial, from the institution's leadership and other important constituencies. Staff often also need someone to be an advocate for their ideas and a promoter of their stock.

Supervisory sessions should be systematic and ongoing throughout a staff member's tenure with the organization. Every staff member is entitled to careful, caring supervision.

Staff Development

Staff development practices should be both institutionally sponsored and individually enabling.

Follow a developmental plan. Each staff member should be treated as a unique resource of the division and the institution. Based on all that is known about each staff member, a deliberate blueprint should be crafted in collaboration with the staff member and followed. The plan, however, should not be rigid. It should be revisited with regularity to make adjustments where indicated based on progress made and new needs that arise from advancing professional demands, such as the use of technology or different scope of responsibilities.

Consider staff development activities as both process and product. New skills are an example of product; the regular, systematic engagement of staff in reflective and purposeful behaviors intended for self- and organizational improvement is a process that, if culturally created and sustained, can become routine, which is healthy for both individuals and the organization.

Incorporate staff development into routine work. *Staff development* is not synonymous with *program* or *workshop*. Often the most effective developmental activities are individually tailored and built into ongoing work assignments.

Employ multiple approaches. No one tactic will work for all staff; the same activity will not work for the same staff all the time. Staff are energized by variety in their opportunities for involvement, so the opportunities should be planned with this in mind.

Ensure recognition of staff maturity and growth. Staff members are uniquely distributed along developmental paths and both the paths and the individuals change with each passing month and year. Staff development plans and activities must recognize this evolution of people and their changing lives and professional pathways.

Performance Appraisal

Performance appraisal is a complex and sensitive institutional system that should be interactively planned and executed.

Recognize the dual focus of staff and organization improvement. The central purpose of performance appraisal is improvement. It is true that institutional needs serve as the underlying justification for creating staff positions in the first place, and that performance appraisal systems include the purpose of guiding staff members toward assisting the institution to achieve its goals. But it need not follow that performance appraisal systems exist solely, or even principally, as a control mechanism. Their overarching purpose is institutional functioning through staff and organization improvement.

Link performance appraisal to institutional productivity and rewards. Individual staff members benefit from performance appraisals and should have a direct and obvious connection to institutional achievement by means of the formal reward system. Consequences of performance appraisal that do not make this connection may have negative consequences on staff morale and productivity.

Recognize contextual constraints on staff performance. Staff members perform in environments often shaped by circumstances beyond their control; thus all performance appraisals should take into account both individual and environmental conditions.

Ensure constant involvement of all stakeholders. Ownership and credibility are important in sustaining effective performance appraisal systems, and the best way to ensure them is to involve all staff in their design, execution, and monitoring. Any system created short of full participation of all staff will be flawed in direct proportion to the level of nonparticipation of staff.

Guarantee system clarity, openness, and fairness. To be effective, staff must understand the system fully and sincerely believe it is fair to all participants. These conditions are best guaranteed when the system is regularly reviewed and rechartered.

Conduct ongoing position analyses. Appraisal of individuals relative to their performance on the job demands that all position requirements be up-to-date. Given that environmental circumstances often change, both appraiser and performer must know the most current expectations at the time of formal appraisal. Of course, where appraisals are conducted frequently, whether formally or not, the requirement for up-to-date information is less problematic.

Demand leadership from appraisers and recognize their unique contribution to the results of appraisals. Appraisers who act as educational and institutional leaders—that is, who recognize that they are behaving in a manner to shape individual and organizational behavior in predetermined directions—are more likely to be effective in carrying out their duties than those who perform their duties perfunctorily. Furthermore, appraiser attributes such as genuineness, sincerity, conscientiousness, and fairness serve to promote effectiveness to at least the same degree as do other system characteristics.

Avoid all systematic biases. The intentional or unintentional inclusion of bias in performance appraisal systems will virtually guarantee system failure. It is unlikely that staff will benefit from a system they do not trust; a system with known or even suspected biases toward certain behaviors or practices will destroy confidence.

General Staffing Principles

Successful staffing requires interactive involvement by all staff on a continuing basis.

In all staffing matters, involvement of current staff is crucial. Staffing practices should be deliberate and usually systemic and, in each functional category—recruitment and selection, orientation, supervision, staff development, and performance appraisal—they should be determined after full participation by all stakeholders in the process. From novice to veteran, all staff have a responsibility and a right to help determine the institutional actions that will affect their individual effectiveness and, ultimately, organization effectiveness.

Staffing should be a conscious and continuous concern of all staff. Formal institutional practices of staffing should be as much a part of day-to-day work agendas as other tasks. Any institutionalized practice that affects the livelihood and professional success of staff deserves ongoing and reflective attention.

Successful staffing requires systematic but not necessarily spectacular approaches.

Written policies should be developed and maintained. Intentions by supervisors and educational leaders about how they propose to treat others within the system should be announced formally through written documents and informally in everyday interactions. At the same time, all formal policies should be subjected to ongoing review and revision where indicated.

Staffing is not recipe-driven nor is it magic; it is creatively fashioned within the institutional and division cultures to maximize human talent and potential. The effectiveness of a given practice is contingent on many local circumstances, so a practice should be fashioned to accommodate these controlling factors. The only universal imperative is the application of certain principles that underlie the tailored structure.

Successful staffing requires naturalness and simplicity.

Within formal policies and purposes, successful staffing processes depend significantly on informality and individual character. These correspond, of course, with formal requirements such as written policies to govern the overall system. The application of formal policies, however, should follow the equally compelling requirement that they be honest, straightforward, and fully understandable by all who are affected.

Improving Staffing Practices

It has been stated repeatedly in this book that staffing practices are embedded in the culture of the institution. Our discussions in previous chapters have been about the compelling reality of how culture shapes and sometimes determines the nature of staffing activities. Now we turn our attention to changing these relationships to improve staffing practices or systems found wanting when judged by the standards or principles of staffing just described. We offer only uncomplicated, straightforward advice.

There is no doubt that institutions of higher education are tremendously complicated organizations; any explicit effort to change them must recognize this. Any aspect of the organization that is modified intentionally may very well affect several others. Care must be exercised to improve the systems, not just to change them. As in the medical profession, the first rule for organizational development is to do no harm. Broken systems should be fixed; workable but inadequate systems should be improved; excellent systems should be monitored and nurtured.

Step one in improving staffing systems is to become thoroughly familiar with existing systems to determine their strengths and weaknesses. This means, of course, studying and eventually making public the findings about all relevant systems and subsystems at the institution, division, and unit levels.

Where existing systems are found inadequate, deliberate or willful behavior is required to initiate restructuring. It is helpful to use all available expertise within the institution pertaining to organizational behavior and change. Perhaps such expertise is available on the student affairs staff or among faculty or administrative staff. If so, such persons definitely should be involved in planning for change of staffing systems. If such expertise is not available, do not panic and, certainly, do not give up. Changing organization systems requires careful, deliberate, thoughtful, cautious, and calculating behaviors, but it does not require complicated, ingenious, or magical acts. Changing organization systems may be more a matter of will than of means, but will must be present along with concerted, long-term effort.

If organizations are to be restructured to achieve participatory and interactive systems—the ideal advocated throughout this book—such characteristics should pervade the methods used to bring about change. Thus, widespread participation should be sought, and planning and change tactics must be collaborative. Professionals must be invested in the staffing systems that to a considerable extent control their productivity and success on the job; the best way to ensure such investment is to allow them to design— and subsequently monitor and redesign—the new systems from the beginning.

Many system changes that will improve staffing have to do with the way people are treated generally within the institution. Attention should be paid to all conditions that affect the way people within the organization relate to one another, so changing a staffing system may not mean following a simple, straightforward set of steps. In fact, it is possible that when institutional systems are modified to ensure full respect of the interests of all staff, the specific staffing practices in student affairs will subsequently change naturally. At the very least, such institutional modifications should be weighed as a prerequisite to extensive effort within the division of student affairs.

While re-creating a cultural structure seems daunting, it may have a simple front door: the use of normative-reeducative teaching and learning strategies. These may be a most suitable approach for changing the way people think about staffing practices, and they are familiar to most current staff. Teaching and learning tactics are common operational tools in higher education. A new approach need not be invented when an old approach with a proven record will achieve desired results. Staff need to know about principles and practices that work in staffing; they can be taught straightforwardly. Staff need to understand and internalize the values of healthy and productive relationships. They need encouragement and coaching about working together and need reinforcement for achieving and sustaining this type of working environment.

Many changes needed in staffing practices are structural; that is, they relate to policies, organizational priorities, and support systems. Again, no magic is involved in making these changes, but a high level of commitment is absolutely necessary. The need for change must be clearly and widely perceived, and the stage must be set for change by educating decision makers about the changes needed. Leadership of the change initiative is key, of course, but chosen tactics simply should include participative style, collaboration, and information sharing. This may be thought of as a process of teaching people about themselves and their preferred manner of relating to one another. It also should be thought of as an explicit and active application of the historic values of the profession of student affairs.

Suggested Changes to Current Staffing Practices

Student affairs has been an identifiable field of work distinguishable from others in higher education for about fifty years. Over the past twenty to twenty-five years, it has become increasingly more specialized, requiring higher levels of skills and command of a larger and more detailed body of knowledge. There has been considerable progress made toward making student affairs a profession through the adoption and promulgation of ethical standards statements and formulation and publication of minimum acceptable standards of practice in most functional areas and in professional preparation programs (Carpenter, 1991; Carpenter, Miller, and Winston, 1980; Winston and Dagley, 1985).

As the profession moves into the next century, the time is propitious for making a quantum leap in professionalization. This is worthy of pursuit, however, if and only if the field's clienteles—higher education institutions and college students—are the direct beneficiaries. We believe that a fully professionalized field would greatly improve the quality of educational experiences colleges and universities provide their students and substantially enhance the educational experiences of individual students.

Important change is possible only if greater attention and care are devoted to staffing practices in student affairs. Greater control needs to be exercised over the educational qualifications of those admitted to practitioner ranks, the quality and extent of ongoing personal and professional development activities, and the rigor of the standards against which staffs' performances are measured. Much greater attention needs to be focused on how student affairs programs and services affect students' academic learning and personal development—higher education's "bottom line." To complete the professionalization of the field requires more rigorous standards for admission to full professional status in the field and continuous monitoring of each staff member's proficiency, knowledge level, and contributions to. accomplishment of institutional goals.

The following proposals are offered as fuel for consideration of important changes needed in the professionalization process in student affairs. These proposals are offered from four perspectives: consideration of alternative staffing patterns, new roles for professional associations in professional development and continuing education, means for greater integration of professional preparation and practice, and new quality assurance mechanisms.

New Staffing Patterns

The typical means of entry into student affairs practice on many campuses is for persons who aspire to work in the field to first complete a master's degree program (although our survey found that 15–25 percent of practitioners below the vice-presidential level hold only a bachelor's degree.) Our survey found that the graduate academic fields through which most entry-level practitioners enter are counseling, higher education, student affairs, and allied fields such as social work, adult education, and psychology. A considerable portion of practitioners, however, enter the student affairs field following graduate study in other disciplines ranging from Russian literature to religion to physics.

Even though it may be appealing to think about restricting entry by controlling the academic preparation programs through which new members are recruited—as has been the model for law and medicine—that does not seem feasible for student affairs, and many people would argue that it is undesirable. The leadership of many colleges and universities would most likely resist such a proposal as unnecessarily restrictive of discretionary powers and as inflationary. Because student affairs does not have (and is unlikely to ever have) control or sanctioning power over the institutions in which its members work, as does law and medicine, there is little likelihood that control of the professional preparation programs' selection processes and curricula can become the primary means of fueling a quantum leap in professionalization. Practitioners will continue to come into the field with a diversity of academic backgrounds for the foreseeable future. If that premise is accepted, then what can be done to promote professionalization?

We recommend the creation of an apprentice-like status in the field as one method of changing the current staffing practices. Instead of thinking about entry into the field as requiring a master's degree, we propose consideration of creating time-limited (perhaps from two to four years maximum) bachelor's-level positions. These initially would be in functional areas—such as admissions, residence life, and student activities—that currently tend to have multiple staff members at entry level and who have experience working with minimally prepared staff. Individuals would be recruited, according to this plan, who have an interest in the student affairs profession, have demonstrated talent or skill in working with people (especially students), and are interested in trying out the field. These positions would afford them an opportunity to explore what the field is all about and to test themselves against the demands and expectations professionals face. Such positions would require more training and closer supervision than is generally required when entry-level personnel who are graduates of reputable preparation programs are employed. An added benefit would be that some of these people would discover early on that student affairs is not an appropriate career.

If, after completing two to four years in the field, these apprentice practitioners wish to become student affairs professionals, they could seek enrollment in a professional preparation program. After completing their master's degree, which generally would be much more valuable because they would be better able to relate theory and research findings to their earlier work with students and organizations, the master's graduates would be prepared to make significantly greater contributions to their employing institutions. This plan would, of course, require restructuring of the present master's degree programs, but the restructured program would allow for greater depth of study and assistance with the acquisition of more sophisticated skills than is currently possible.

Such a proposal, if adopted, would place greater responsibilities on the institutions that employ the apprentice practitioners to provide a basic introduction to the field, its ethics, and careful and thorough training in basic skills such as programming, supervis-

ing, crisis intervention, paraprofessional-level counseling, and organizing. These responsibilities would necessitate having supervising
professionals on hand with the necessary skills and knowledge to
teach these basics and a restructuring of some position responsibilities. Professional preparation programs and professional associations could assist institutions in the apprentice practitioners'
initial orientation to the field by providing four- to six-week summer programs at conveniently located sites across the country.

This staffing schema would address a number of problems currently experienced in the field. A frequently heard complaint from
new professionals is that many of them find that their first jobs
require them to spend most of their time performing organizational
maintenance and other mundane tasks that, while undeniably necessary to the smooth functioning of the institution, do not generally
require the use of the more complex skills and knowledge they
learned in their graduate programs. From talent utilization and cost
perspectives, such assignments of master's-level credentialed staff is
not an efficient use of institutional resources. These kinds of tasks
that new professionals currently perform are important to the institution, but could as effectively be done by apprentice practitioners.

This approach would also conserve resources of preparation
programs and those enrolled therein. Frequently, students with
minimal experience in student affairs complete preparation programs only to discover that they have made mistakes; either they
are not well-suited temperamentally for student affairs practice or
they do not find the work as rewarding or interesting as they anticipated. By requiring (or at least strongly encouraging) practical
experience through an apprentice practitioner position prior to
beginning graduate study, those who enroll should have a clearer
vision of what they seek professionally and a better understanding
of themselves as student affairs professionals and of what is
required to build a career in the field.

This proposal is not a return to staffing patterns of the 1940s
and 1950s, when few practitioners held graduate degrees in the
field. In no way does this proposal advocate less preparation for
practice in the field. Instead, the proposal addresses a problem of
handling certain duties of student affairs through a more highly
differentiated staffing pattern. It envisions another rung on the
ladder of professional growth by inserting a staffing category at the

entry level, but its intentions are to limit time in this category and to encourage movement from it with enhanced potential for later professionalism and contributions to the field.

New Roles for Professional Associations

From their inception, professional associations in student affairs have sought to keep their members informed about developments in the field and to stimulate continued professional growth. To a significant extent, this is accomplished through annual conventions and conferences. The approach generally used is similar to a smorgasbord: a broad array of programs and activities are laid before members who select what they like and participate to the degree they choose. Much of what has been offered lacked depth because of the time limitations imposed by a convention format and the desire to cover as many topics as possible. Although this approach is likely to satisfy many diners' appetites, it does nothing to assure that they receive a balanced, nutritious diet that will sustain their health.

If practitioners were skilled at assessing their professional development needs and self-disciplined enough to seek what they need rather than what suits their individual preferences, this approach might be an effective means of continuing professional education. For many people, such is not the case; from our observations, professionals are similar to students in that they tend to seek out programs that build on their strengths rather than address their weaknesses (Hess and Winston, 1995).

We propose that professional associations develop means to assist practitioners in assessing their professional development needs, especially in identifying their weaknesses, and in tailoring educational programs to strengthen inadequate areas. Perhaps this can be accomplished through a consortium of professional associations, which will be discussed later in this chapter. If our proposal for experimentation with apprentice practitioner-type staffing were adopted, then professional associations would be morally obligated to assist in the development of a training curriculum and in providing the initial training of these staff.

The fact is, however, that professional associations must develop means for continuing professional education that go beyond current practice that is centered on group gatherings at workshops, conferences, and conventions with loosely defined and almost totally uncontrolled expectations for learning. Some system that focuses on individualized learning is absolutely necessary, in our opinion. We envision a system that is self-motivated and self-regulated and open routinely for participation by all members of the profession. The rudiments of a model for this type of practice exists in CAS, where standards of practice are promulgated to be employed as self-regulating and self-assessing mechanisms for program improvement. Of course, setting up a system that would provide access to all members of the student affairs field—perhaps 40,000 or more individuals—is a daunting task. But that is precisely the challenge for the professional associations.

No doubt this proposal, if adopted, would require extensive cooperation and participation by employing institutions if it is to work. They have the most powerful hold over rewards for individual improvement; they normally provide support for staff development activities. It is the professional associations, however, that have the knowledge and expertise and, in our opinion, the ethical and moral obligation to provide the content of programs, and to a considerable extent the motivation for, individual staff growth and constant improvement. This strongly suggests the need for the establishment of several quality assurance mechanisms at a national level.

Greater Integration of Professional Preparation and Practice

Since the emergence of professional preparation programs in student affairs, there has been a certain level of tension between the faculty who teach in the programs and professional practitioners. Practitioners maintain that academic programs are too theoretical in their orientation and unsympathetic to the political realities of practice. Academics counter that practitioners are too utilitarian in their orientation, overly concerned with accomplishment of tasks without sound theoretical foundation, and too conservative to take risks for the sake of enhancing students' development.

To bridge these differences a model that assures collaboration is needed. We propose the adoption of a practice audit model developed originally by Queeney and Smutz (1990) that offers a conceptual framework for bridging this gap. We believe that the Queeney and Smutz seven-phase model would work in student affairs as it seems to have done in the pharmacy field where it was originally formulated:

- Create a professional team composed of faculty members and representatives of professional associations.
- Develop practice descriptions that outline the scope of practice (identification of all the tasks practitioners can be called upon to perform, even though no single practitioner is required to perform all of them).
- Develop performance assessment materials designed to determine practitioner strengths and weaknesses (the team creates exercises that measure practitioners' performance and establish performance standards that define the point at which practitioners' performance as a group is deemed acceptable).
- Administer a practice audit to a representative sample of practitioners.
- Analyze performance indicators and compare performance and standards.
- Design and plan continuing professional education programs that are directly related to the necessary skills and knowledge identified in the practice audit.
- Implement continuing professional education programs and evaluate their effectiveness.

It is likely, of course, that certain modifications to this model would need to be made to accommodate contingencies of the student affairs field, but an approach similar to the practice audit model would ensure that the content of continuing education is clearly and directly tied to daily practice and would increase opportunities to help practitioners understand existing theories and to develop their own theories of professional practice. This approach also would have the ultimate effect of creating specific knowledge for a continuing education curriculum for the profession. Professionals must take the lead in development of such an initiative.

New Quality Assurance Mechanisms

Consideration is due to ways of documenting the levels of skill and knowledge possessed by those who work in the field. As use of professional preparation programs does not seem capable of performing this function for persons entering the field and no mechanism exists for determining levels of competence for experienced practitioners, other strategies need to be considered.

We propose the establishment of a professional development institute, with the goals of providing volunteer professionals with a broad-based, multifaceted assessment of their knowledge and skills related to a functional level (for example, assessments normed for persons at entry-, mid-, and senior-level leadership, which might be further refined by functional area of specialty); coordinating continuing professional education activities and programs that would allow professionals to remedy identified weaknesses; and recording activities and accomplishments of the continuing education of professionals. The last might be accomplished by the establishment of a professional registry for individual student affairs practitioners, but we envision a more comprehensive initiative embodied in the academy.

This proposal is based on the principles enumerated by the joint ACPA-NASPA Quality Assurance Task Force Report (see Appendix C): "Professional associations, while necessarily operating interdependently with employing institutions, are the entities most responsible for quality assurance of professional practice; and . . . professional associations, working in concert with employing institutions, are the entities most likely to bring about change toward improved professional practice" (Creamer and others, 1992, p. 15). According to this view, professional associations have an ethical responsibility to create appropriate mechanisms to assure quality practice in the field. They are, in fact, the only existing agencies with the capabilities to handle such a responsibility.

It seems unlikely that any one professional association could undertake such an important and massive project alone. As the experience of creating minimum professional practice standards through the Council for the Advance of Standards in Higher Education (CAS) has clearly demonstrated, through collaboration and consensus seeking it is possible to speak for the whole profession. No single association can do so.

Therefore, CAS or some similar consortium of professional associations is urged to consider the idea of the professional development institute and to assume leadership in exploring ways to improve the quality of programs and services offered students through improved staffing practices. Through this mechanism, professional associations could maintain their own identities and autonomy while cooperating through coordination of continuing education activities and lending expertise and financial support to the undertaking.

Proposed Research Agenda for Staffing Practices

Research on staffing practices in student affairs, and for that matter all of higher education, remains virtually virgin territory. Scholarly investigations into any aspect of staffing might be helpful to further establish baseline descriptive data and to provide the foundation for the study of causal relationships in the practices. Despite all that we have learned and reported here, there is much more that needs to be explored through systematic study. As we have noted repeatedly, there is little in the student affairs literature about staffing, and not much more in higher education except for faculty appraisal information on promotion and tenure. There is a considerable body of knowledge in the business literature, but much of it has limited application in higher education.

Beyond more descriptive studies of staffing practices, we see specific need for further research into the role of institution-specific conditions or variables and the role of individual behavior in staffng practices.

Regarding institutional conditions, we propose studies that seek to answer research questions such as the following:

- What are the effects of institutional leadership, culture, policy, values, and structure on staffing practices in student affairs?
- What is the relationship between institutional type, such as research universities, comprehensive state universities, small liberal arts colleges, and two-year community colleges, and student affairs staffing practices?
- Are distinctive staffing practices associated with demographic factors such as institutional size or geographical location?

Regarding individual behavior and staffing practices, we suggest studies that investigate research questions such as the following:

- How do individual characteristics such as personality attributes affect specific staffing practices, such as supervision and performance appraisal?
- How do gender and ethnicity affect staffing practices, especially in supervision, staff development, and performance appraisal?
- We know that different types of people are attracted to different functional areas in student affairs (seldom would someone seeking a student activities position be equally attracted to a position in financial aid, for instance); what is the relationship between personal attributes of staff and their effectiveness in specific functional areas of student affairs?
- Does the application of conceptual models of staffing such as synergistic supervision improve staff performance?
- Does the use of behaviorally anchored performance data improve approaches to staff evaluation and improvement?

Evaluation studies also are needed. We need program evaluation models, and we need to test different models for their effectiveness in all staffing areas discussed in this book. We also need models of training, and we need to test them for effectiveness, especially regarding supervision, staff development, and performance appraisal.

Concluding Remarks

Despite the vital link between staffing practices and the achievement of quality in higher education, staffing practices have been neglected by scholars and educational leaders far too long. They have been treated within institutions and professional associations as if no special knowledge or expertise is required to create and sustain them. While acknowledging their essential nature, staffing practices in student affairs have been managed perfunctorily and without the aid of scholarship. This book is an attempt to begin correcting this condition.

Our approach was multifaceted if not completely comprehensive; through it we gained much knowledge about staffing practices, and we share our insights throughout this book. As with most research projects, however, the conclusion of one phase is but the beginning of others. We now urge a concerted and widespread involvement of professionals in the field to advance our knowledge and to sharpen our skills in this vital aspect of the higher-education enterprise. What we discovered and report here must now be used to further practice and to expand scholarship in all aspects of staffing in student affairs.

Appendix A

Staffing Survey
Methodology, Instruments, and Supplemental Data

Following is a description of the survey research strategy reported in Chapter Four.

The research plan called for collecting data from four categories of institutions (research universities, comprehensive colleges and universities, liberal arts colleges, and two-year colleges) from three geographical regions of the United States. Within each region, however, there were fewer than fifty institutions in certain categories. When this was so, all available institutions were chosen. In one instance in the Northeast region, fifty-one liberal arts colleges were selected; two colleges had combined and appeared in the Integrated Postsecondary Education Data System (IPEDS) as a single institution but still had two deans of students, and at their requests that institution was treated as two separate institutions.

The final sample was drawn by Darryl E. Harris of Pinkerton Computer Consultants, Inc., who had access to the IPEDS[1] data files and agreed to help with the selection. (The complete list of

Note: We gratefully acknowledge grants received from the College of Education at Virginia Polytechnic and State University and the School of Professional Studies in the College of Education at the University of Georgia, which enabled us to conduct the surveys reported herein.

[1] IPEDS data are compiled from reports made to the National Center for Educational Statistics, U.S. Department of Education, Office of Educational Research and Improvement.

151 institutions that actually provided data is shown in Exhibit A.1 at the end of the appendix; they are displayed by region and institutional type.)

The first step in the data collection plan involved contacting by mail the chief student affairs administrator (referred to hereafter as the vice president) of each of the identified institutions. The letters contained a short description of the proposed study and a request for the vice president's participation and support, with the option to decline. Many did decline, often citing arrival of the request at a very busy time for them (Spring 1994). Several noted that financial shortfalls in their budgets were forcing them to restructure their organizations and that this resulting instability of their organizations and a lack of time to assist us was the basis of their decision to decline.

Participation for the vice presidents included indicating whether any part of five functional areas were a part of the student affairs division at that institution, providing a list (preferably a set of labels) of all the professional staff in student affairs by functional area, and agreeing to answer (at a later date) an extensive set of questions about institutional policies related to staffing and a scale concerning their approach to supervising staff. By agreeing to participate, the vice presidents also agreed to assist in the distribution of questionnaires to as many as ten staff members (identified by the researchers) on their campuses.

Of the 491 institutions in the original sample, vice presidents at 194 institutions (31 percent) agreed to participate. Of the 194 vice presidents, responses from staff at 151 institutions (78 percent) actually completed questionnaires. In the end, 121 usable questionnaires were received from vice presidents and 816[2] from staff members.

Responses were sought from the vice president at each institution in the sample and from two staff members from each of five functional areas in student affairs. The five areas entailed grouping of the following units:

- Enrollment services: admissions, financial aid, registrar, and retention services and programs

---

[2]Because not all instruments were complete, the total number of responses to any given question varies by as much as 10 percent.

- Housing: housing, residential life, and dining services
- Campus activities: student union, student activities, recreational sports and intramurals, concerts and lectures, Greek life, community service programs, judicial services and discipline, new-student orientation, and student media
- Student health: medical and dental services, wellness programs, sex education programs, and drug and alcohol education programs
- Student support services: counseling, career services, academic advising, academic assistance, international student services, minority student programs, women's programs, chaplains, and child care

When the lists of staff names by functional area were returned, samples were drawn systematically from each so as to yield at least one (if the functional area existed on the campus) and not more than two persons in each area. Questionnaires were placed in envelopes with the staff member's name affixed.

Instruments

Three questionnaires were designed for use in the staffing study. The Vice President's Staffing Practices Survey was sent to all vice presidents in the sample. The Student Affairs Staffing Survey was divided into two forms, A and B. This device was used to reduce the overall length of the staffing survey for any one staff member. It was reasoned that the sampling selection procedures used by the researchers would not yield any known differences among respondents. Staff members selected were randomly sent either Form A or Form B, but not both, to accomplish this purpose.

Ideally, it was planned that one staff member in each functional area would receive Form A of the questionnaire and one staff member would receive Form B. In many instances, however, either no staff were reported in a particular area or only one was listed. In these cases, attempts were made to equalize the number of Form A and Form B surveys sent to a particular campus.

Next, a package was sent to each vice president who agreed to participate and who provided a list of staff members by functional area containing one Vice President's Staffing Practices Survey and

Forms A and B of the Student Affairs Staffing Survey with the names of selected staff members affixed on each form. The vice presidents were asked to distribute the forms to the staff members named and to request that the completed surveys be returned in sealed envelopes marked "staffing survey" either to the vice presidents' office or directly to the researchers. The vice presidents returned all completed surveys that were sent to them in a single package.

Categories

The following categories of information were included in the study: institutional and personal demographics, staff recruitment and selection, position orientation, approaches to supervision, supervision received, supervision given, performance evaluations, staff development, and job satisfaction. These categories varied by form:

- Vice President's Staffing Practices Survey included demographic information, institutional policy and practices in the areas of staff recruitment and selection, staff development, and performance evaluation; personal approach to supervising staff.
- Student Affairs Staffing Survey Form A included demographic information, personal approaches to supervision, job satisfaction, and staff development activities.
- Student Affairs Staffing Survey Form B included demographic information, topics covered in supervision received and supervision given, position orientation activities experienced, and performance appraisal experiences.

Exhibit A.1. Colleges and Universities That Participated in Staffing Survey.

REGION: MIDWEST
Research Universities
Case Western Reserve University
Indiana University
Ohio State University
University of Illinois-Chicago
University of Illinois-Urbana/Champaign
University of Iowa
University of Minnesota-Twin Cities
University of Missouri-Columbia
Washington University
Wayne State University
Liberal Arts Colleges
Beloit College
Calumet College of St. Joseph
Carthage College
Coe College
Concordia College (Minnesota)
Grace College
Grand View College
Illinois College
Malone College
Oberlin College
Siena Heights College
Upper Iowa University
Wheaton College
Comprehensive Colleges and Universities
Anderson University
Ashland University
Augsburg College
Baldwin-Wallace College
Cedarville College
Central Missouri State University
Drury College
Illinois Wesleyan University
Indiana University-Kokomo

Indiana University/Purdue University-Fort Wayne
Lawrence Technical University
Mankato State University
Maryville University
Southeast Missouri State University
University of Northern Iowa
University of St. Thomas
Webster University
Community Colleges
Anoka-Ramsey Community College
Belmont Technical College
College of DuPage
Firelands College of Bowling Green State University
Hawkeye Community College
Joliet Junior College
Itasca Community College
Kishwaukee College
Lakeshore Technical College
Longview Community College
Mesabi Community College
Northcentral Technical College
Ohio State University-Lima
Rainy River Community College
Southeastern Community College
Southwest Wisconsin Technical College
Triton College
Truman College-City Colleges, Chicago
University of Minnesota-Crookston
Washington State Community College
Waukesha County Technical College (Ohio)
Worthington Community College
REGION: NORTHEAST
Research University
State University of New York-Albany
Liberal Arts Colleges
Bradford College
D'Youville College
Gordon College
Keuka College

Long Island University-Southhampton
Purchase College-State University of New York
University of Maine-Presque Isle
Vassar College
Comprehensive Colleges and Universities
Bridgewater State College
Dominican College of Blauvaldt
Dowling College
Keane State College
Merrimack College
Plymouth State College
Providence College
Rivier College
Saint Bonaventure University
Saint Francis College
Salem State College
Simmons College
Springfield College
State University of New York-Geneseo
Community Colleges
Adirondack Community College
Bunker Hill Community College
Capital Community Technical College
Dutchess Community College
Manchester Community-Technical College
Mater Dei College
Naugatuck Valley Community-Technical College
Niagara County Community College
North Shore Community College
State University of New York-Morrisville
Westchester Community College
REGION: WEST
Research Universities
Arizona State University
Oregon State University
University of California-Irvine
University of California-Santa Barbara
University of Oregon
Washington State University

Liberal Arts Colleges
California Baptist College
College of Notre Dame
Holy Names College
Marylhurst College of Lifelong Learning
Pacific University
Reed College
Saint Martin's College
Western Baptist College
Westmont College
Comprehensive Colleges and Universities
Boise State University
California State University-Bakersfield
California State University-Chico
California State University-Hayward
California State University-Los Angeles
California State University-Northridge
California State University-Sacramento
California State University-Stanislaus
Chapman University
Eastern Oregon State College
Eastern Washington University
Point Loma Nazarene College
San Jose State University
Santa Clara University
Seattle University
Southern Oregon State College
University of LaVerne
University of Nevada-Las Vegas
University of the Pacific
University of Puget Sound
University of Redlands
University of San Diego
Western Washington University
Whittier College
Community Colleges
Bassist College
Canada College
Chaffey College

Citrus College
College of the Redwoods
Fresno City College
Laney College
Mira Costa College
North Seattle Community College
Northern Nevada Community College
Tacoma Community College
Victor Valley College
Walla Walla Community College
Western Nevada Community College

Exhibit A.2. Vice President's Staffing Practices Survey.

Institution Name: _____

Source of primary support: *(Check one.)*
___ Public
___ Private—Does it have an affiliation?
     ___ No
     ___ Yes—With? _____

Approximate headcount credit enrollment during Fall 1993: _____

Approximate full-time-equivalent credit enrollment during
Fall 1993:_____

Please indicate the total number of staff members in the Student Affairs
Division in each of the following categories: [See definitions in the
cover letter.]
____ Professionals
____ Allied Professionals
____ Support Staff
____ Graduate Assistants
____ Undergraduate Student Paraprofessional, such as resident
     assistants or tutors [Do not include part-time student workers,
     such as desk clerks, file clerks, or maintenance staff.]
____ Other—Specify: _____

What percentage of the total institutional budget was assigned to the Student Affairs Division in academic year 1992–1993? *(Check one.)*
___ 5% or less
___ 6–10%
___ 11–15%
___ 16–20%
___ 21% or more

Does the institution operate residence halls? *(Check one.)*
___ No
___ Yes—Housing how many residents? _____

What is the approximate population of the city, town, or area in which your institution is located? *(Check one.)*
___ 10,000 or less
___ 10,001–25,000
___ 25,001–50,000
___ 50,001–75,000
___ 75,001–100,000
___ 100,001–150,000
___ 150,001–200,000
___ More than 200,000

Staff Recruitment and Selection

Who usually prepares position descriptions in student affairs? *(Check one.)*
___ Vice President for Student Affairs
___ Department Head who has staff vacancy
___ Search committee named by the Vice President for Student Affairs
___ Search committee named by the Department Head
___ Staff within the department where the vacancy occurred
___ Institutional Personnel Office
___ Other—Specify: _____

Who usually prepares position announcements? *(Check one.)*
___ Vice President for Student Affairs
___ Department Head who has staff vacancy
___ Search committee named by the Vice President for Student Affairs
___ Search committee named by the Department Head
___ Staff within the department where the vacancy occurred
___ Institutional Personnel Office
___ Other—Specify: _____

Where are position announcements usually published for mid-level student affairs administrators (e.g., Department Heads)? *(Check all that apply.)*
___ Institutional house organ
___ Local public media
___ National public media
___ *Chronicle of Higher Education*
___ Regional professional media (including job banks and placement services)
___ National professional media (including job banks and placement services)
___ Professional student affairs conferences
___ Other—Specify: _____

Where are position announcements usually published for entry-level student affairs staff? *(Check all that apply.)*
___ Institutional house organ
___ Local public media
___ National public media
___ *Chronicle of Higher Education*
___ Regional professional media (including job banks and placement services)
___ National professional media (including job banks and placement services)
___ Professional student affairs conferences
___ Other—Specify: _____

Where are position announcements usually published for allied professional staff? *(Check all that apply.)*
___ Institutional house organ
___ Local public media
___ National public media
___ *Chronicle of Higher Education*
___ Regional professional media (including job banks and placement services)
___ National professional media (including job banks and placement services)
___ Professional student affairs conferences
___ Allied professional conferences (e.g., medicine, nursing, accounting)
___ Other—Specify: _____

If search committees usually are employed in hiring, what are their responsibilities? *(Check all that apply).* ( )**Do not use search committees** [Go to next question].
___ Prepare position announcement
___ Publish announcement
___ Establish screening process
___ Publish screening procedures
___ Establish selection process
___ Publish selection process
___ Screen applicants to determine if minimum qualifications are satisfied
___ Select who is to be interviewed
___ Recommend a list to be interviewed
___ Coordinate on-campus interviews
___ Recommend a candidate to be hired
___ Submit a rank-ordered list of qualified candidates
___ Submit an unranked list of qualified candidates
___ Select a candidate to whom to make an offer
___ Contact candidate and make an offer
___ Negotiate hiring terms/salary with candidate
___ Other—Specify: _____

Which policies and procedures govern the staff recruitment and selection process? *(Check all that apply.)*
___ Written institutional policies
___ Written student affairs division policies
___ Written student affairs department policies
___ Ad hoc policies formulated by the Vice President each time there is a search
___ Ad hoc policies formulated by the department in which there is a vacancy each time there is a search
___ Policies formulated by each search committee
___ Other—Specify: _____

Who is usually the *primary* decision maker about selection/hiring of each category of staff? Record your response by entering the appropriate single number in the space before each category of staff.
1 = President
2 = Vice President for Student Affairs
3 = Department Head
4 = Search Committee
5 = Department staff as a group
6 = Direct Supervisor
7 = Other (identify in margin)

____ Department Heads/Director
____ Mid-Level Professional Staff (e.g., Associate/Assistant Department Heads/Directors)

____ Entry-Level Professional Staff
____ Allied Professionals (e.g., physicians, lawyers, accountants)
____ Support Staff (full-time)
____ Student paraprofessionals (e.g., resident assistants, tutors, peer counselors)
____ Student Support Staff (e.g., desk clerks, security staff, file clerks)

Approximately what percent of the total Student Affairs budget in 1992–93 was spent on recruitment and selection of staff in all categories? *(Check one.)*
____ Nothing
____ Less than 1%
____ 1–2%
____ 3–4%
____ 5–6%
____ 7–8%
____ 9% or more

Is there a written Division statement of ethics governing selection and hiring of staff? *(Check one.)*
____ No
____ Yes [Please attach a copy.]

Is there a written Student Affairs Division affirmative action policy statement or action plan? *(Check one.)*
____ No
____ Yes [Please attach a copy.]

How are applicants for professional and allied professional staff vacancies who already are employed by the institution handled? *(Check the single best response.)*
____ In-house applicants are treated exactly as other applicants
____ Decision is made about hiring/promoting in-house applicants before publicly announcing vacancies
____ In-house applicants are discouraged from applying for vacancies
____ In-house applicants are placed in applicant pool and are given preference
____ In-house applicants are not given preference, but always are interviewed
____ Other—Specify: _____

Staff Development

Does the Student Affairs Division have an annual budget (planned budget line) specifically for staff development? *(Check one.)*
___ No
___ Yes

Approximately what percentage of the total Student Affairs budget was spent in 1992–93 for *on-campus* staff development activities?
___ Nothing
___ Less than 1%
___ 1–2%
___ 3–4%
___ 5–6%
___ 7% or more

Approximately what percentage of the total Student Affairs budget was spent in 1992–93 for off-campus staff development activites? [*Exclude* attendance at professional association conventions.]
___ None (0%)
___ Less than 1%
___ 1–2%
___ 3–4%
___ 5–6%
___ 7% or more

Identify on-campus staff development activities that were conducted in 1992–93. (Specify the number of times each activity took place. Place a zero (0) in the space if the activity did not take place.)
___ Division social event (reception, holiday party, etc.)
___ Invited speaker (spoke to total Division)
___ Workshop for Division volunteers (2–4 hours in duration)
___ Workshop for Division volunteers (5–8 hours in duration)
___ Workshop for Division volunteers (9+ hours in duration)
___ Workshop for department staff (2–4 hours in duration)
___ Workshop for department staff (5–8 hours in duration)
___ Workshop for department staff (9+ hours in duration)
___ Other—Specify: _____

Does the Student Affairs Division have a written policy about staff development? *(Check one)*

___ No
___ Yes [Please attach a copy.]

How is Division staff development managed? *(Check the single best response.)*
___ Division committee plans and organizes
___ Division staff member responsible for staff development activities
___ Staff development is solely the responsibility of departments
___ Staff development is solely an individual responsibility
___ Staff development is a coordinated effort between the division and departments
___ Staff development at division level and in departments is conducted independently
___ Other—Specify: _____

Approaches to Supervision

Based on your experience supervising staff during the *previous twelve months,* select the response (1, 2, 3, or 4) that best describes your approach to supervising each of three categories of staff. If more than one response describes your approach to supervision, select the single response that you consider the most important or that you make most frequently. Write the number that corresponds to your chosen response in the space provided to the left of each item. If you did not *directly* supervise a category of staff, leave the corresponding spaces blank. Please identify your actual approach in each category and do not worry if some of your choices are repeated across staff categories.

Professionals & Allied Professionals	Support Staff	Paraprofessionals	
___	___	___	The fundamental principle upon which I based supervision was 1. sharing responsibility with staff 2. providing freedom for staff to work 3. maintaining attentive oversight of staff 4. sustaining warm personal relations with staff
___	___	___	The most important goal of supervision was to 1. establish a shared commitment to goals 2. establish rapport between people

Professionals &
Allied Professionals

Support Staff

Paraprofessionals

3. respect individual abilities
4. honor organizational authority

___ ___ ___   As a supervisor, I strived to
1. keep a watchful eye on all actions of staff
2. support friendly relations among staff
3. collaborate with staff on important work-related matters
4. provide adequate leeway for staff to conduct their work

___ ___ ___   My supervisory actions
1. advocated collaborative generation of information for decision making
2. allowed staff autonomy to generate information for decision making
3. provided information for decision making
4. discussed with staff the use of information in decision making

___ ___ ___   My supervision was most concerned with achieving goals of
1. departmental cohesion
2. the organization
3. individual professionals
4. upper level administrators

___ ___ ___   My supervision occurred
1. frequently, as a part of everyday interactions
2. irregularly, on an as-needed schedule
3. regularly and systematically
4. infrequently, when requested

___ ___ ___   I view supervision in the context of my own work as interactions to
1. enhance productivity
2. solidify relationships
3. encourage professonal autonomy
4. maintain clear work instructions

Professionals & Allied Professionals	Support Staff	Paraprofessionals

___ ___ ___   I felt most successful as a supervisor when the staff was fully knowledgeable about
1. the relationships among staff
2. the organization and its goals
3. the work-related concerns of the staff
4. the instructions I provided about work expectations

___ ___ ___   My relationship with staff who I supervise is based primarily on
1. shared commitment to excellence
2. desire to allow maximum individual autonomy of action and style
3. institutional definitions of responsibilities
4. camaraderie and esprit d'corp

___ ___ ___   A central focus of my supervisory sessions with staff was
1. encouraging both personal and professional growth
2. sharing personal and job-related experiences
3. solving job-related problems
4. auditing job performance

___ ___ ___   Conflicts between the staff and me were handled by my
1. assuming responsibility and directing compliance
2. seeking consensus
3. finding common ground for achieving agreed-upon goals
4. yielding liberty to staff with accountability

___ ___ ___   In my experience, poor staff performance resulted in
1. failure to achieve staff goals
2. jeopardizing my authority to get the necessary work done
3. endangering of personal relationships within the department
4. creating disequilibrium in productivity among individual staff

Professionals & Allied Professionals	Support Staff	Paraprofessionals	
___	___	___	I handled poor staff performance by 1. helping staff design better strategies 2. encouraging staff to find solutions to problems 3. instructing staff about how to avoid the problem or handle the situation 4. showing personal support for continued effort at improved performance
___	___	___	In my supervision, I held to the belief that the single most important attribute of my relationship with staff was 1. respect for authority 2. harmony among people 3. commitment to mutually derived goals 4. independence of action
___	___	___	My communications with staff during supervision sessions were typified by 1. deliberation about duties and assignments 2. dialogue about personal concerns 3. discussions about how our goals/responsibilities might be better accomplished 4. exchanges about equivalent responsibilities
___	___	___	When the "system" or organizational structure got in the way of accomplished goals, I acted to 1. join in devising ways to overcome the barriers 2. allow methods to get around the organizational barriers 3. explain how the organization works and what accommodations are required of staff 4. help staff to understand the limitations of the organization and commended them to continued effort
___	___	___	When conflicts occurred between a staff member whom I supervised and other units of the organization, I 1. intervened to achieve compliance with institutional policies and procedures

Professionals &
Allied Professionals

Support Staff

Paraprofessionals

2. supported and defended my staff member
3. mediated the dissension
4. allowed the staff member to deal with the matter

___ ___ ___ My values as a supervisor are most attuned to principles of
1. respect for authority
2. humanism
3. democratic decision making
4. professional autonomy

___ ___ ___ When making difficult personnel decisions as a
supervisor, I found it most helpful when
1. commitment to goals was mutually shared
2. institutional policies and procedures were fairly
administered
3. relations among staff were cordial
4. respect for independence among professionals was
honored

___ ___ ___ Personal and professional development needs of staff
were determined by
1. establishing discrepancies between institutional
requirements and current staff attributes
2. supervisor and staff collaboratively
3. staff preferences for future growth
4. staff member's personal interest

___ ___ ___ The context of planning for future growth of staff was
1. combined institutional and individual need
2. individual self-assessed interests
3. individual need
4. institutional need

___ ___ ___ In my supervision of staff, individual fit with the
institutional culture was viewed as
1. a significant determinant for success

Professionals &
Allied Professionals

Support Staff

Paraprofessionals

   2. a matter of staff member choice
   3. irrelevant, so long as a sense of community is achieved
   4. optional, so long as a sense of community is achieved

___ ___ ___   When things went wrong for staff members, I tended to
   1. look for an explanation jointly between the organization and the staff member
   2. offer direct advice for corrective action
   3. champion the staff member to bolster confidence
   4. expect the staff member to find a solution or ask for help

Performance Evaluations

How frequently are performance evaluations usually conducted in the Student Affairs Division? Use the following code:

   1 = Never   4 = Twice a year
   2 = Irregularly   5 = Three times a year
   3 = Once a year   6 = Four or more times a year

___ Professional staff
___ Allied professional staff
___ Support staff

Are performance evaluations of professional and allied professional staff regularly reviewed by administrators above the one who performed the initial evaluation? *(Check one.)*
___ No
___ Yes

Is training provided for conducting performance evaluations of student affairs professionals?
___ No
___ Yes—Explain: _____

Are there specific policies/procedures in place for following up performance evaluations?

___ No
___ Yes—Explain: _____

Demographic Information

Highest degree earned: *(Check one.)*
___ High school and/or technical school diploma   ___ Master's
___ Associate   ___ Doctorate
___ Baccalaureate

Major field of highest degree earned: *(Check one.)*
___ Student Affairs
___ Counseling or Counseling Psychology
___ Higher Education
___ Allied Field (such as medicine, nursing, law, recreation, etc.)
___ Other Fields (such as English, biology, Russian literature, or
    philosophy)

Are you currently pursuing further degrees? *(Check one.)*
___ Yes ___ No

Sex *(Check one.)*
___ Female   ___ Male

Racial/Ethnic Background *(Check single best response.)*
___ African American   ___ Asian American or Pacific Islander
___ Caucasian/White American (non-Hispanic)
___ Hispanic American ___ Other: Specify: _____

Age *(Check one.)*
___ 25 or younger   ___ 31–35 ___ 41–45 ___ 51–55 ___ 61–65
___ 26–30   ___ 36–40 ___ 46–50 ___ 56–60 ___ 66 or
                                                      older

Years (including the current year) worked in Student Affairs as a
professional or allied professional *(Check one.)*
___ 1–3   ___ 7–9   ___ 13–15   ___ 19–21
___ 4–6   ___ 10–12   ___ 16–18   ___ 22 or more

Years (including the current year) worked in student affairs as a
professional or allied professional at current institution *(Check one.)*
___ 1–3   ___ 7–9   ___ 13–15   ___ 19–21
___ 4–6   ___ 10–12   ___ 16–18   ___ 22 or more

Current membership in *national* professional organizations *(Please do not use acronyms.)*

_____

_____

_____

_____

_____

Current membership in *regional* professional organizations *(Please do not use acronyms.)*

_____

_____

_____

How many staff members in each of the following categories do you personally/directly supervise currently? *(See cover letter for definitions. Write in total number for each category.)*

____ Student Affairs Professionals

____ Allied Professional Student Affairs Staff

____ Full-Time Support Staff

____ Part-Time Support Staff (including students such as work study)

____ Graduate Assistants

____ Undergraduate Paraprofessionals

Nomination of Noteworthy Programs

We plan to conduct a limited number of interviews or case studies of student affairs divisions or departments that have noteworthy staffing practices. Could you identify exemplary staffing practices (whether at your institution or at another with which you are familiar)? The practice may be for all aspects of staffing or for a particularly impressive aspect such as staff selection, staff development, or performance evaluation. (Please provide information on a separate sheet.)

• Briefly describe the practice/program.

• Please identify a contact person, including address, and telephone number.

Please return survey, staff manual, copies of requested policy statements (if available) and your staff's responses to:

Dr. Don G. Creamer
College of Education
Virginia Tech
Blacksburg, VA 24061-0302

Exhibit A.3. Student Affairs Staffing Survey, Form A.

Employing Institution: _____

Position title: *(Check one best response.)*
___ Vice President
___ Associate/Assistant Vice President
___ Dean
___ Associate/Assistant Dean
___ Department Head/Director
___ Associate/Assistant Department Head/Director
___ Coordinator
___ Nonadministrative position (e.g., physician, psychologist, or accountant)

Position classification: (Definitions provided in the cover letter.) *(Check one best response.)*
___ Professional Staff   ___ Support Staff
___ Allied Professional Staff   ___ Paraprofessional Staff

Number of administrators/levels of administration between you and the Vice President for Student Affairs: *(Check one.)*
___ 0   ___ 1   ___ 2   ___ 3   ___ 4 or more

Highest degree earned: (Check one.)
___ High school and/or technical school diploma   ___ Master's
___ Associate   ___ Doctorate
___ Baccalaureate   ___ Other—Specify _____

Major field of highest degree earned: *(Check one.)*
___ Student Affairs
___ Counseling or Counseling Psychology
___ Higher Education
___ Allied Field (such as medicine, nursing, law, recreation, etc.)
___ Other Fields (such as English, biology, Russian literature, or philosophy)

Are you currently pursuing further degrees? *(Check one.)*
___ Yes   ___ No

Sex *(Check one.)*
___ Female   ___ Male

Racial/Ethnic Background *(Check single best response.)*
___ African American   ___ Asian American or Pacific Islander
___ Caucasian/White American (non-Hispanic)
___ Hispanic American ___ Native American
___ Other: Specify: _____

Age *(Check one.)*
___ 25 or younger   ___ 31–35 ___ 41–45 ___ 51–55 ___ 61–65
___ 26–30   ___ 36–40 ___ 46–50 ___ 56–60 ___ 66 or
                                                        older

Years (including the current year) worked in Student Affairs as a professional or allied professional: *(Check one.)*
___ 1–3   ___ 7–9   ___ 13–15   ___ 19–21
___ 4–6   ___ 10–12   ___ 16–18   ___ 22 or more

Years (including the current year) worked in Student Affairs as a professional or allied professional at current institution: *(Check one.)*
___ 1–3   ___ 7–9   ___ 13–15   ___ 19–21
___ 4–6   ___ 10–12   ___ 16–18   ___ 22 or more

Current membership in *national* professional organizations *(Please do not use acronyms.)*

_____
_____
_____
_____
_____

Current membership in *regional* professional organizations *(Please do not use acronyms.)*

_____

_____

_____

How many staff members in each of the following categories do you personally/directly supervise currently? *(See cover letter for definitions. Write in total number for each category.)*

____ Student Affairs Professionals
____ Allied Professional Student Affairs Staff
____ Full-Time Support Staff
____ Part-Time Support Staff (including students such as work study)
____ Graduate Assistants
____ Undergraduate Paraprofessionals

Indicate the functional areas in which you have assigned responsibility by ranking them. Assign 1 for the most time consuming, 2 for less time consuming, and 3 for the least time consuming responsibility. (Do not rank all the functional areas. Many staff members will work in a single functional area; if that is the case, enter a 1 before that functional area.)

____ Academic Assistance
____ Academic Advising
____ Admissions
____ Alcohol/Drug Education
____ Campus Activities
     (including Greek Life)
____ Career Planning &
     Placement
____ Child Care
____ Community Service
____ Counseling and Testing
____ Facilities Management
     (across functional areas)
____ Financial Aid
____ Housing and Residence Life
____ International Students

____ Judicial (discipline)
____ Minority Student Programs
____ Orientation
____ Registrar
____ Research and/or Evaluation
____ Recreational Sports
____ Staff Development and Training
____ Student Affairs Division
     Administration (across areas)
____ Student Health
____ Student Union
____ Women's Programs
____ Other: _____

Approaches to Supervision

Based on your experience supervising staff during the *previous twelve months,* select the response (1, 2, 3, or 4) that best describes your approach to supervising each of three categories of staff. If more than one response applies to your approach to supervision, select the single response that you consider the most important or that you make most frequently. Write the number that corresponds to your chosen response in the space provided to the left of each item. If you did not *directly* supervise a category of staff, leave the corresponding spaces blank. Please identify your actual approach in each category and do not worry if some of your choices are repeated across staff categories.

Professionals & Allied Professionals   Support Staff   Paraprofessionals

___ ___ ___   The fundamental principle upon which I based supervision was
1. sharing responsibility with staff
2. providing freedom for staff to work
3. maintaining attentive oversight of staff
4. sustaining warm personal relations with staff

___ ___ ___   The most important goal of supervision was to
1. establish a shared commitment to goals
2. support rapport between people
3. respect individual abilities
4. honor organizational authority

___ ___ ___   As a supervisor, I strived to
1. keep a watchful eye on all actions of staff
2. support friendly relations among staff
3. collaborate with staff on important work-related matters
4. provide adequate leeway for staff to conduct their work

___ ___ ___   My supervisory actions
1. advocated collaborative generation of information for decision making
2. allowed staff autonomy to generate information for decision making
3. provided information for decision making
4. discussed with staff the use of information in decision making

Professionals &
Allied Professionals

Support Staff

Paraprofessionals

___ ___ ___ My supervision was most concerned with achieving goals of
1. departmental cohesion
2. the organization
3. individual professionals
4. upper level administrators

___ ___ ___ My supervision occurred
1. frequently, as a part of everyday interactions
2. irregularly, on an as-needed schedule
3. regularly and systematically
4. infrequently, when requested

___ ___ ___ I view supervision in the context of my own work as
interactions to
1. enhance productivity
2. solidify relationships
3. encourage professional autonomy
4. maintain clear work instructions

___ ___ ___ I felt most successful as a supervisor when the staff was
fully knowledgeable about
1. the relationships among staff
2. the organization and its goals
3. the work-related concerns of the staff
4. the instructions I provided about work expectations

___ ___ ___ My relationship with staff who I supervise is based
primarily on
1. shared commitment to excellence
2. desire to allow maximum individual autonomy of
action and style
3. institutional definitions of responsibilities
4. camaraderie and esprit d'corp

___ ___ ___ A central focus of my supervisory sessions with staff was
1. encouraging both personal and professional growth

Professionals &
Allied Professionals

Support Staff

Paraprofessionals

2. sharing personal and job-related experiences
3. solving job-related problems
4. auditing job performance

___ ___ ___ Conflicts between the staff and me were handled by my
1. assuming responsibility and directing compliance
2. seeking consensus
3. finding common ground for achieving agreed-upon goals
4. yielding liberty to staff with accountability

___ ___ ___ In my experience, poor staff performance resulted in
1. failure to achieve staff goals
2. jeopardizing my authority to get the necessary work done
3. endangering of personal relationships within the department
4. creating disequilibrium in productivity among individual staff

___ ___ ___ I handled poor staff performance by
1. helping staff design better strategies
2. encouraging staff to find solutions to problems
3. instructing staff about how to avoid the problem or handle the situation
4. showing personal support for continued effort at improved performance

___ ___ ___ In my supervision, I held to the belief that the single most important attribute of my relationship with staff was
1. respect for authority
2. harmony among people
3. commitment to mutually derived goals
4. independence of action

Professionals &
Allied Professionals

Support Staff

Paraprofessionals

___ ___ ___ My communications with staff during supervision
sessions were typified by
1. deliberation about duties and assignments
2. dialogue about personal concerns
3. discussions about how our goals/responsibilities
   might be better accomplished
4. exchanges about equivalent responsibilities

___ ___ ___ When the "system" or organizational structure got in the
way of accomplished goals, I acted to
1. join in devising ways to overcome the barriers
2. allow methods to get around the organizational
   barriers
3. explain how the organization works and what
   accommodations are required of staff
4. help staff to understand the limitations of the organization and commended them to continued effort

___ ___ ___ When conflicts occurred between a staff member whom
I supervised and other units of the organization, I
1. intervened to achieve compliance with institutional
   policies and procedures
2. supported and defended my staff member
3. mediated the dissension
4. allowed the staff member to deal with the matter

___ ___ ___ My values as a supervisor are most attuned to
principles of
1. respect for authority
2. humanism
3. democratic decision making
4. professional autonomy

___ ___ ___ When making difficult personnel decisions as
supervisor, I found it most helpful when
1. commitment to goals was mutually shared

Professionals &
Allied Professionals
Support Staff
Paraprofessionals

2. institutional policies and procedures were fairly administered
3. relations among staff were cordial
4. respect for independence among professionals was honored

____ ____ ____ Personal and professional development needs of staff were determined by
1. establishing discrepancies between institutional requirements and current staff attributes
2. supervisor and staff collaboratively
3. staff preferences for future growth
4. staff member's personal interest

____ ____ ____ The context of planning for future growth of staff was
1. combined institutional and individual need
2. individual self-assessed interests
3. individual need
4. institutional need

____ ____ ____ In my supervision of staff, individual fit with the institutional culture was viewed as
1. a significant determinant for success
2. a matter of staff member choice
3. irrelevant, so long as a sense of community is achieved
4. optional, so long as a sense of community is achieved

____ ____ ____ When things went wrong for staff members, I tended to
1. look for an explanation jointly between the organization and the staff member
2. offer direct advice for corrective action
3. champion the staff member to bolster confidence
4. expect the staff member to find a solution or ask for help

Job Satisfaction

Circle the number that best represents your level of satisfaction with your current position.
1 = very dissatisfied (I will leave at the first opportunity.)
2 = dissatisfied (I will leave if a genuine opportunity arises.)
3 = neutral (I can take it or leave it.)
4 = satisfied (I like my position.)
5 = very satisfied (My position fulfills my highest expectations.)

What is the single most rewarding aspect of your current position?
(Check only one.)
___ working directly with students   ___ teaching through
___ creating educational programs   eduational programs
___ being a member of an   ___ dealing with intellectual
    educational community   matters
___ handling administrative duties   ___ solving complicated problems
___ managing budgets   ___ my own personal development
___ handling personnel matters   ___ salary
              ___ fringe benefits of working
                  in an academic community
              ___ Other: _____

Are you planning a career or job change within the next 12 months?
(Check one.)
___ No
___ Yes—Is the change to another position in student affairs or to a
    position outside student affairs?
    ___ **Another student affairs position**—*Check the single most*
    important reason for desiring to leave your current position.
      ___ desire for better pay
      ___ desire for more responsible position
      ___ incompatibility with institutional culture
      ___ conflict/disagreement with supervisor
      ___ better opportunities to help students
      ___ desire to get out of "live-in" requirements
      ___ spouse/significant other is moving
      ___ desire to change functional areas (e.g., go from
        housing to admissions)
      ___ desire to change type institution (e.g., go from public
        to private college or from four-year to two-year)

(Responses to this question continue on the next page.)

___ desire to live in another part of the country
___ need to move nearer to family/parent(s)
___ personal crisis or life change (e.g., death, divorce, or child birth)
___ desire to begin work on doctorate
___ Other: _____
___ **Position outside of student affairs**—*Check the single most important reason for leaving student affairs field.*
___ poor prospects for more advanced position in student affairs
___ other career opportunities available
___ dual career problems
___ unwilling/unable to relocate
___ inadequate pay in the field
___ lack of prestige/respect for student affairs practitioners and the work they do
___ inflexibility of work requirements (e.g., not compatible with raising family)
___ dissatisfied with field (e.g., not what I thought it would be like)
___ dislike dealing with institutional politics
___ lack of professionalism in the field
___ desire to work in another area of higher education
___ Other: _____

Staff Development

Indicate how many times you participated in the following staff development activities during the previous 12 months. (Enter zero (0) if you did not participate in a given activity.)
___ Attended off-campus (not part of convention program) workshop
___ Attended professional association convention
___ Attended on-campus professional development workshop of 4 hours or more
___ Received coaching from senior staff member
___ Received personal consultation to solve a specific problem
___ Performed independent research on a topic
___ Authored/coauthored a manuscript for publication
___ Read a book directly related to student affairs
___ Read a professional journal article
___ Participated in summer professional development program/institute

___ Attended preconvention workshop
___ Attended on-campus professional development speaker program
___ Enrolled in graduate class directly related to field
___ Volunteered to assume responsibility in area in order to get
     new/additional experience
___ Conducted data-based research study
___ Attended program/workshop to enhance personal growth
___ Attended program/workshop to develop personal skills (e.g., time
     management, speaking, writing)
___ Acquired new technical skill (e.g., use of computer program)
___ Other: _____

To what extent was your decision about participation in various staff
development activities influenced by the supervision you received?
(Check one.)
___ Not at all ___ Slightly ___ Moderately ___ Considerably
___ Completely

Briefly describe the most meaningful/helpful professional
development activity in which you have participated within the past 36
months. (The activity may not have been a formal workshop or
convention program.)

_____
_____
_____
_____
_____

How frequently is the following knowledge and/or skills used in your
daily work activities? Use the following scale to record your response:

0 = Never **1** = Rarely **2** = Occasionally **3** = Frequently **4** = Every Day

0 1 2 3 4 Conflict management skills
0 1 2 3 4 Crisis intervention skills
0 1 2 3 4 General knowledge of higher education
0 1 2 3 4 General technical knowledge (e.g., accounting, higher
            education law, computers, institutional regulations)
0 1 2 3 4 Knowledge of research and evaluation methodologies
0 1 2 3 4 Knowledge of group dynamics
0 1 2 3 4 Knowledge of program design and implementation
(This question continues on the next page.)

0 1 2 3 4   Knowledge of history of institution and its leaders
0 1 2 3 4   Specific knowledge about college student development
0 1 2 3 4   Technical knowledge of functional area (e.g., housing,
                student center, food service, admissions)
0 1 2 3 4   Skill in organizing work for others to perform
0 1 2 3 4   Basic human relations skills
0 1 2 3 4   Detailed knowledge in allied professional area (e.g.,
                medicine, child care, law)
0 1 2 3 4   Counseling/helping skills and techniques
0 1 2 3 4   Knowledge of organizational theory and behavior
0 1 2 3 4   Knowledge of characteristics or needs of student populations
                (e.g., minorities, disabled, adults)
0 1 2 3 4   Supervisory skills
0 1 2 3 4   Conflict resolution skills
0 1 2 3 4   Other (specify) _____

How much did the institution contribute directly to you for your
professional development during the academic year 1992–93?
$ _____   ( ) I was not employed at this institution during 1992–93.

Did you spend from personal (unreimbursed) funds on professional
development (other than professional association membership dues)
during the academic year 1992–93? *(Check one.)*
___ No
___ Yes—Approximately how much? $ _____

How much did you spend from personal funds on professional
association memberships in the past 12 months? $ _____

Thank you for your assistance with this research study.
Please
1. *Place your questionnaire in an envelope and seal it.*
2. *Sign your name across the flap.*
3. *Write "Staffing Survey" on the front.*
4. *Return envelope to the Vice President's Office.*

The Vice President's Office will collect the questionnaires
*and return them **unopened** to the researchers in a package.*
(We don't have enough money for individual postage. Sorry!)

Exhibit A.4. Student Affairs Staffing Survey, Form B.

Employing Institution: _____

Position title: *(Check one best response.)*
___ Vice President
___ Associate/Assistant Vice President
___ Dean
___ Associate/Assistant Dean
___ Department Head/Director
___ Associate/Assistant Department Head/Director
___ Coordinator
___ Nonadministrative position (e.g., physician, psychologist, or accountant)

Position classification: (Definitions provided in the cover letter.) *(Check one best response.)*
___ Professional Staff   ___ Support Staff
___ Allied Professional Staff   ___ Paraprofessional Staff

Number of administrators/levels of administration between you and the Vice President for Student Affairs: *(Check one.)*
___ 0   ___ 1   ___ 2   ___ 3   ___ 4 or more

Highest degree earned: *(Check one.)*
___ High school and/or technical school diploma   ___ Master's
___ Associate   ___ Doctorate
___ Baccalaureate   ___ Other—Specify _____

Major field of highest degree earned: *(Check one.)*
___ Student Affairs
___ Counseling or Counseling Psychology
___ Higher Education
___ Allied Field (such as accounting, medicine, nursing, law, or recreation)
___ Other Fields (such as English, biology, Russian literature, or philosophy)

Are you currently pursuing further degrees? *(Check one.)*
___ Yes   ___ No

Sex *(Check one.)*
___ Female   ___ Male

Racial/Ethnic Background *(Check single best response.)*
___ African American   ___ Asian American or Pacific Islander
___ Caucasian/White American (non-Hispanic)
___ Hispanic American ___ Native American
___ Other: Specify: _____

Age *(Check one.)*
___ 25 or younger   ___ 31–35 ___ 41–45 ___ 51–55 ___ 61–65
___ 26–30   ___ 36–40 ___ 46–50 ___ 56–60 ___ 66 or
                                                        older

Years (including the current year) worked in Student Affairs as a
professional or allied professional: *(Check one.)*
___ 1–3   ___ 7–9   ___ 13–15   ___ 19–21
___ 4–6   ___ 10–12   ___ 16–18   ___ 22 or more

Years (including the current year) worked in student affairs as a
professional or allied professional at current institution: *(Check one.)*
___ 1–3   ___ 7–9   ___ 13–15   ___ 19–21
___ 4–6   ___ 10–12   ___ 16–18   ___ 22 or more

Current membership in *national* professional organizations *(Please do
not use acronyms.)*

_____

_____

_____

_____

_____

Current membership in *regional* professional organizations *(Please do not
use acronyms.)*

_____

_____

_____

How many staff members in each of the following categories do you
personally/directly supervise currently? *(See cover letter for definitions.
Write in total number for each category.)*
_____ Student Affairs Professionals
_____ Allied Professional Student Affairs Staff

_____ Full-Time Support Staff
_____ Part-Time Support Staff (including students such as work study)
_____ Graduate Assistants
_____ Undergraduate Paraprofessionals

Indicate the functional areas in which you have assigned responsibility by ranking them. Assign 1 for the most time consuming, 2 for less time consuming, and 3 for the least time consuming responsibility. (Do not rank all the functional areas. Many staff members will work in a single functional area; if that is the case, enter a 1 before that functional area.)

_____ Academic Assistance	_____ Judicial (discipline)
_____ Academic Advising	_____ Minority Student Programs
_____ Admissions	_____ Orientation
_____ Alcohol/Drug Education	_____ Registrar
_____ Campus Activities	_____ Research and/or Evaluation
(including Greek Life)	_____ Recreational Sports
_____ Career Planning &	_____ Staff Development and Training
Placement	_____ Student Affairs Division
_____ Child Care	Administration (across areas)
_____ Community Service	_____ Student Health
_____ Counseling and Testing	_____ Student Union
_____ Facilities Management	_____ Women's Programs
(across functional areas)	_____ Other: _____
_____ Financial Aid	
_____ Housing and Residence Life	
_____ International Students	

Supervision Received

Indicate by circling the appropriate number before each item how frequently each of the following topics were discussed during supervisory sessions you had with your supervisor in the past twelve months.

If you have not had a supervisory session in the past 12 months, check below and then go to section entitled "Supervision Given." ( ) *I did not have a supervisory session in past 12 months.*

1 = never 2 = seldom 3 = sometimes 4 = often 5 = always

0 1 2 3 4 5 Work assignments to be accomplished in near future (in days or weeks)

334 Improving Staffing Practices in Student Affairs

0 1 2 3 4 5   Work assignments to be accomplished during current term/year

0 1 2 3 4 5   Short-term personal goals (e.g., increase exercise)

0 1 2 3 4 5   Short-term professional development goals (e.g., join professional association committee)

0 1 2 3 4 5   Long-term personal goals (e.g., assertiveness, procrastination, avoidance)

0 1 2 3 4 5   Long-term professional development goals (e.g., improve supervisory skills)

0 1 2 3 4 5   Personal attitudes (e.g., cooperation, sarcasm)

0 1 2 3 4 5   Professional skills (e.g., report writing, program evaluation)

0 1 2 3 4 5   Personal skills (e.g., time management, public speaking)

0 1 2 3 4 5   Interpersonal relationships

0 1 2 3 4 5   Work attitudes (e.g., thoroughness, enthusiasm)

0 1 2 3 4 5   Values of the profession (e.g., altruism, human dignity, equity)

0 1 2 3 4 5   New knowledge and/or information

0 1 2 3 4 5   Professional ethical issues

0 1 2 3 4 5   Progress toward position(s) of greater responsibility

0 1 2 3 4 5   Mistakes or instance(s) of faulty/poor judgment

0 1 2 3 4 5   Inadequate work performance

0 1 2 3 4 5   Exemplary (outstanding) work performance/production

0 1 2 3 4 5   Short-term career goals

0 1 2 3 4 5   Long-term career goals

0 1 2 3 4 5   Other _____

Indicate by circling the appropriate number how satisfied you are with the following attributes of the supervision you received in the past twelve months.

1 = Very dissatisfied   **2** = Dissatisfied   **3** = Satisfied   **4** = Very satisfied

0 1 2 3 4   Frequency of supervisory sessions

0 1 2 3 4   Skills used in supervision

0 1 2 3 4   Helpfulness of supervision

How (if at all) would you like to change the style, content, or frequency of the supervision you received in the past twelve months?

_____

_____

_____

Supervision Given

In the past 12 months, approximately how frequently did you have
individual sessions (exclusively for the purpose of supervision) with the
staff for whom you have supervisory responsibility? Circle the
appropriate number before each staff category. If you do not supervise
a category of staff place an X in the space provided.

If you do not supervise any staff, check and go to section entitled
"Position Orientation." ( ) *I do not supervise any staff.*

> **0** = Gave no supervision this year
> **1** = Once a year
> **2** = Twice a year
> **3** = Four times a year
> **4** = Six times a year
> **5** = Monthly or more frequently
> **X** = Did not supervise this category of staff

0 1 2 3 4 5 X   Professional Staff
0 1 2 3 4 5 X   Allied Professional Staff
0 1 2 3 4 5 X   Support Staff
0 1 2 3 4 5 X   Paraprofessional Staff

Indicate how frequently each of the following topics were discussed
during the supervisory sessions you conducted this year with student
affairs professionals and/or allied professionals.

1 = Never   **2** = Seldom   **3** = Sometimes   **4** = Often   **5** = Always

0 1 2 3 4 5   Work assignments to be accomplished in near future (in
days or weeks)
0 1 2 3 4 5   Work assignments to be accomplished during current
term/year
0 1 2 3 4 5   Short-term personal goals (e.g., increase exercise)
0 1 2 3 4 5   Short-term professional development goals (e.g., join
professional association committee)
0 1 2 3 4 5   Long-term personal goals (e.g., increase assertiveness)
0 1 2 3 4 5   Long-term professional development goals (e.g., improve
supervisory skills)
0 1 2 3 4 5   Personal attitudes (e.g., cooperation, sarcasm)

0 1 2 3 4 5   Professional skills (e.g., writing, program evaluation)
0 1 2 3 4 5   Personal skills (e.g., time management, public speaking)
0 1 2 3 4 5   Interpersonal relationships
0 1 2 3 4 5   Work attitudes (e.g., thoroughness, enthusiasm)
0 1 2 3 4 5   Values of the profession (e.g., altruism, human dignity, equity)
0 1 2 3 4 5   New knowledge and/or information
0 1 2 3 4 5   Professional ethical issues
0 1 2 3 4 5   Progress toward position(s) of greater responsibility
0 1 2 3 4 5   Mistakes or instance(s) of faulty/poor judgment
0 1 2 3 4 5   Inadequate work performance
0 1 2 3 4 5   Exemplary (outstanding) work performance/production
0 1 2 3 4 5   Short-term career goals
0 1 2 3 4 5   Long-term career goals
0 1 2 3 4 5   Other _____

Indicate how satisfied you are with the following attributes of your
supervision of others by circling the appropriate number.

1 = Very dissatisfied   2 = Dissatisfied   3 = Satisfied   4 = Very satisfied

0 1 2 3 4   Frequency of supervisory sessions
0 1 2 3 4   Skills possessed and used in supervision
0 1 2 3 4   Overall effectiveness of supervision delivered

Have you received formal training in the supervision of staff? *(Check one.)*
____ Yes [Continue]
____ No [Please go to "Position Orientation" Section]

When was your training in supervision acquired? *(Check all that apply.)*
____ In graduate preparation
____ Prior to assuming your current role by another institution
____ Prior to assuming your current role by this institution
____ Concurrent to assuming your current role by your immediate
supervisor
____ Concurrent to assuming your current role by others at this
institution
____ Subsequent to assuming your current role by others at this
institution

Rate the quality of your training in supervision from all sources
checked above. *(Check one.)*
____ Excellent   ____ Good   ____ Fair   ____ Poor

Position Orientation

Respond to this section only if you assumed your current position in the past three years. Answer Part A if you came to your current position from another institution or from graduate school. Answer Part B if you assumed your position after holding another position in the institution.

If you have been in your current position for over three years, check below and then skip the remainder of this section and go to section entitled "Performance Appraisal." ( ) *I have been in my current position for more than three years.*

Part A (Came to the institution new.)

Did you have an orientation to your current position? *(Check one.)*
( ) Yes [please continue]   ( ) No [Please skip to "Performance Evaluation" Section.]

Was the orientation formally structured? *(Check one.)*
( ) Yes   ( ) No Please briefly describe the orientation process:
_____
_____

Who had primary responsibility for your orientation? *(Check one.)*
___ Department/Division head
___ Direct supervisor (if not head)
___ Peer(s)
___ Different staff addressed topics
___ Other: _____

How well were the following topics addressed in your orientation to the institution and your new position? *(Circle the appropriate letter before each item.)*

E = Excellent   **G** = Good   **F** = Fair   **P** = Poor   **N** = Not addressed at all

E G F P N   Explained institution's personnel policies
E G F P N   Gave detailed explanation of job expectations
E G F P N   Explained "unwritten" institutional expectations
E G F P N   Explained benefits plan
E G F P N   Explained office procedures and policies
E G F P N   Identified relevant resources (e.g., library, professional literature, equipment)

E G F P N Introduced you to staff with whom you would generally
work
E G F P N Described student body characteristics
E G F P N Described faculty characteristics
E G F P N Explained expectations for performance
E G F P N Discussed institutional culture
E G F P N Discussed office/department/division culture(s)
E G F P N Described performance evaluation process
E G F P N Explained staff development policies
E G F P N Described potential/real problem situations/relationships

Part B (Assumed position within same institution)

Rate how well the following topics were addressed in the orientation to
your new position/role *only* if you assumed the new position within the
same institution. *(Circle the appropriate letter before each item.)*

E = Excellent **G** = Good **F** = Fair **P** = Poor **N** = Not addressed at all

E G F P N New job description
E G F P N Productivity expectations
E G F P N Explained potential problem situations/relationships
E G F P N Introduction to staff outside of Student Affairs with whom
you will work
E G F P N Performance evaluation procedures
E G F P N Explanation of institutional procedures unique to new
position

Performance Evaluation

During the past 12 months, how frequently did your supervisor provide
a *formal* work performance evaluation? *(Check one.)*
___ Zero   ___ Three or more times
___ Once   ___ Other: _____
___ Twice

During the past 12 months, how many times did your supervisor
provide an *informal* work performance evaluation? *(Check one.)*
___ Zero   ___ Three or more times
___ Once   ___ Other: _____
___ Twice

Check all the sources of data that were considered in your formal work performance evaluation(s) conducted in the past 12 months. *(Check all that apply.)*

___ No formal evaluation conducted to my knowledge.—**Return questionnaire.**

___ Supervisor's observations
___ Students' evaluations
___ Evaluations of programs for which you were responsible
___ Data provided by you related to preestablished goals
___ Peers' observations/evaluations
___ Budget information
___ Your self-evaluations
___ Support staff evaluations
___ Other: _____

As a result of your performance evaluation(s), which of the following resulted as follow-up? *(Check all that apply.)*
___ Recommendations for professional development activities
___ Changes in supervision procedures/process
___ Salary adjustment for next year determined
___ Establishment of new position goals
___ Reassignment of position responsibilities
___ Establishment of new personal and/or professional goals
___ Recommendations for behavior changes
___ Nothing related to performance
___ Other: _____

Thank you for your assistance with this research study.

Please

1. *Place your questionnaire in an envelope and seal it.*
2. *Sign your name across the flap.*
3. *Write "Staffing Survey" on the front.*
4. *Return envelope to the Vice President's Office.*

The Vice President's Office will collect the questionnaires and return them **unopened** *to the researchers in a package.*
(We don't have enough money for individual postage. Sorry!)

Table A.1. Demographic Characteristics of Sample by Position Title.

Variable	VPSA		Deans		Directors		Coordinators		Nonadministrative	
	n	percent	n	percent	n	percent	n	percent	n	percent
Sex										
Male	77	64	16	62	32	23	206	43	47	31
Female	43	36	10	38	107	77	277	57	107	69
Ethnicity										
African American	16	13	1	4	14	1	29	6	12	8
Asian American	3	2	1	4	1	1	5	1	23	
Caucasian American	99	82	23	88	118	84	427	89	127	84
Hispanic American	3	2	0	0	5	1	15	3	5	3
Native American	0	0	0	0	0	0	2	1	4	3
Biracial	0	0	0	0	2	1	4	1	0	0
Age										
30 or under	3	2	0	0	12	7	68	14	37	25
31–40	16	13	5	19	52	38	146	30	50	33
41–50	63	52	11	42	41	30	164	34	48	32
51–60	31	25	10	38	26	19	83	17	15	10
61 and older	9	7	0	0	7	5	20	4	1	1
Years in the profession										
1–6 years	15	13	0	0	47	35	113	24	78	53
7–12 years	21	18	2	8	42	31	130	27	33	22
13–18 years	23	20	5	19	29	21	115	24	17	11
19+ years	58	50	19	73	17	13	79	17	20	14

Variable	VPSA		Deans		Directors		Coordinators		Nonadministrative	
	n	percent	n	percent	n	percent	n	percent	n	percent
Years in current position										
1–6	50	42	7	27	61	45	223	46	88	59
7–12	30	25	2	8	41	30	126	26	31	21
13–18	18	15	3	12	14	10	81	17	14	9
19+ years	22	18	14	54	19	14	50	10	15	10
Memberships in national professional organizations										
None	23	19	0	0	46	33	80	17	47	32
One	26	22	12	46	43	31	174	36	57	38
Two	27	23	5	19	26	19	124	26	25	17
Three	19	16	4	15	15	11	65	14	14	9
Four	13	11	5	19	6	3	24	5	4	3
Five or more	12	10	0	0	4	3	13	3	1	1
Highest degree earned										
High school	0	0	0	0	9	7	2	1	7	5
Associate	0	0	0	0	8	6	8	2	4	3
Bachelor's	2	2	4	16	31	23	98	21	48	32
Master's	48	40	11	44	68	50	314	67	86	57
Doctoral	69	58	10	40	19	14	49	10	7	5

Table A.1. Demographic Characteristics of Sample by Position Title (cont.).

Variable	VPSA		Deans		Directors		Coordinators		Nonadministrative	
	n	percent	n	percent	n	percent	n	percent	n	percent
Field of highest degree earned										
Student affairs	17	14	1	4	12	9	69	15	18	12
Counseling or counseling psychology	21	18	11	42	35	26	118	25	33	22
Higher education	47	39	7	27	16	12	66	14	23	15
Allied field	7	6	4	15	44	33	116	25	32	21
Other	28	23	4	15	28	21	99	21	43	29
Functional area of primary responsibility[a]										
Academic assistance			0	0	0	0	6	1	4	1
Academic advising			0	0	0	0	8	1	7	1
Admissions			0	0	7	1	20	2	8	1
Alcohol, drug education			0	0	2	1	3	1	8	1
Campus activities			0	0	4	1	41	5	20	2
Career planning and placement			0	0	4	1	32	4	4	1
Child care			0	0	0	0	3	1	2	1
Community service			0	0	0	0	0	0	2	1
Counseling			2	1	18	2	24	3	3	1
Facilities management			2	1	0	0	7	1	2	1

Variable	VPSA		Deans		Directors		Coordinators		Nonadministrative	
	n	percent	n	percent	n	percent	n	percent	n	percent
Financial aid			1	1	5	1	41	5	12	1
General administration			3	1	2	1	0	0	1	1
Housing and residence life			4	1	11	1	68	8	13	1
International students			0	0	1	1	7	1	2	1
Judicial programs, student discipline			1	1	1	1	5	1	3	1
Minority student services			1	1	1	1	8	1	1	1
New-student orientation			0	0	1	1	4	1	5	1
Registrar			0	0	2	1	15	2	2	1
Research, evaluation			0	0	1	1	0	0	4	1
Recreational sports			0	0	0	0	1	1	1	1
Staff development			0	0	0	0	1	1	1	1
Student health			1	1	38	5	41	5	9	1
Student union			1	1	1	1	9	1	3	1
Women's programs			0	0	1	1	1	1	0	0
Other			0	0	2	1	37	5	11	1

Note: VPSA = chief student affairs administrator. Deans = staff with titles of associate or assistant vice president and dean (not VPSA). Directors = staff with titles of department head or director and associate or assistant dean. Coordinators = staff with titles of associate or assistant department head or director and coordinator. Nonadministrative = staff with titles such as physician, psychologist, nurse, day-care worker, or accountant. 1 percent is entered for the range .01–1.4 percent in this table.

[a]Does not apply to VPSAs.

Table A.2. Advertising and Recruiting Methods for Entry-level, Mid-level, and Allied Professionals by Institutional Type (percentages).

Advertisement and Recruiting Vehicle	Entry-level Professionals				Mid-level Professionals				Allied Professionals			
	RU	Comp. C.	LA	CC	RU	Comp. C.	LA	CC	RU	Comp. C.	LA	CC
House organ	100	81	79	82	100	86	75	82	79	70	57	63
Local media	79	84	79	97	100	81	79	97	79	72	87	74
National media	7	7	13	5	36	23	25	13	7	7	13	8
Chronicle of Higher Education	36	35	50	16	86	74	63	53	29	14	22	11
Regional professional media[a]	36	58	50	45	36	67	68	56	36	44	30	29
National professional media[a]	29	33	29	3	71	42	50	8	29	26	9	0
Professional conferences	79	63	54	18	64	74	50	26	21	23	13	3
Other	7	14	13	8	14	19	17	11	43[b]	33[b]	17[b]	11[b]

Note: RU = research university, Comp. C. = comprehensive college or university, LA = liberal arts college, CC = community college.

[a]Includes newsletters, web pages, listservs, and telephone message listings.

[b]Includes professional media and conferences of profession other than student affairs, such as law, medicine.

Table A.3. Who Makes Final Hiring Decisions by Institutional Type (percentages).

Decision Maker and Institutional Type	Position Being Filled			
	Department Director	Mid-level Professional	Entry-level Professional	Allied Professional
President				
RU	0	0	0	0
Comp. C.	3	0	0	3
LA	22	4	0	5
CC	28	14	12	17
Vice president				
RU	86	0	0	0
Comp. C.	92	25	3	42
LA	74	23	8	63
CC	64	39	15	20
Department director				
RU	NA	100	54	90
Comp. C.	NA	72	89	52
LA	NA	57	71	16
CC	NA	33	53	20
Others				
RU	14	0	46	10
Comp. C.	6	3	13	3
LA	4	17	20	10
CC	6	15	21	24

Note: NA = not applicable, Vice president = vice president for student affairs, RU = research university, Comp. C. = comprehensive college or university, LA = liberal arts college, CC = two-year or community college. "Others" include a selection committee, the department's staff as a group, or the direct supervisor.

**Table A.4. Subjects Addressed in Orientation to New Positions
for Persons Hired from Another Institution
(percentages).**

Subject	Addressed Well	Addressed Poorly	Not Addressed at All
Job expectations	47	43	9
Performance expectations	54	38	9
Personnel policies	49	40	12
Benefits plan	50	34	16
Office procedures and policies	46	49	5
Relevant resources (such as library, professional literature, equipment)	32	47	17
Introduction to staff with whom generally work	79	18	3
Potential or real problem situations or relationships	41	43	16
Institutional culture	49	36	15
"Unwritten" institutional expectations	29	37	22
Office, department, division culture	47	31	22
Performance evaluation process	37	43	20
Staff development policies	30	32	38
Student population characteristics	55	36	9
Faculty characteristics	32	41	18

Note: $n = 67$. "Addressed well" is the sum of *excellent* and *good* responses;
"addressed poorly" is the sum of *fair* and *poor* responses.

**Table A.5. Satisfaction with Supervision Received
by Position Classification (percentages).**

Position Classification	Frequency of Supervision	Skills Used in Supervision	Helpfulness of Supervision
Deans ($n = 7$)	71	71	71
Directors ($n = 52$)	85	73	75
Coordinators ($n = 189$)	83	75	77
Nonadministrative ($n = 68$)	87	81	75

Note: Table reports combined responses of satisfied and very satisfied. Deans = staff with titles of associate or assistant vice president and dean (not VPSA); Directors = staff with titles of department head or director and associate or assistant dean; Coordinators = staff with titles of associate or assistant department head or director and coordinator; Nonadministrative = staff with titles such as physician, psychologist, nurse, day care worker, or accountant.

Table A.6. Frequency per Year of Staff Development Activities by Institutional Type (percentages).

Activity Type	Frequency per Year				
	None	Once	Twice	Three Times	Four or More Times
Social event	13	27	19	18	24
Research universities	21	14	14	21	28
Comprehensive colleges or universities	3	39	16	19	23
Liberal arts colleges	0	27	32	14	27
Community colleges	15	28	18	18	23
Invited speaker	38	27	23	6	7
Research universities	36	14	21	7	21
Comprehensive colleges or universities	33	33	26	2	9
Liberal arts colleges	35	26	26	9	4
Community colleges	48	25	18	8	3
Division workshop of 2–4 hours	64	13	8	5	9
Research universities	50	7	21	7	14
Comprehensive colleges or universities	61	14	5	5	16
Liberal arts colleges	70	4	13	9	4
Community colleges	70	20	5	3	3
Division workshop of 5+ hours	85	11	3	1	3
Research universities	57	21	14	0	7
Comprehensive colleges or universities	81	12	2	0	5
Liberal arts colleges	83	9	4	4	0
Community colleges	90	8	3	0	0

Frequency per Year

Activity Type	None	Once	Twice	Three Times	Four or More Times
Department workshop of 2–4 hours	31	25	9	9	25
Research universities	25	33	0	0	33
Comprehensive colleges or universities	33	23	5	5	35
Liberal arts colleges	35	17	13	13	22
Community colleges	30	30	15	10	15
Department workshop of 5+ hours	67	20	3	7	4
Research universities	64	21	0	7	7
Comprehensive colleges or universities	65	19	0	7	7
Liberal arts colleges	78	13	4	4	0
Community colleges	88	8	3	0	3

Table A.7. Frequency of Performance Appraisals (percentages).

Variable	Deans	Directors	Coordinators	Nonadministrative
Frequency of formal performance appraisals in previous 12 months				
None	33	37	27	26
1	56	54	53	57
2	0	5	10	12
3 or more times	11	0	2	0
Other	0	3	3	4
Frequency of informal performance appraisals in previous 12 months				
None	25	45	38	35
1	38	29	12	16
2	13	11	13	19
3 or more times	25	15	37	29

Table A.8. **Single Most Rewarding Aspect of Current Position
by Position Title (n = 431, percentages).**

Reward	Deans	Directors	Coordinators	Nonadministrative
Working directly with students	63	65	52	57
Creating educational programs	13	13	3	7
Being a member of an educational community	0	4	17	12
Handling administrative duties	0	4	4	4
Managing budgets	0	0	1	0
Teaching through educational programs	0	0	2	2
Dealing with intellectual matters	0	0	0	2
Solving complicated problems	13	6	8	5
My own personal development	13	4	2	5
Salary	0	0	1	1
Fringe benefits of working in an academic community	0	4	2	1
Other	0	0	9	1

Note: Deans = staff with titles associate or assistant vice president and dean (not VPSA). Directors = staff with titles department head or director and assistant or associate dean. Coordinators = assistant or associate department director and coordinator. Nonadministrative = staff with titles such as physician, psychologist, accountant, nurse.

Quality Assurance in College Student Affairs
A Proposal for Action by Professional Associations

Executive Summary

There is little agreement in the student affairs profession about how to ensure quality practice—the core function of the field. Accreditation, credentialing, self-regulation, and no regulation approaches are advocated by different constituencies. Most agree, however, that something should be done to improve the quality of professional practice and to offer better assurances to the public that student affairs practice is conducted ethically and effectively.

A recent study group appointed by the American College Personnel Association (ACPA) and the National Association of Student Personnel Administrators (NASPA) concluded that professional associations of the field should assume the principal role of guarantor of quality assurance in college student affairs. The study group also concluded that accrediting and credentialing options

Note: This material was originally a report prepared for the American College Personnel Association and the National Association of Student Personnel Administrators and presented on November 1, 1992. The study group members who prepared it were Don G. Creamer (chair), Roger B. Winston, Jr., John H. Schuh, Donald D. Gehring, Marylu K. McEwen, Deanna S. Forney, D. Stanley Carpenter, and Dudley B. Woodard.

currently practiced by specialized accrediting agencies, such as the Council for the Accreditation of Counseling and Related Professions (CACREP), and credentialing bodies, such as the National Board of Certified Counselors (NBCC), may not be the best or most appropriate strategies to assure quality for college student affairs.

The study group posited a Quality Assurance Model (QAM) that is recommended for adoption and implementation by ACPA, NASPA, and the Council for the Advancement of Standards (CAS) for Higher Education. The model incorporates the centrality of practice, the use of standards for self-regulation, and continuing professional education as hallmarks of quality assurance in the field. The study group also formulated a Professional Development Implementation Model (PDIM) to demonstrate access to a variety of pathways for continuing professional education and to recognize excellent performance by an ever more diverse body of professionals. The implementation model reflects a clear preference for the professional preparation route of entry into the profession.

Specific recommendations of the study group include (a) new roles for professional associations, (b) new roles for CAS, (c) widespread dissemination and discussion of materials on quality assurance, and (d) need for immediate action on further study of certain aspects of the proposed Quality Assurance Model.

Introduction

Concerns for quality in student affairs practice have taken several forms. Some professionals believe that concerns for quality practice should be addressed through formal accreditation of preparation programs coupled with formal credentialing of individual practitioners, though even among proponents of this approach there is no agreement about which agency should do the job (Ebbers and Kruempel, 1992). Others believe that the profession is too diverse for such approaches and should rely instead on the approach of the Council for the Advancement of Standards (CAS) that is based solely on self-assessment and self-regulation of preparation programs and programs of service delivery. Some believe that the quality of educational programs is the business of the institution and that professional associations should have no role in their implementation. No consensus among professional organizations in student affairs is yet apparent regarding which approach is best for the long-term health of the student affairs profession or will produce the greatest benefit to students.

It is the lack of consensus among professional association leaders and, to some extent, the lack of understanding of accrediting and credentialing practices themselves that has led to formal calls for study of quality assurance issues in college student affairs. Two recent examples of formal calls for study can be found in the report of the Joint Task Force on Professional Preparation and Practice (1989) and the report of Creamer and Woodard (1992) on accrediting and credentialing in college student affairs. Both reports point to the importance of quality preparation and practice in the profession and both call for formal study of alternative approaches to quality assurance. These reports, coupled with a growing concern among individual leaders of the profession that formal and systematic action is needed by professional associations to address quality assurance issues, led directly to the formation of a small study group to consider approaches to quality assurance for the profession and to make specific recommendations for action to the American College Personnel Association (ACPA) and the National Association of Student Personnel Administrators (NASPA).

Members of the study group included Don G. Creamer (Chair), Virginia Tech; Roger B. Winston, Jr., University of Georgia; John H. Schuh, Wichita State University; Donald D. Gehring, Bowling Green State University; Marylu K. McEwen, University of Maryland-College Park; Deanna S. Forney, Western Illinois University; D. Stanley Carpenter, Texas A & M University; and Dudley B. Woodard, University of Arizona. Creamer, Winston, Schuh, and Gehring also served ACPA as Senior Scholars wherein they assumed a special group role to study quality assurance issues. McEwen, Forney, and Carpenter also served ACPA as Commission XII (Professional Preparation) members wherein they assumed a similar role. Woodard earlier served NASPA in the study of quality assurance issues and continued in this capacity on this study group. Schuh also served on the NASPA Board of Directors.

This report is issued as a call for action by all professional organizations concerned with preparation and practice in student affairs; however, the declarations of the study group specifically call for action by ACPA, NASPA, and CAS. The members of the study group believe that while much more work is required from many concerned professionals to direct the efforts of these national professional organizations, certain steps should be taken now and that plans should be drafted now for longer-term action.

The report begins with a conceptual model for quality assurance, continues with a discussion of beliefs and principles inherent in the model, proposes a conceptual scheme for the implementation of the model, and concludes with specific recommendations for action by ACPA, NASPA, and CAS.

Quality Assurance Model

The core function of college student affairs is professional practice. As shown in Figure B.1, professional practice forms the nucleus of the Quality Assurance Model (QAM) around which entry into the profession is depicted and the major conditions that lead to quality practice are shown. Recognition of multiple routes into the profession is displayed in the model and the role of professional ethics and standards are characterized. Following entry into the profession, assessment of professional competences and needs, continuing professional education, and recognition and reporting systems are shown as ongoing crucial aspects of quality assurance. Professional ethical standards and CAS standards currently exist as tools for quality assurance. Reliable and widely acknowledged systems of professional assessment, continuing professional education, and recognition and reporting systems for student affairs do not exist currently. The model is dynamic, allowing for evolving professional standards and expectations.

The terminology of QAM avoids the language of most accrediting and credentialing bodies. Instead, its language was chosen deliberately to encourage creative thinking about approaches to quality assurance and reflects straightforward concepts associated with professional practice in all higher education settings.

Professional Preparation Programs refers to formal education in theory and research about student development and the effects of college attendance, student affairs application skills, values, and professional practices and to formal education in other related disciplines, such as psychology, allied health, and recreation.

Other Avenues refers to the reality of entry into student affairs

Figure B.1. Quality Assurance Model.

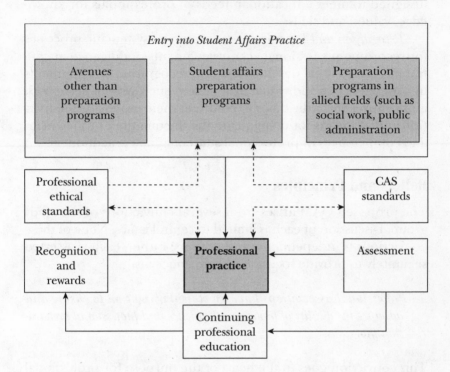

based on personal attributes and competence gained through study in other disciplines rather than to entry based on formal education in student affairs alone.

Professional Ethical Standards refers to published statements of ACPA (1989), NASPA (1992–93), and other professional associations intended to prescribe appropriate standards of conduct for members.

CAS Standards (1988) refers to the published standards of the Council for the Advancement of Standards for Higher Education related to professional practice and academic preparation.

Assessment refers to an ongoing act of supervision and appraisal of individual professional performance capabilities to determine current status and future needs of the employing institution and the individual professional for education and training.

Continuing Professional Education refers to systems of instruction designed to meet educational needs of professionals for knowledge, values, and skills.

Recognition and Reporting Systems refers to systematic processes for recording professional acknowledgments of diligence in continuing professional development and recognition of attainments in competence or individual proficiency. Such systems serve both as incentives for individuals to continue their professional education and as means for recognizing the documented proficiencies and competences of professional student affairs practitioners.

Beliefs and Principles

The proposed QAM arises from several convictions of the study group. Discussion of each is limited to central issues. None of these convictions is independent of the others; rather, each is asserted separately to provide focus on certain concerns.

1. *Professional associations have an ethical obligation to ensure and advance the quality of professional practice and professional preparation programs.*

This conviction goes to the heart of the purpose for professional associations. We recognize that many professional associations may not now be appropriately constituted to fulfill this obligation; however, we believe that the absence of such constitutional character, where it exists, should not stand. We believe that certain formal training (although not necessarily through degree programs) should be required for membership in professional associations, that membership in professional associations should imply certain expertise, and that members in professional associations should agree to adhere to prescribed ethical standards and standards of practice. Professional associations have the collective responsibility to the public to establish mechanisms for disciplining practitioners who act in an unethical manner because such behavior degrades the entire profession. It is the duty, in our opinion, of professional associations to offer assurances to the public of quality professional preparation programs, competence of their members, and quality educational services and programs at the institutional level.

2. *Quality assurance in whatever form must embrace diverse programs and practitioners.*

The system of American higher education fundamentally is pluralistic. Any plan for assuring quality in student affairs practice must be sensitive to the vast diversity of institutions and student affairs programs and to the diversity of professional assignments and professional interests. The approach must be inclusive and multifaceted, not exclusive and myopic.

3. *Specialized preparation program accreditation, in its present form, has a multitude of problems.*

Among these problems are failure of accreditation agencies to recognize legitimate diversity in professional preparation and practice, controversies over who prepares the standards used by the accrediting agencies, controversies over the appropriateness of the published standards, costs of the accreditation process, intrusiveness of the accrediting process, redundancy of accreditation services by multiple specialized agencies, and controversies over the role of external agencies determining internal institutional quality standards. Currently, the public cannot assume that the best preparation programs are accredited and the worst are unaccredited. The process of self-selection for taking part in the process may be, and often is, self-serving. The public's interests may, or may not, be served by the available process.

4. *Current credentialing processes, such as professional certification as practiced in counseling and psychology, will not work in student affairs.*

While it may be asserted that a relatively homogeneous profession, such as counseling, may benefit from appropriate certification processes that offer sensible assurances of proficiency, the same cannot be said for a profession, such as student affairs, that is characterized by its heterogeneity. The notion of certifying individual professional proficiency of persons engaged in such diverse activities as recruiting, admissions, advising, financial aid, career planning, campus activities, recreation, residence halls management, residence education, dining services, judicial services, commuter affairs, student unions, multicultural programs, minority student services, and other special services is beyond current capabilities of a national certification system as evident in counseling and psychology. This is not to argue that individual credentialing is impossible in student affairs, but the perspective recognizes that another model would be required.

5. *The Council for the Advancement of Standards has developed standards for professional practice that could be used for quality assurance for both professional practice and for preparation programs.*

A current and anticipated future strength of student affairs is its commitment to the application of standards to preparation and practice. CAS has a distinguished record of consensus building among professionals and professional associations to derive these standards. The current practice of promulgating standards for self-assessment and self-regulation is well received by the profession in general. We recognize, however, that CAS may be able to play an even greater role in the implementation of a comprehensive QAM. For example, we believe that it could be beneficial if the staff requirements of the CAS functional area standards were strengthened to specifically require possession of certain knowledge, values, and skills basic to student affairs.

6. *Certain skills and competencies are required for practice in student affairs no matter how one enters the field.*

Professional practice, the core function of the profession, compels proficient performance by individuals. Professionals are expected to possess certain knowledge, hold certain values, and execute certain skills. When these attributes are absent or lacking in some manner, the employing institution currently must assume complete responsibility for educating its underqualified staff. To assist in meeting this obligation, supervisors should have access to a professionally derived and sanctioned plan to remedy the deficiencies. The goal is competence in all professionals regardless of their prior education and training. Professional associations collectively thus have the responsibility to make available well-conceptualized, low-cost, basic and advanced professional education programs.

7. *Practitioners enter student affairs from a variety of backgrounds that include professional preparation programs, related degree programs, unrelated degree programs, and no formal academic training.*

Corollary to the preceding conviction, this statement emphasizes the need for effective assessment and prescription of professional continuing education that can be configured to fit the variety of previous education and training while ensuring acquisition of fundamental knowledge, values, and skills of student affairs. Consistent with the concern for inclusiveness, competence in student affairs can, and should, be built upon regardless of the academic and professional background of the individual. Entry into the profession via formal graduate preparation programs is preferred; however, appropriate accommodations should be made to determine the status of professional attributes and to prescribe effective continuing professional education.

8. *Practitioners are at unique levels of professional development.*

Regardless of the route of original entry into the field and regardless of the character of previous education and training, practitioners may still possess uneven professional attributes and deserve assistance from their supervisors, their institutions, and their professional associations to seek continuous improvement in professional capabilities. It is especially important that supervision of student affairs professionals be done by persons capable of making appropriate assessments of strengths and weaknesses. Professional associations can support institutions and aid individual practitioners by providing high-quality assessment and appraisal services designed to diagnose areas in which additional education or training is needed.

9. *Practitioners must be assisted by national professional associations in their continuing professional education efforts.*

Consistent with the principle that membership in professional associations implies certain professional competence, associations should provide educational and training opportunities to permit qualification for membership and continuous enhancement of professional skills. Such educational and training opportunities need not be offered independent of institutionally based programs of continuing education; rather, they may well be coordinated in some manner consistent with the principle that all members, and potential members, have access to the opportunities and receive appropriate recognition for their achievements.

10. *Assessment necessarily precedes continuing professional education.*

One of the principal roles of supervisors in student affairs is to help professionals working under their guidance to appraise their individual talents needed for competent professional practice and to arrange for further education and training where indicated. We also believe that neither institutional nor professional association-based assessment processes adequate to accomplish these purposes are available currently. A crucial need in the immediate future is for professional associations to construct useful, effective, and transportable assessment systems to accomplish these needs. This could be accomplished most effectively through consortium arrangements involving professional preparation programs, regional groups of colleges and universities (public and private), and professional associations. CAS, as the coordinator of member professional associations, seems to be the logical leader in initiating such programs.

11. *We believe that (a) quality professional practice requires lifelong continuing professional education, (b) principles of adult education should form the basis for continuing professional education, and (c) continuing professional education can take place in many forms and arenas.*

Continuous learning goes to the heart of professional practice. Continuing professional education is an irrefutable ethical responsibility of practicing professionals. It is incumbent upon professional associations, however, to assist in the process of individual continuing professional education. Legitimate educational opportunities must be accessible to all professionals and should recognize their status as adult learners. Principles of adult learning should be applied in the design of continuing professional educational systems. These continuing education programs should be directly applicable to practitioners' work with students and fulfillment of institutional goals and missions.

12. *Professionals practicing in student affairs may, in addition to participating in continuing professional education programs in student affairs, have their identity in a related profession and participate in allied continuing professional education.*

Such dual allegiance is not a threat to student affairs, but a strength. We believe its advantages should be recognized and built upon, taking care only to guarantee basic student affairs knowledge, values, and skills in the process. All "allied professionals" should be fully schooled in student affairs philosophy and educated as to how the practice of their specialized skill and knowledge fits into the overall institutional goals and the student affairs division's mission.

13. *Practitioners who engage in improving their professional practice should receive recognition for those achievements.*

Achievement deserves recognition and leads to motivation for further achievement. It is in the best interests of supervisors, departments, institutions, and professional associations to implement systems of reward tied to improvement in professional practice. Improved individual performance leads to increased departmental effectiveness, and so on throughout the institution and the profession. A plan also needs to be constructed to report these achievements and rewards so that others within the department, the institution, and the profession are informed. It is possible that a repository for such reports could be a national registry of proficient professionals in student affairs, though the precise mechanism is less important than the goal of an informed public. Considerable additional study is needed on this topic, but instituting such a system is essential to any substantial improvement in professional practice.

Implementation of QAM

The presentation of the QAM and the discussion of beliefs and principles highlights many of our ideas for quality assurance in student affairs. We recognize, however, that the QAM may be seen as overly abstract and our discussion overly abbreviated. Consequently, we offer another view of the process focusing on how the QAM might be implemented in the field. Figure B.2 portrays entry into the profession from one of three tracks and several pathways to quality practice. The Professional Development Implementation Model (PDIM) demonstrates that all professionals can achieve competence and recognition, but that differing avenues, especially of continuing professional education, may be required.

The implementation model reflects the diversity of the profession and the common goal of full performance of all members of the profession. Notice, however, that the arrows used to depict movement within the profession are of two dimensions—one is bolder than the other. This distinction, which is intentional, is designed to underscore a value or a preference for entry into the profession via the route of professional preparation programs. The pathways toward full proficiency in the field following the professional preparation entry route are, therefore, more logical and require less remediation through continuing professional education than may be required by entry via the alternative routes.

Certain attributes of professional practice are highlighted in the model. Notice that practice includes supervision, mentoring, and professional involvement. We believe that these aspects of practice have not received enough attention to date and we wish to underscore them. Some of us oversee the work of others and it is absolutely incumbent upon the overseers to supervise, evaluate, and assist those to whom guidance is offered and to insist upon their personal professional involvement. Supervision and mentoring imply certain high-level skills of professional practice and should themselves be constantly strengthened through continuing professional education.

Recommendations for Action

Our discussion of beliefs and principles may be summarized succinctly:

Figure B.2. Professional Development Implementation Model.

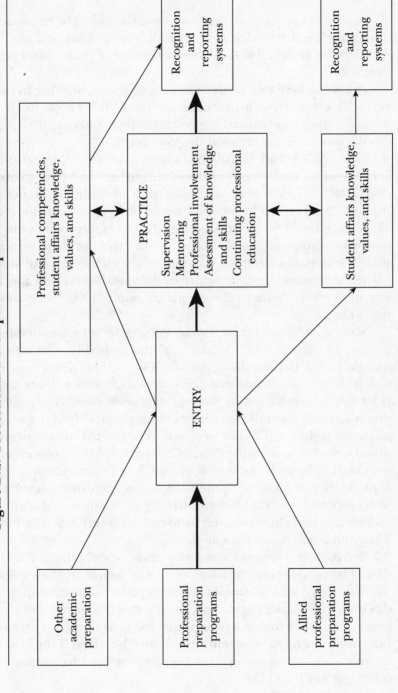

Other academic preparation

Professional preparation programs

Allied professional preparation programs

ENTRY

PRACTICE
Supervision
Mentoring
Professional involvement
Assessment of knowledge and skills
Continuing professional education

Professional competencies, student affairs knowledge, values, and skills

Student affairs knowledge, values, and skills

Recognition and reporting systems

Recognition and reporting systems

(a) We believe that professional associations, while necessarily operating interdependently with employing institutions, are the entities most responsible for quality assurance of professional practice; and

(b) We believe that professional associations, working in concert with employing institutions, are the entities most likely to bring about change toward improved professional practice.

We therefore recommend the following.

First, ACPA and NASPA should create an organizational arrangement, codependent upon volunteers and paid professional staff, to guarantee continuing study of quality assurance in student affairs and to formulate specific plans to achieve the goal. The creation of a new unit to address these responsibilities might be considered or CAS might be asked to carry out these responsibilities. Initiatives to meet the goal might include careful study of the current and desired nature of the associations with special attention given to their roles in quality assurance for the profession at large.

Second, CAS should be invited to consider an expanded role beyond its current function in any plans for quality assurance in student affairs. Certain changes, such as strengthened staff requirements in functional area standards, would offer immediate assistance toward greater quality assurance; however, other changes that might alter the overall boundaries of responsibility of the entity might be considered if they were well coordinated with its professional association membership. ACPA's and NASPA's representatives should be instructed to request CAS to discuss assuming a leadership role in development of comprehensive assessment processes and coordinated continuing professional education. Included in that charge should be to further investigate a national recognition and reporting system.

Third, consciousness among all professionals in student affairs should be raised about the issues of quality assurance. Widespread discussion of the issues should be accomplished. Dissemination of this report and other papers and reports that complement or challenge it should provide a substantive focus to these discussions. Programs at annual conventions should be offered on how to strengthen in-service education on campuses and to accomplish other goals of the QAM.

Fourth, more study of certain components of the QAM should be conducted, especially of the assessment, continuing professional education, and recognition and reporting systems elements. We believe that it would prove beneficial to conduct a national symposium on quality assurance in student affairs. The content of the symposium might be derived by inviting all member associations of CAS to submit papers on assessment, continuing professional education, and recognition and reporting systems that thoughtfully consider each aspect in the total model.

References

American College Personnel Association. (1989). *Statement of ethical principles and standards.* Washington, D.C.: Author.

Council for the Advancement of Standards for Higher Education. (1988). *CAS standards and guidelines for student services/development programs.* College Park, MD: University of Maryland.

Creamer, D. G., & Woodard. D. B. (1992). *Accrediting and credentialing in college student affairs: The role of ACPA and NASPA.* An unpublished paper commissioned by ACPA and NASPA. Washington, D.C.: American College Personnel Association/National Association of Student Personnel Administrators.

Ebbers, L. H., & Kruempel, B. J. (1992). Student affairs preparation programs: Should they be accredited? *NASPA Journal, 30,* 59–65.

Joint Task Force on Professional Preparation and Practice. (1989). *The recruitment, preparation, and nurturing of the student affairs professional.* Washington, D.C.: National Association of Student Personnel Administrators.

National Association of Student Personnel Administrators. (1992–1993). Standards of professional practice. In *Member handbook* (pp. 17–18). Washington, D.C.: Author.

│ **Case Interview Protocol**

Document Analysis

1. Acquire policy statements, manuals, and division regulations that pertain to personnel matters.
2. Acquire descriptive material pertaining to all in-service or training activities, both of a continuous or periodic nature.
3. Read these written materials prior to conducting interviews to become familiar with any formal staffing practices pertaining to staff recruitment and selection, personnel orientation, supervision, personnel appraisal and performance reviews, staff development, and personnel evaluation.
4. Notes from these document analyses will be used as probe questions during interviews.

Interviews

1. Interview individually the vice president for student affairs and one student affairs unit director and one mid-level or entry-level staff member (representing the five categories of staff designated on our original letter to the vice presidents) following these questions generally:
   a. Please describe your general approach to staff selection, supervision, development, and evaluation.
   b. What is your evidence that your approach is effective?
   c. What staffing practices in your unit(s) do you consider distinctively effective? Why?
2. Interview, in sets of five to six, two groups of staff selected randomly from among all student affairs personnel. Avoid sets

where staff from one unit may dominate the discussions. Follow these questions generally:

a. Please describe your experiences in your current position or other positions in student affairs at this institution regarding professional staff.
   • Selection
   • Supervision
   • Development
   • Evaluation
b. What is your evidence of effectiveness of the staffing practices in student affairs at this institution?
c. What staffing practices in student affairs do you consider distinctively effective? Why?

3. Interview individually any member of student affairs who specifically requests to be heard regarding his or her views of staffing practices at this institution. Follow these questions generally:
   a. Please describe your experiences in your current position or other positions in student affairs at this institution regarding staff selection, supervision, development, and evaluation.
   b. What is your evidence of effectiveness of the staffing practices in student affairs at this institution?
   c. What staffing practices in student affairs do you consider distinctively effective? Why?
   d. If you had the power, how would you change staff practices here? Why?

Recorded and Written Report

1. Audio record all interview sessions.
2. Review (listen) to all recorded conversations and transcribe excerpts (taking care to note the specific context of the excerpted comments).
3. Write a narrative of the reports that focus on distinctive aspects of staffing practices at the institution.
4. Review narrative in two steps. (a) Winston or Creamer will write the first draft of the narrative; the other member of the team will critique the narrative for clarity and coherence. (b) The second draft will be forwarded to the vice president at the case site to be reviewed for factual accuracy.
5. Write the final narrative of the case.

References

American College Personnel Association. (1993). Statement of ethical principles and standards. *Journal of College Student Development, 34,* 89–92.

American Council on Education (ACE). (1937/1994). The student personnel point of view. In A. L. Rentz (Ed.), *Student affairs: A profession's heritage* (2nd ed.). Washington, DC: American College Personnel Association.

American Council on Education (ACE). (1949/1994). The student personnel point of view (Rev. ed.). In A. L. Rentz (Ed.), *Student affairs: A profession's heritage* (2nd ed.). Washington, DC: American College Personnel Association.

Astin, A. W. (1985). *Achieving educational excellence.* San Francisco: Jossey-Bass.

Astin, A. W., & Chang, M. J. (1995). Colleges that emphasize research and teaching: Can you have your cake and eat it too? *Change, 27*(5), 44–49.

Atkinson, R. C., & Tuzin, D. (1992). Equilibrium in the research university. *Change, 24*(3), 20–31.

Bacharach, S. B., & Lawler, E. J. (1980). *Power and politics in organizations: The social psychology of conflict, coalitions, and bargaining.* San Francisco: Jossey-Bass.

Baier, J. L. (1985). Recruiting and training competent staff. In M. J. Barr, L. A. Keating, & Associates, *Developing effective student services programs.* San Francisco: Jossey-Bass.

Baird, L., Beatty, R. W., & Schneier, C. E. (Eds.) (1982). *The performance appraisal sourcebook.* Amherst, MA: Human Resource Development Press.

Barnes, S. F., & O'Donnell, J. A. (1985). *Organizational vitality in student affairs.* Paper presented at the Annual Conference of the National Association of Student Personnel Administrators, Portland, OR, March 31–April 3. (ERIC Document Reproduction Service No. ED 261 330)

Barr, R. B., & Tagg, J. (1995, November/December). From teaching to learning: A new paradigm for undergraduate education. *Change, 27,* 12–25.

Baskett, H. K., & Marsick, V. J. (Eds.). (1992). *Professionals' ways of knowing: New findings on how to improve professional education.* New Directions for Adult and Continuing Education, No. 55. San Francisco: Jossey-Bass.

Batchelor, S. W. (1993). Mentoring and self-directed learning. In M. J. Barr & Associates, *The handbook of student affairs administration.* San Francisco: Jossey-Bass.

Beeler, K. D. (1977a). Mini-U: A promising model for student affairs staff development. *NASPA Journal, 14,* 38–43.

Beeler, K. D. (1977b). Staff development in student affairs: The referral process. *NASPA Journal, 15,* 14–23.

Bergquist, W. H., Greenberg, E. M., & Klaum, G. A. (1993). *In our fifties: Voices of men and women reinventing their lives.* San Francisco: Jossey-Bass.

Biglan, A. (1973). The characteristics of subject matter in different academic areas. *Journal of Applied Psychology, 57,* 195–203.

Birnbaum, R. (1988). *How colleges work: The cybernetics of academic organizations and leadership.* San Francisco: Jossey-Bass.

Blackburn, R. T., & Pitney, J. A. (1988). *Performance appraisal for faculty: Implications for higher education.* (Technical Report No. 88-D-002.0). Ann Arbor, MI: School of Education, University of Michigan. (ERIC Document Reproduction Service No. ED 316 066)

Bland, C. J., & Holloway, R. L. (1995, September/October). A crisis of mission: Faculty roles and rewards in an era of health-care reform. *Change, 27,* 30–35.

Blimling, G. S. (1993a). The context of conflict in the academy: An educational dialectic on faculty and student affairs educators. *College Student Affairs Journal, 13*(1), 4–12.

Blimling, G. S. (1993b). New challenges and goals for residential life programs. In R. B. Winston, Jr., S. Anchors, & Associates, *Student housing and residential life: A handbook for professionals committed to student development goals.* San Francisco: Jossey-Bass.

Bloland, P. A., & Moore, P. L. (1982). The ubiquitous search committee and its deployment in student affairs. *Journal of College Student Personnel, 23,* 252–257.

Borland, D. T. (1983). The impact of collective bargaining: Professional dilemma or panacea? In T. K. Miller, R. B. Winston, Jr., W. R. Mendenhall, & Associates, *Administration and leadership in student affairs: Actualizing student development in higher education.* Muncie, IN: Accelerated Development.

Bowen, H. R. (1977). *Investment in learning: The individual and social value of American higher education.* San Francisco: Jossey-Bass.

Braskamp, L. A., & Ory, J. C. (1994). *Assessing faculty work: Enhancing individual and institutional performance.* San Francisco: Jossey-Bass.

Brown, R. D. (1988). *Performance appraisal as a tool for staff development.* New Directions for Student Services, No. 43. San Francisco: Jossey-Bass.

Bullington, R., & Ponterotto, J. G. (1990). Affirmative action: Definitions and philosophy. In J. G. Ponterotto, D. E. Lewis, & R. Bullington (Eds.), *Affirmative action on campus.* New Directions for Student Services, No. 52. San Francisco: Jossey-Bass.

Bunker, D. R., & Wijnberg, M. H. (1988). *Supervision and performance: Managing professional work in human service organizations.* San Francisco: Jossey-Bass.

Burke, T. H., & Randall, K. P. (1994). Developing an organizational commitment to employee success: The student affairs staff development model. *College Student Affairs Journal, 13,* 73–81.

Campbell, J. P., Dunnette, M. D., Lawler, E. E., III, & Weick, K. E. (1970). *Managerial behavior: Performance and effectiveness.* New York: McGraw-Hill.

Carpenter, D. S. (1991). Student affairs profession: A developmental perspective. In T. K. Miller, R. B. Winston, Jr., & Associates, *Administration and leadership in student affairs: Actualizing student development in higher education* (2nd ed.). Muncie, IN: Accelerated Development.

Carpenter, D. S., Miller, T. K., & Winston, R. B., Jr. (1980). Toward the professionalization of student affairs. *NASPA Journal, 18,* 16–22.

Chichester, J. H. (1996). *Making connections: Matching Virginia higher education's strengths with the commonwealth's needs.* Richmond: Commission on the Future of Higher Education in Virginia.

Chickering, A. W., & Havighurst, R. J. (1981). The life cycle. In A. W. Chickering & Associates, *Modern American college: Responding to the new realities of diverse students and a changing society.* San Francisco: Jossey-Bass.

Chronicle of Higher Education Almanac. (1995, September 1). The nation. Washington, DC: Author.

Clement, L. M., & Rickard, S. T. (1992). *Effective leadership in student services: Voices from the field.* San Francisco: Jossey-Bass.

Cohen, M. D., & March, J. G. (1974). *Leadership and ambiguity: The American college president.* New York: McGraw-Hill.

Condition of Education. (1995). Washington, DC: National Center for Education Statistics.

Cooper, J. F., & Garmon, J. F. (1990). *Personnel selection: The holistic approach.* Brownsville, TX: Texas Southmost College. (ERIC Document Reproduction Service No. ED 321 794)

Council for the Advancement of Standards in Higher Education. (1986).

Standards and guidelines for student services/development programs. Washington, DC: Author.

Cox, D. W., & Ivy, W. A. (1984). Staff development needs of student affairs professionals. *NASPA Journal, 22,* 26–33.

Creamer, D. G. (1988). A model of in-service education: Professional initiative for continuous learning. In R. B. Young & L. V. Moore (Eds.), *The state of the art of professional education and practice* (pp. 62–70). Monograph # 1: Generativity Project. Washington, DC: American College Personnel Association.

Creamer, D. G. (1995). Report of initial meetings. Unpublished manuscript of Recommendations for Professional Association Action, Interassociation Committee for Continuing Professional Education. Blacksburg, VA: Virginia Polytechnical Institute.

Creamer, D., & Shelton, M. (1988). Staff development: A literature review of graduate preparation and in-service education of student affairs professionals. *Journal of College Student Development, 29,* 407–414.

Creamer, D. G., Winston, R. B., Jr., Schuh, J. H., Gehring, D. D., McEwen, M. K., Forney, D. S., Carpenter, D. S., & Woodard, D. B., Jr. (1992). *Quality assurance in college student affairs: A proposal for action by professional associations.* Unpublished manuscript. Blacksburg: Virginia Polytechnical Institute.

Creamer, D. G., & Woodard, D. B. (1992). *Accrediting and credentialing in college student affairs: The role of ACPA and NASPA.* An unpublished manuscript. Blacksburg: Virginia Polytechnical Institute.

Cummings, L. L., & Schwab, D. P. (1973). *Performance in organizations.* Glenview, IL: Scott, Foresman.

Cummings, L. L., & Schwab, D. P. (1978). Methods of appraisal. In C. Schneir and R. Beatty (Eds.), *Personnel administration today: Readings and commentary.* Reading, MA: Addison-Wesley.

Cyert, R. M., & March, J. G. (1963). *A behavioral theory of the firm.* Englewood Cliffs, NJ: Prentice-Hall.

Dalton, J. C. (1988). Employment and supervision of student affairs personnel. In M. J. Barr & Associates, *Student services and the law: A handbook for practitioners.* San Francisco: Jossey-Bass.

Dalton, J. C. (1989). Enhancing staff knowledge and skills. In U. Delworth, G. R. Hanson, & Associates, *Student services: A handbook for the profession.* San Francisco: Jossey-Bass.

Dalton, J. C. (1996). Managing human resources. In S. R. Komives, D. B. Woodard, Jr., & Associates, *Student services: A handbook for the profession* (3rd ed.). San Francisco: Jossey-Bass.

Daughtrey, A. S., & Ricks, B. R. (1989). *Contemporary supervision: Managing people and technology.* New York: McGraw-Hill.

DeCoster, D. A., & Brown, S. S. (1991). Staff development: Personal and professional education. In T. K. Miller, R. B. Winston, Jr., & Associates, *Administration and leadership in student affairs: Actualizing student development in higher education* (2nd ed.). Muncie, IN: Accelerated Development.

Delworth, U. (Ed.). (1978). *Training competent staff.* New Directions for Student Services, No. 2. San Francisco: Jossey-Bass.

DeVries, D. L., Morrison, A. M., Shullman, S. L., & Gerlach, M. L. (1981). *Performance appraisal on the line.* New York: Wiley.

Eaton, J. S. (1995). *Investing in American higher education: An argument for restructuring.* New York: Council for Aid to Education.

Eble, K. E. (1978). *The art of administration.* San Francisco: Jossey-Bass.

Fortunato, R., & Elliott, J. (1988). *A handbook for developing higher education personnel policies.* Washington, DC: College and University Personnel Association.

Fortunato, R. T., & Waddell, D. G. (1981). *Personnel administration in higher education: Handbook of faculty and staff personnel practices.* San Francisco: Jossey-Bass.

Foxley, C. H. (Ed.). (1980). *Applying management techniques.* New Directions for Student Services, No. 9. San Francisco: Jossey-Bass.

French, J.R.P., & Raven, B. H. (1959). The bases of social power. In D. Cartwright (Ed.), *Studies in social power.* Ann Arbor: University of Michigan Press.

Fulk, J., Brief, A. P., & Barr, S. H. (1985). Trust-in-supervisor and perceived fairness and accuracy of performance evaluations. *Journal of Business Research, 13*(4), 301–313.

Gehring, D. D. (1993). Understanding legal constraints on practice. In M. J. Barr & Associates, *The handbook of student affairs administration.* San Francisco: Jossey-Bass.

Gilbert, S. P. (1992). Ethical issues in the treatment of severe psychopathology in university and college counseling centers. *Journal of Counseling and Development, 70,* 695–699.

Gordon, S. E., Borders Strode, C., & Mann, B. A. (1993). The mid-manager in student affairs: What are CSAOs looking for? *NASPA Journal, 30,* 290–297.

Guskin, A. E. (1996). Facing the future: The change process in restructuring universities. *Change, 28*(4), 27–37.

Haro, R. P. (1991). Selecting a dean of student services in the far west: When right may be wrong. *NASPA Journal, 28,* 149–155.

Henderson, R. (1980). *Performance appraisal: Theory to practice.* Reston, VA: Reston Publishing.

Hersey, P., & Blanchard, K. H. (1977). *Management of organizational behavior: Utilizing human resources* (3rd ed.). New York: Prentice-Hall

Herzberg, G. (1968). One more time: How do you motivate employees? *Harvard Business Review, 46*(1), 53–62.

Hess, W. D., & Winston, R. B., Jr. (1995). Developmental task achievement and students' intentions to participate in developmental activities. *Journal of College Student Development, 36,* 314–321.

Hodkinson, H. L. (1974). Adult development: Implications for faculty and administrators. *Educational Record, 55,* 263–274.

Hollander, P. A., & Young, D. P. (1991). Legal issues and employment practices in student affairs. In T. K. Miller, R. B. Winston, Jr., & Associates, *Administration and leadership in student affairs: Actualizing student development in higher education* (2nd ed.). Muncie, IN: Accelerated Development.

Hyman, R. E. (1988). Graduate preparation for professional practice: A difference of perceptions. *NASPA Journal, 26,* 143–150.

Jarvis P. (1983). *Professional education.* London: Croom-Helm.

Kaplin, W. A., & Lee, B. A. (1995). *The law of higher education: A comprehensive guide to legal implications of administrative decision making* (3rd ed.). San Francisco: Jossey-Bass.

Kearney, W. J. (1976). The value of behaviorally based performance appraisals. *Business Horizons, 19*(3), 75–83.

Kirkpatrick, D. L. (1993). *How to train and develop supervisors.* New York: American Management Association.

Klevans, D. R., Smutz, W. D.. Shuman, S. B., & Bershad, C. (1992). Self-assessment: Helping professionals discover what they do not know. In H. K. Baskett and V. J. Marsick (Eds.), *Professionals' ways of knowing: New findings on how to improve professional education.* New Directions for Adult and Continuing Education, No. 55. San Francisco: Jossey-Bass.

Krager, L. (1985). A new model for defining ethical behavior. In H. J. Canon & R. D. Brown (Eds.), *Applied ethics in student services.* New Directions for Student Services, No. 30. San Francisco: Jossey-Bass.

Kuh, G. D., & Hall, J. E. (1993). Cultural perspectives in student affairs. In G. D. Kuh & Associates, *Cultural perspectives in student affairs work.* Washington, DC: American College Personnel Association.

Lawing, M. A., Moore, L. V., & Groseth, R. (1982). Enhancement and advancement: Professional development for student affairs staff. *NASPA Journal, 20*(2), 22–26.

Lenney, E., Mitchell, L., & Browning, C. (1983). The effect of clear evaluation criteria on sex bias in judgments of performance. *Psychology of Women Quarterly, 7,* 313–328.

Levinson, D. J., Darrow, C. N., Klein, E., Levinson, M. H., & McKee, B. (1978). *The seasons of a man's life.* New York: Knopf.

Levinson, D. J., with Levinson, J. D. (1996). *The seasons of a woman's life.* New York: Knopf.

Levy S. R. (1990). Challenges and limits: A view from a chief student affairs office. *The Counseling Psychologist, 18,* 614–618.

Masey, W. F., & Wilger, A. K. (1995, July/August). Improving productivity: What faculty think about it—and its effect on quality. *Change, 27,* 10–20.

Matthews, R. S., Cooper, J. L., Davidson, N., & Hawkes, P. (1995, July/August). Building bridges between cooperative and collaborative learning. *Change, 27,* 34–40.

McGregor, D. (1966). *Leadership and motivation.* Boston: MIT Press.

McIntire, D. D., & Carpenter, D. S. (1981). Employment practices in student affairs. *NASPA Journal, 18*(3), 18–24.

McIntyre, J. P. (1974). The management of student personnel programs. *NASPA Journal, 15,* 487–491.

Meabon, D. L., Sims, O. S., Suddick, D. E., & Alley, B. (1978). Management techniques in student affairs: A national study. *Journal of College Student Personnel, 19,* 221–224.

Merkle, H. B., & Artman, R. B. (1983). Staff development: A systematic process for student affairs leaders. *NASPA Journal, 21,* 55–63.

Meyer, H. H. (1975). The pay for performance dilemma. *Organizational Dynamics, 3,* 39–50.

Meyer, H. H., Kay, E., & French, R. P., Jr. (1965, January-February). Split roles in performance appraisal. *Harvard Business Review,* 123–129.

Miller, D. B. (1990). Organizational, environmental, and work design strategies that foster competence. In S. L. Willis, S. S. Dubin, & Associates, *Maintaining professional competence: Approaches to career enhancement, vitality, and success throughout a work life.* San Francisco: Jossey-Bass.

Miller, T. K. (1975). Staff development activities in student affairs programs. *Journal of College Student Personnel, 16,* 258–264.

Miller, T. K, Winston, R. B., Jr., & Associates. (1991). *Administration and leadership in student affairs: Actualizing student development in higher education* (2nd ed.). Muncie, IN: Accelerated Development.

Mills, D. B. (1993). The role of the middle manager. In M. J. Barr & Associates, *The handbook of student affairs administration.* San Francisco: Jossey-Bass.

Moore, P. L. (1993). The political dimension of decision making. In M. J. Barr & Associates, *The handbook of student affairs administration.* San Francisco: Jossey-Bass.

Mosley, D. C., Megginson, L. C., & Pietri, P. H., Jr. (1993). *Supervisory management: The art of empowering and developing people* (3rd ed.). Cincinnati, OH: South-Western.

Mouton, J. S., & Blake, R. R. (1984). *Synergogy: A new strategy for education, training, and development.* San Francisco: Jossey-Bass.

Nicklin, J. L. (1995, January 27). The hum of corporate buzzwords. *The Chronicle of Higher Education*, A33–34.

Nordvall, R. C. (1977). Evaluation of college administrators: Where are we now? *NASPA Journal, 15*, 53–60.

O'Malley, K., Wheeler, I., Murphey, J., O'Connel, J., & Waldo, M. (1990). Changes in levels of psychopathology being treated in college and university counseling centers. *Journal of College Student Development, 31*, 464–465.

Ostroth, D. D. (1981). Competencies for entry-level professionals: What do employers look for when hiring new staff? *Journal of College Student Personnel, 22*, 5–11.

Pascarella, E. T., & Terenzini, P. T. (1991). *How college affects students: Findings and insights from twenty years of research*. San Francisco: Jossey-Bass.

Pfeffer, J. (1981). Management as symbolic action: The creation and maintenance of organizational paradigms. *Research in Organizational Behavior, 3*, 1–52.

Phillips, J. J. (1985). *Improving supervisors' effectiveness*. San Francisco: Jossey-Bass.

Ponterotto, J. G. (1990). Affirmative action: Current status and future needs. In J. G. Ponterotto, D. E. Lewis, R. Bullington (Eds.), *Affirmative action on campus*. New Directions for Student Services, No. 52. San Francisco: Jossey-Bass.

Queeney, D. S., & Smutz, W. D. (1990). Enhancing the performance of professionals: The practice audit model. In S. L. Willis, S. S. Dubin, & Associates, *Maintaining professional competence: Approaches to career enhancement, vitality, and success throughout a work life*. San Francisco: Jossey-Bass.

Reilly, A. J., & Jones, J. E. (1974). Team-building. In J. W. Pfeiffer & J. E. Jones (Eds.), *The 1974 annual handbook for group facilitators*. La Jolla, CA: University Associates.

Rhatigan, J. J., & Crawford, A. E. (1978). Professional development preferences of student affairs administrators. *NASPA Journal, 15*, 45–52.

Rickard, S. T. (1981). Effective staff selection. *Personnel Journal, 60*, 475–478.

Rickard, S. T. (1984). Staff selection in student affairs: Common problems and their prevention. *NASPA Journal, 22*, 17–25.

Robinson, D. C., & Delbridge-Parker, L. (1991). A model job rotation plan: A 10-year follow-up. *NASPA Journal, 28*, 172–178.

Rokeach, M. (1973). *The nature of human values*. New York: Free Press.

Sagaria, M. A., & Johnsrud, L. K. (1991). Recruiting, advancing, and retaining minorities in student affairs: Moving from rhetoric to results. *NASPA Journal, 28*, 105–120.

Sandeen, A. (1991). *The chief student affairs officer: Leader, manager, mediator, educator.* San Francisco: Jossey-Bass.

Schein, E. H. (1978). *Career dynamics: Matching individual and organizational needs.* Reading, MA: Addison-Wesley.

Schneier, C. E., & Beatty, R. W. (1978). *Personnel administration today: Readings and commentary.* Reading, MA: Addison-Wesley.

Schroeder, C. C. (Guest Editor). (1996). The student learning imperative. [Special issue]. *Journal of College Student Development, 37*(2).

Schuh, J. H., & Carlisle, W. (1991). Supervision and evaluation: Selected topics for emerging professionals. *Administration and leadership in student affairs: Actualizing student development in higher education* (2nd ed.). Muncie, IN: Accelerated Development.

Scott, W. R. (1969). Professional employees in a bureaucratic structure. In A. Etzioni (Ed.), *The semiprofessions and their organization.* New York: Free Press.

Seldin, P. (1988). *Evaluating and developing administrative performance: A practical guide for academic leaders.* San Francisco: Jossey-Bass.

Sims, J. M., & Foxley, C. H. (1980). Job analysis, job descriptions, and performance appraisal systems. In C. H. Foxley (Ed.), *Applying management techniques.* New Directions for Student Services, No. 9. San Francisco: Jossey-Bass.

Snyder, D. (1989). Hiring support staff can be a win/win affair. *College & University, 64,* 300–305.

Sprunger, B. E., & Bergquist, W. H. (1978). *Handbook for college administration.* Washington DC: Council for the Advancement of Small Colleges.

Stamatakos, L. C. (1981). Student affairs progress toward professionalism: Recommendations for action, parts 1 and 2. *Journal of College Student Personnel, 22,* 105–113, 197–207.

Stamatakos, L. C., & Oliaro, P. M. (1972). In-service development: A function of student personnel. *NASPA Journal, 9,* 269–273.

Stimpson, R. F. (1993). Selecting and training competent staff. In M. J. Barr & Associates, *The handbook of student affairs administration.* San Francisco: Jossey-Bass.

Stone, G. L., & Archer, J., Jr. (1990). College and university counseling centers in the 1990s: Challenges and limits. *The Counseling Psychologist, 18,* 539–607.

Stronge, J. H., & Helm, V. M. (1992). A performance evaluation system for professional support personnel. *Educational Evaluation and Policy Analysis, 14,* 175–180.

Terry, G., & Franklin S. (1982). *Principles of management.* Homewood, IL: Richard D. Irwin.

Truitt, J. W., & Gross, R. A. (1970). In-service education. In O. R. Herron (Ed.), *New dimensions in student personnel administration.* Scranton, PA: International Textbook.

Upcraft, M. L. (1971). Does training make a difference? *NASPA Journal, 9,* 134–137.

Upcraft, M. L. (1988). Managing right. In M. L. Upcraft & M. J. Barr (Eds.), *Managing student affairs effectively.* New Directions for Student Services, No. 41. San Francisco: Jossey-Bass.

Upcraft, M. L., & Barr, M. J. (Eds.). (1988). *Managing student affairs effectively.* New Directions for Student Services, No. 41. San Francisco: Jossey-Bass.

Westefeld, J. S., Whitchard, K., & Range, L. M. (1990). College and university student suicide: Trends and implications. *The Counseling Psychologist, 18,* 464–476.

Wexler, A. (1995). *Conditions of interpersonal trust reported by two-year college student affairs professionals of their performance evaluators.* Unpublished doctoral dissertation. Blacksburg: Virginia Polytechnic Institute and State University.

Wingspread Group on Higher Education. (1993). *An American imperative: Higher expectations for higher education.* Racine, WI: The Johnson Foundation.

Winston, R. B., Jr., & Dagley, J. C. (1985). Ethical standards statements: Uses and limitations. In H. J. Canon, & R. D. Brown (Eds.), *Applied ethics in student services.* New Directions for Student Services, No. 30. San Francisco: Jossey-Bass.

Winston, R. B., Jr., & Ender, S. C. (1988). Use of student paraprofessionals in divisions of college student affairs. *Journal of Counseling and Development, 66,* 466–473.

Winston, R. B., Jr., & Miller, T. K. (1991). Human resource management: Professional preparation and staff selection. In T. K. Miller, R. B. Winston, Jr., & Associates, *Administration and leadership in student affairs: Actualizing student development in higher education* (2nd ed.). Muncie, IN: Accelerated Development.

Winston, R. B., Jr., Ullom, M. S., & Werring, C. J. (1984). Student paraprofessionals in residence halls. In S. C. Ender & R. B. Winston, Jr., (Eds.), *Students as paraprofessional staff.* New Directions for Student Services, No. 27. San Francisco: Jossey-Bass

Wood, L., Winston, R. B, Jr., & Polkosnik, M. C. (1985). Career orientations and professional development of young student affairs professionals. *Journal of College Student Personnel, 26,* 532–539.

Woodard, D. B., Jr., & Komives, S. R. (1990). Ensuring staff competence. In M. J. Barr, M. L. Upcraft, & Associates, *New futures for student affairs: Building a vision for professional leadership and practice.* San Francisco: Jossey-Bass.

Woodard, D. B., Jr., & von Destinon, M. (1993). Identifying and working with key constituent groups. In M. J. Barr & Associates, *The handbook of student affairs administration.* San Francisco: Jossey-Bass.

Young, R. B. (1987). A model of professional education. In L. V. Moore & R. B. Young (Eds.), *Expanding opportunities for professional education.* New Directions for Student Services, No. 37. San Francisco: Jossey-Bass.

Young, R. B. (1988). Advancing the concepts of continuing professional education. In R. B. Young and L. V. Moore (Eds.), *The state of the art of professional education and practice* (pp. 71–78). Monograph No. 1: Generativity Project. Washington, DC: American College Personnel Association.

Young, R. B. (Ed.). (1993a). *Identifying and implementing the essential values of the profession.* New Directions for Student Services, No. 61. San Francisco: Jossey-Bass.

Young, R. B. (1993b). The essential values of the profession. In R. B. Young (Ed.), *Identifying and implementing the essential values of the profession.* New Directions for Student Services, No. 61. San Francisco: Jossey-Bass.

Young, R. B. (1996). Guiding values and philosophy. In S. R. Komives, D. B. Woodard, Jr., & Associates, *Student services: A handbook for the profession* (3rd ed.). San Francisco: Jossey-Bass.

Young, R. B., & Elfrink, V. L. (1991). Essential values of student affairs work. *Journal of College Student Development, 32,* 47–55.

Zemsky, R., Massey, W. F., & Oedel, P. (1993). On reversing the ratchet. *Change, 25*(3), 56–62.

Index

Psychological services, 9–10
Public institutions, 9, 22–23, 149

Q

Quality, and staffing practices, 273–277
Quality assurance, 292–294, 353–367; recommendations on, 365, 366–367
Quality Assurance Model (QAM), 354, 356–358; beliefs and principles of, 358–363; implementation of, 364, 365
Queeney, D. S., 291–292

R

Randall, K. P., 230–231
Range, L. M., 10
Ranking, for performance appraisal, 255
Raven, B. H., 34
Recommendations: on orientation to new position, 176–177; on performance appraisal, 269–271; on quality assurance, 364, 366–367; on recruitment and selection, 156–158; on staff development, 241–242; on supervision, 212–218
Recruitment procedures: literature on, 131–133. *See also* Recruitment and selection
Recruitment and selection, 40–41, 123–159; in case studies, 51, 58, 65–66, 72, 75; and economy, 23; literature on, 128–134; principles of, 277–278; problems and issues in, 123–128; and professional preparation, 139–141; recommendations on, 156–158; staffing model in, 141–157; survey on, 99–107, 135–139, 346–349
Regulations: antidiscrimination, 150, 151; and orientation to new position, 167; and recruitment and selection, 149–151; and staffing practices, 22, 26

Rehabilitation Act, 151
Reilly, A. J., 190
Resources, institutional, 28–29
Rewards, 85, 265; of position, 117, 120, 311
Rhatigan, J. J., 229, 232
Richmond College, 64, 79. *See also* University of Richmond
Rickard, S. T., 133–134, 213, 214
Ricks, B. R., 249–250, 256
Robinson, D. C., 229
Rokeach, M., 15

S

Sagaria, M. A., 129, 158
Salaries, and performance appraisals, 258–259
Samford University, 46, 48; case study, 67–70; institutional culture, 68, 69–70, 77, 80–81, 82; leadership, 83, 85; organizational structures, 87–88; performance appraisal, 259; supervision, 90; values, 78–79, 89–90
Sandeen, A., 129, 213
Schein, E. H., 201
Schneier, C. E., 251
Schuh, J. H., 183, 184, 194, 248, 355
Schwab, D. P., 251, 254
Scott, R., 56, 57, 58, 59, 84
Scott, W. R., 181
Screening applicants, 153–154
Search committees, 102–105, 144–148; literature on, 132–133, 134
Seldin, P., 249
Selection process, literature on, 133–134. *See also* Recruitment and selection
Shelton, M., 225, 226
Shullman, S. L., 251–252
Shuman, S. B., 228
Sims, J. M., 129, 130, 131, 144, 248, 252, 254, 256
Sims, O. S., 252
Smutz, W. D., 228, 291–292